ROGER HICKS

AND NGAKPA CHOGYAM

GREAT OCEAN

*An Authorized Biography
of the Buddhist Monk Tenzin Gyatso
His Holiness the Fourteenth
Dalai Lama*

Penguin Books

PENGUIN BOOKS

Published by the Penguin Group
27 Wrights Lane, London w8 5tz, England
Viking Penguin Inc., 40 West 23rd Street, New York, New York 10010, USA
Penguin Books Australia Ltd, Ringwood, Victoria, Australia
Penguin Books Canada Ltd, 2801 John Street, Markham, Ontario, Canada l3r 1b4
Penguin Books (NZ) Ltd, 182–190 Wairau Road, Auckland 10, New Zealand

Penguin Books Ltd, Registered Offices: Harmondsworth, Middlesex, England

First published in Great Britain by Element Books 1984
Published in Penguin Books 1990
1 3 5 7 9 10 8 6 4 2

Made and printed in Great Britain by
Richard Clay Ltd, Bungay, Suffolk

PENGUIN BOOKS
GREAT OCEAN

Roger Hicks has been fascinated by Tibet and Tibetan culture since he was seven years old; among the earliest books he can remember reading are Hillary's *The Ascent of Everest*, Harrier's *Seven Years in Tibet*, and a boys' adventure story set in Tibet, called *Lost City of Light*. Over the past few years, his involvement with the Tibetan movement in exile has been steadily growing; he numbers among his friends several prominent Tibetans in His Holiness's Government in Exile.

Ngakpa Chögyam is a practitioner of the Nyingma ('Ancient Ones') school of Tibetan Buddhism. He has been studying Buddhism since he was a teenager in England, and his teacher in India (Lama Khamtrül Yeshe Dorje Rinpoche) has instructed him in the *Ngakpa* (sorcerer) traditions. He is a professional counsellor, and teaches Buddhism at several centres in England.

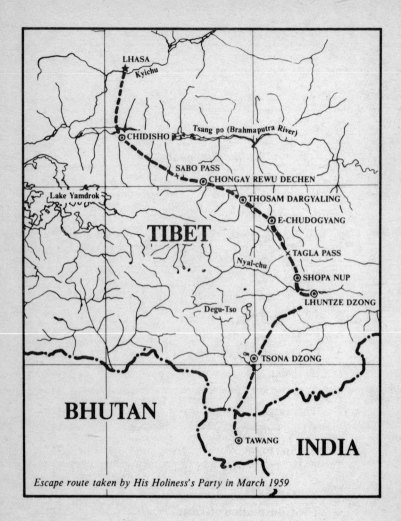

LHASA

Kyichu

Tsang po (Brahmaputra River)

CHIDISHO

SABO PASS

CHONGAY REWU DECHEN

Lake Yamdrok

THOSAM DARGYALING

E-CHUDOGYANG

TIBET

TAGLA PASS

Nyal-chu

SHOPA NUP

LHUNTZE DZONG

Degu-Tso

TSONA DZONG

BHUTAN

INDIA

TAWANG

Escape route taken by His Holiness's Party in March 1959

Contents

Foreword

Remarks by His Holiness the Fourteenth Dalai Lama
of Tibet on being Awarded the Nobel Peace Prize

I am deeply touched to be chosen as this year's recipient of the Nobel Peace Prize. I believe my selection reaffirms the universal values of non-violence, peace and understanding between all members of our great human family. We all desire a happier, more humane and harmonious world, and I have always felt that the practice of love and compassion, tolerance and respect for others is the most effective manner in which to bring this about.

I hope this prize will provide courage to the six million people of Tibet. For some forty years now Tibetans have been undergoing the most painful period in our long history. During this time, over a million of our people perished and more than six thousand monasteries – the seat of our peaceful culture – were destroyed. There is not a single family, either in Tibet or among the refugees abroad, which has gone unscathed. Yet our people's determination and commitment to spiritual values and the practice of non-violence remain unshaken. This prize is a profound recognition of their faith and perseverance.

The demonstrations which have rocked Tibet for the past two years continue to be non-violent despite brutal suppression. Since the imposition of martial law in Lhasa last March, Tibet has been sealed off, and while global attention has focused on the tragic events in China, a systematic effort to crush the spirit and national identity of the Tibetan people is being pursued by the Government of the People's Republic.

Tibetans today are facing the real possibility of elimination as a people and a nation. The Government of the People's Republic of China is practising a form of genocide by relocating millions of

Chinese settlers into Tibet. I ask that this massive population transfer be stopped. Unless the cruel and inhuman treatment of my people is brought to an end, and until they are given their due right to self-determination, there will always be obstacles in finding a solution to the Tibetan issue.

I accept the Nobel Peace Prize in a spirit of optimism despite the many grave problems which humanity faces today. We all know the immensity of the challenges facing our generation: the problem of overpopulation, the threat to our environment and the dangers of military confrontation. As this dramatic century draws to a close, it is clear that the renewed yearning for freedom and democracy sweeping the globe provides an unprecedented opportunity for building a better world. Freedom is the real source of human happiness and creativity. Only when it is allowed to flourish can a genuinely stable international climate exist.

The suppression of the rights and freedoms of any people by totalitarian governments is against human nature, and the recent movements for democracy in various parts of the world are a clear indication of this.

The Chinese students have given me great hope for the future of China and Tibet. I feel that their movement follows the tradition of Mahatma Gandhi's *ahimsa* or non-violence which has deeply inspired me ever since I was a small boy. The eventual success of all people seeking a more tolerant atmosphere must derive from a commitment to counter hatred and violence with patience. We must seek change through dialogue and trust. It is my heartfelt prayer that Tibet's plight may be resolved in such a manner and that once again my country, the Roof of the World, may serve as a sanctuary of peace and a resource of spiritual inspiration at the heart of Asia.

I hope and pray that the decision to give me the Nobel Peace Prize will encourage all those who pursue the path of peace to do so in a renewed spirit of optimism and strength.

5 October 1989
Newport Beach, CA

Preface

Writing biographies is a dangerous game. No two people can ever agree completely on the character of a third, and, when the person in question is both alive and an internationally known figure, it is almost impossible to write a description which everyone will recognize. The most difficult goal is objectivity, especially when you know and admire your subject. In the end we decided that we could not be wholly objective; our biography had to reflect the love which we feel for His Holiness. Although this will be evident throughout the book, we do not feel that it is necessarily a flaw. The attraction of the Dalai Lama is his immense warmth and humanity, as well as his wisdom and spirituality, and no one who has met him could fail to be moved by these qualities.

It is also clear throughout the book that the Chinese come out very badly. Given our declared bias, it might seem that we were propagandizing, but we do not believe that this is the case – except in so far as one can propagandize by telling the truth. Endless Tibetan witnesses can be found to Chinese atrocities, and with both the International Commission of Jurists and the United Nations calling attention to Chinese genocide in Tibet (the International Commission of Jurists' words) and gross disregard of human rights, we believe that we have nowhere distorted the facts.

Because of the Dalai Lama's unique position, we have had to write three books in one. The first is a biography of the Buddhist monk Tenzin Gyatso, the Fourteenth Dalai Lama, the One whose Wisdom is as great as the Ocean, the Holder of the White Lotus, the spiritual and temporal leader of all Tibetans everywhere. The second is a biography of the previous thirteen incarnations: it would have been meaningless to write about the Fourteenth Dalai Lama in isolation, both from the viewpoint of historical context and in the light of the fact that the previous thirteen lives are also, by orthodox Tibetan reasoning, the lives of the Fourteenth. And the third is a story of a small and peaceful country, which was ruled by the Dalai Lama in this and previous incarnations for over three hundred years.

Tibet was not a perfect country, but what country ever was? It was materially backward, but it was considered by many to have been the most spiritually advanced in the world. The most interesting aspect, though, is that the Dalai Lamas were usually in the forefront of progress and change. This is particularly true of the three Dalai Lamas who took most part in the running of their country – the Fifth, Thirteenth, and Fourteenth. The first two are generally known as the Great Fifth and the Great Thirteenth, and already many refer to the Great Fourteenth. Since they invaded Tibet in 1950, the Chinese have waged a constant propaganda war against the 'reactionary oppressors of the people', and the 'chief bandit' the Dalai Lama. Countless others, in Europe and America and elsewhere, have had the opportunity of hearing the Dalai Lama's teaching, and believe that Tibet's loss has been the world's gain. We hope that this book will help the reader judge who is right.

ROGER W. HICKS
NGAKPA CHOGYAM

Bristol, Cardiff, and Dharamsala
1984

Acknowledgements

His Holiness the Dalai Lama was both the inspiration for this book and a major force in ensuring its completion. In addition to granting us several audiences, he effected many introductions and smoothed the way for us generally.

In the Private Office of His Holiness in Dharamsala, both his younger brother Tendzin Choegyal and Tempa Tsering were endlessly helpful. Not only did Tendzin Choegyal furnish many anecdotes and read the entire manuscript, he also proved a warm and hospitable friend.

The Dalai Lama's elder brother, Lobsang Samten, and his younger sister, Mrs Pema Gyalpo, were also very helpful. Both contributed information and anecdotes which would have been difficult or impossible to obtain elsewhere. Lobsang Samten is in charge of the Tibetan Medical Centre in Dharamsala, and Mrs Pema Gyalpo runs the Tibetan Children's Village.

Tenzing Geyche, his former Private Secretary, provided a good deal of information about the Dalai Lama's travels, and Lodi Gyari Gyaltsen (Gyari Rinpoche) of the Office of Information was also a mine of information, as were his colleagues and staff. In England, Phuntsog Wangyal of the Office of His Holiness was a great help.

It would be impossible to name all the others who gave us both specific information and a general feeling for Tibet and things Tibetan, but particular thanks are due to Jamyang Norbu, Director of the Tibetan Institute of Performing Arts; Lama Yeshi Dorje Rinpoche (Ngakpa Rinpoche, Ngakpa Chögyam's teacher); Tsering Wangyal, Editor of the *Tibetan Review;* Rinchen Khando, Tendzin Choegyal's wife; and the staff and librarians of the Library of Tibetan Works and Archives at Gangchen Kyishong.

The manuscript was read in whole or in part by Tendzin Choegyal, Gyari Rinpoche, Lobsang Samten, Mrs Pema Gyalpo, Tenzing Geyche, Jamyang Norbu, Paul and Elisabeth Butkovich,

ACKNOWLEDGEMENTS

Herr Prof. Dr. Hanns-Peter Wolff, and Frances Schultz. We are grateful for their comments and input, but emphasise that any errors are our own.

The pictures in this book were gleaned from a number of Tibetan sources, and it has not always been possible to find or contact the photographer. If we have inadvertently infringed copyright, we apologise.

R.H.
N.C.

I

The Holder of the White Lotus

The lotus is one of the most important symbols of Buddhism. It is rooted in mud, and it grows through water – often muddy and polluted water – but its pure white blossoms open in the air, untouched by the two elements which gave it birth. Similarly, the teachings of the Buddha are rooted in the mundane world, but they blossom in a realm which transcends the mundane.

In the Tibetan pantheon of awareness-beings, often referred to as 'deities' in English, compassion is symbolised by Chenrezi. Like many Tibetan awareness-beings, he appears in a number of different forms, some very strange to Western eyes. In one form, he has a thousand arms and a thousand heads, with extra eyes on the palms of his hands and the soles of his feet. This recalls the legend that he was contemplating the task of working for the happiness of all sentient beings when his head exploded into a thousand fragments with the realisation of the enormity of the undertaking. Amitabha, the Buddha of Limitless Light, restored him to life and also gave him this form. The thousand heads and the extra eyes symbolise the all-seeing nature of his compassion; the thousand arms symbolise the ever-present and all-encompassing nature of his help.

Often, too, Chenrezi is shown holding a white lotus flower. Because of this he is known as the Holder of the White Lotus. Millions of people believe that Chenrezi is represented on earth by the Buddhist monk Tenzin Gyatso, so the monk too is known as the Holder of the White Lotus. Tibetans mostly call him Yeshi Norbu, which means Precious Jewel or The Precious One. Those who are close to him call him simply Kundun, which means Presence. In the West, he is best known as the Dalai Lama.

Both Tibet and the Dalai Lama belongs, as far as many people are concerned, to myth and legend rather than to the modern world. But His Holiness the Fourteenth Dalai Lama exists, and the country over which he ruled can be found on the map. Often, Tibet is shown as a part of China, but until the Chinese invaded in 1950 it was unmistakeably a separate and independent country. Even since 1959, when the Dalai Lama was forced to flee by Chinese shells falling near his Summer Palace, the Tibetan people have maintained their identity. The Chinese have relentlessly claimed that Tibet is a part of China and has always been so, and also that the Chinese army 'liberated' the Tibetans. In the absence of alternative information many people have accepted this, but six million Tibetans, including one hundred thousand who have fled Tibet, feel otherwise.

After his flight, the Dalai Lama lived briefly in Mussoorie. For over a year he lived in a bungalow in this former British hill station just outside Dehra Dun. After a while, though, it became obvious that there was little chance of an early return to Tibet. Almost daily there were new stories of Chinese massacres and atrocities in Tibet, and the Dalai Lama realised that he could best serve his people by publicising their cause from a base in a free country. India generously provided that base.

The Dhauladur range is a southern spur of the Himalayas, and scattered across one face of the mountain, just before it descends into the plains, is a collection of settlements jointly known as Dharamsala. One of the highest of these is called McLeod Ganj – a tribute to the Scottish influence in British India – and it was, for a while, a fashionable hill station. Even before the British left in 1947, it was beginning to decay and, by the late 1950s, it was all but deserted. Since 1961, when the Dalai Lama moved there, it has become a Tibetan village of several thousand people. In its streets, you will hear more Tibetan than Hindi; you will see women in the traditional *chuba* dress with (if they are married) brilliantly-coloured aprons; you will see prayer-wheels being turned, monks in maroon robes, and adorable Tibetan children. You will smell Tibetan incense, hear the unearthly chants and rhythms of Tibetan sacred rituals, and see Tibetan handicrafts for sale in all the shops. If you are hungry, you can eat *momo* (meat dumplings) or *thukpa* (noodle soup), and if you know where to go you can buy *chang* (barley beer) to drink with it. It is sometimes known as Little Lhasa; although it is a poor substitute for the real Lhasa, the capital of Tibet, it is the nearest you will find nowadays to a large Tibetan town. It is also the seat of the Tibetan Administration in Exile, led by the Dalai Lama, which accounts for the name.

In Tibet, the Dalai Lama was the absolute spiritual and temporal head of his country. Its borders were ill-defined, and there had never been a proper census, but a fair estimate of the population would have been about six million people spread across the three provinces of U-Tsang, Kham, and Amdo. At the edges of the realm, there were many more people who recognised the spiritual and sometimes the temporal authority of the Dalai Lama, even to the extent of paying taxes, as in Ladakh and even parts of India. On the other hand, parts of Eastern Tibet had been occupied by the Chinese for many years and were effectively Chinese-administered, despite being ethnically and culturally Tibetan and strongly resenting Chinese rule.

This somewhat ramshackle nation may not have been very clearly defined in Western terms, but that was not very important to the vast majority of its inhabitants. Their life continued sub-stantially unchanged from generation to generation, farming and trading, and the exact question of who ruled them politically did not worry most people. Their devotion to the Dalai Lama was for the most part unquestioning, and they paid their modest taxes in kind and in labour to the local monastery and the local governor, whoever he might be. The idea of paying taxes to a monastery may seem strange to a modern Westerner, but mediaeval tithing was familiar to our forefathers, and few doubted the spiritual benefits the monasteries brought. From time to time there would be a harsh or greedy abbot, but this was by no means an indictment of the whole system. Tibetans were and still are intensely religious, and in their eyes anyone who devoted his or her entire life to religion deserved support. There were material benefits too: in times of famine, the monasteries' granaries ensured that no one starved.

It was this very lack of definition, this *laissez-faire* attitude to life, that made Tibet such an easy prey for the Chinese. They could say or do anything, and find some justification for it. For example, the Chinese give the population of Tibet as under two million rather than six. In order to do so, they divide the country into 'inner Tibet', the eastern provinces in which the majority of the people live, and 'outer Tibet', the province of U-Tsang, and then call 'inner Tibet', a part of China. It is certainly true that there are only about two

million people in U-Tsang; and although Amdowas and Khambas
do not take kindly to being called Chinese, if there are no clear maps
and no census figures the average Western politician will not listen
to this argument. Of course, the Chinese rather spoil one of their
own arguments by this approach: if the population is only two
million, then the 100,000 refugees who have left since 1950 amount
to five per cent of the population, rather than one and a half per cent.
That would mean that one Tibetan in twenty was prepared to risk a
Chinese bullet and to leave behind everything he had, rather than
one in sixty.

Again, the Chinese could point to maladministration, corruption, and bribery. The Incarnate Lamas who ruled large parts of
Tibet were by no means always honest, and even if they were, it
was customary for a Lama who devoted his life to more spiritual
pursuits to have a sort of 'business manager' to look after the secular
side of his affairs. Many of these were not above enriching themselves at others' expense, and then hiding behind their master's
robes, or 'wiping their dirty hand on his sleeve' as the Tibetan
saying has it, when questions were asked. No matter that these
were isolated cases, and that the majority were above this sort of
thing; no matter that the Great Thirteenth had instituted a campaign
to clean up local administration, which had become corrupt during
the long period of Chinese influence that had preceded his reign; no
matter that far worse corruption and cruelty was almost syn-
onymous with Chinese provincial administration; the evidence
could be found.

The Fourteenth Dalai Lama was just fifteen when the Chinese
invaded, so the country had been ruled by Monks-Regent since the
death of the Great Thirteenth in 1933. He was the fourteenth in a
spiritual line which stretched back into the fourteenth century of the
Christian era, and the ninth Dalai Lama to have held the temporal
power in Tibet since it became concentrated in the hands of the
Great Fifth Dalai Lama (1617-1682). An inevitable flaw of such a
system of succession is that there are long periods between reigns,
between the death of one and the coming of age of the next incarnation. Each gap or interregnum might last twenty years, during
which time the leadership might be weak or fragmented, or might
fall away from the high standards set by such giants as the Great
Fifty Dalai Lama, or the Great Thirteenth.

Nevertheless, there was in Tibet a genuine attempt to put into practice the teachings of the Lord Buddha, and herein lies one of the fundamental paradoxes of both Tibet and the Dalai Lama. Buddhism is not a religion of dogma and rules; rather, it is based upon compassion, logic, and a desire to implement wisdom. Every case is a special case: as the Tibetan proverb puts it, "A hundred valleys, a hundred dialects; a hundred monks, a hundred religions." But nations are not ruled as assemblies of special cases: they demand laws and regulations. Similarly, Buddhism stresses love, compassion and non-violence: "Hate the deed, not the doer." What happens when you are invaded, when machine-guns and artillery are turned upon you? The deed ceases to be abstract; you are brought face to face with the doer.

Most politicians are skilled in the art of compromise: after all, a fair definition of politics is the 'art of the possible'. What the Dalai Lama tries to do, though, goes beyond that. Like Marxism, Buddhism believes in the greatest good of the greatest number. But 'good' can be interpreted in many ways; could it be said in any way that 'good' might accrue from the wiping out of the Tibetan people and the Tibetan culture? A hard-line Marxist might say that, by ridding the world of reactionary elements, 'good' was done; but if every case is a special case and every person desires his or her own 'good', can this be so? His Holiness likens religion to food for the mind: just as different people like different kinds of food, and just as different diets suit different ways of life, so is there a need for different belief-systems – including Marxism as well as Buddhism.

Most monks are not faced with such problems; even fewer are faced with them at the age of fifteen. This book was written as the Dalai Lama approached his fiftieth birthday, with over three decades of meditation, bitter experience, and learning since that invasion. Before we go on to consider the Dalai Lama himself in more detail, it is worth examining briefly the Buddhist tradition in which he was brought up.

The Lord Buddha was born about five hundred years before Christ, at Lumbini in what is now Nepal. Given the racial mix in that part of the world, it is quite possible that he had some Tibetan blood. He was born into a minor royal family, though 'minor' is a relative term: the wealth and power of even a minor Indian potentate in those days was immense. Astrologers and soothsayers who were consulted at his birth foretold that he would be either a great secular leader or a great religious leader. His father, understandably, wanted him to succeed to the throne, and so the young Gautama was brought up shielded from any influences which might develop a religious inclination in him. In particular, he was shielded from any sign of old age, suffering, poverty, disease and death.

He was a young man already married, and the father of a son, when chance first showed him suffering in its various forms. Outside the palace he saw the suffering, the dying, and the dead. At first he did not understand what they were: even after he had been told, he did not know what to do about them. Then, he met a holy man and recognised in him the path that he should follow: only in a spiritual search would he find what he was looking for. He left his wife and child, left his luxurious palace, and became a wandering *saddhu* in the forests. Even today, many Indians follow this path; they are known in the West by many names, including *fakir,* but a word often used in India is *sannyasin,* 'follower' or 'seeker'.

For seven years, he followed the path of renunciation. Like Indian holy men to the present day, he begged for his food, symbolising his indifference to the world and his willingness to accept whatever it gave him. At the end of seven years, the world had proved so indifferent to Gautama that he was nearly dead from starvation and exhaustion. When he recovered consciousness after a long period of dead faint, he understood that this Way of renunciation was no better than the Way of luxury that he had abandoned. So, he set out upon a Middle Way, neither tormenting his body nor pandering to it. Only when the body was a fit vehicle for the mind, he reasoned, could the mind have free play.

He sat under the famous Bodhi tree at Bodh Gaya and meditated upon the nature of this Middle Way; and in May, five hundred and forty four years before the birth of Christ, he achieved realisation – or enlightenment, as it is sometimes called. He rose, and slowly walked southwards towards the holy city of Benares. By the time he had reached the Deer Park at Sarnath, just outside Benares and two hundred miles from Bodh Gaya, he had worked out a way of teaching.

The core of his teaching is simple. All sentient beings desire happiness and the causes of happiness, and want to avoid suffering and the cause of suffering. This is equally true of all beings, whether human or animal or even in the spirit realms. But existence is inextricably bound up with suffering: pain, discomfort, unhappiness, old age and death come to all of us, and poverty and disease are the lot of many. The first of the Four Noble Truths is therefore the Noble Truth of Suffering. This is also known as the Noble Truth of Pain, though a more accurate rendition than either would be the Noble Truth of Unsatisfactoriness – for no matter how well things are going, life is seldom wholly satisfactory, and even more seldom remains so for long.

The Noble Truth of the Cause of Suffering is the second of the Four Noble Truths. This states that pain and suffering, and indeed all unsatisfactoriness, are the product of our own will. 'Will' is normally translated as 'desire', but this is not very helpful; few people desire unhappiness and suffering. Traditionally, 'will' is divided into attraction, aversion, and indifference.

This requires a little explanation. All through our lives, we cling to what we want (or think we want) and desperately try to avoid what we do not want (or think we do not want). But, of course, we are all familiar with the person who spends more time and effort avoiding work than it would take to do the work itself, and with the person who is constantly striving for goals which everyone else can see will bring him no good at all. We all function at this level in some ways, and the ultimate expression of it is the ego. This is nothing more than a bundle of desires and aversions (and indifferences, often to what is most valuable), but to itself the ego is the last and most fundamental possession. Even after we die, the ego rolls on; this is what is reborn. It changes, of course, as the balance of desires and aversions changes, but it is the core of 'I'. If only we could rid ourselves of this bundle of desires and aversions, we would lose the ego, and then we could see ourselves for what we truly are: limitless and undifferentiated, the Clear White Light of Reality. This is what Gautama did, thereby becoming the Buddha or 'Enlightened One'.

The Noble Truth of the Cessation of Suffering, the third of the Four Noble Truths, is simple to grasp: it states that if we can get rid of the causes of suffering, which as we have seen are internal rather than external, then we can also rid ourselves of the suffering itself. The difficulty, though, comes in understanding the 'illusoriness' of suffering: surely, suffering is real. But there is a story of a disciple of the Buddha which shows how mental attitude affects suffering. He told the Buddha that he wanted to go and teach in an area where the natives were well known to be wild and cruel. The Buddha asked him what he would do if they laughed and ignored him, or jeered at him. "I shall be grateful," he said, "because at least they will not be attacking me." Next, the Buddha asked him what he would do if they did attack him, with fists and sticks. "I shall be grateful," he answered, "because they are not using swords and axes." "And if they use swords and axes?" asked the Buddha. "Then I shall be grateful that they do not kill me." "And if they kill you?" "Then I shall be grateful, because they will have liberated me from the Wheel of Suffering." The Lord Buddha smiled at him and gave him his blessing. "Go," he said. "You could teach anywhere." This may seem an extreme case, but perhaps Shakespeare put it more succinctly in *Hamlet:* "There is nothing either good or bad, but thinking makes it so."

The Noble Truth of the Way that Leads to the Cessation of Suffering is the last of the Four Noble Truths. This is the Eightfold Path of Buddhism, often represented as an eight-spoked wheel in which all spokes lead to the hub. The spokes are Right Understanding, Right Aspiration, Right Speech, Right Conduct, Right Vocation, Right Effort, Right Alertness and Right Concentration (sometimes translated as Right Absorption).

There are many thousands of commentaries on the nature of Buddhism, including several by the present and past Dalai Lamas, but even the brief summary given here is enough to show that Buddhism is not a religion in the conventional sense. It makes no mention of God, and, when the Lord Buddha was asked about God, he replied that he did not know anything about Him. What he did know was about suffering, and the means to be rid of it, and on that he was willing to teach all that he knew. He dealt with many other 'spiritual' questions in the same way.

When the first Dalai Lama was born, Buddhism was already close to two thousand years old. It had all but vanished in its native India when the Moslems invaded and established what was to become the Mogul empire, but it had been transmitted in its entirety into Tibet – the only country to receive the whole body of Buddhist thought at the peak of its development in India. There were innumerable schools and subdivisions, but three broad strands were detectable: the Hinayana, or Lesser Vehicle; the Mahayana, or Greater Vehicle; and the Vajrayana, or Thunderbolt Vehicle. The Fourteenth Dalai Lama quotes the old Tibetan saying:

> Outwardly, practice Hinayana
> Inwardly, practice Mayahana
> Secretly, practice Vajrayana.

Hinayana, also known as Theravada or 'the way of the Elders', is the oldest, simplest, and most direct form of Buddhism. As the Lord Buddha said, on his deathbed, to Ananda, his most faithful disciple, "All compound things decay; work out your own salvation with diligence." Only you can free yourself from the cycle of life and death, and ultimately each man and woman is responsible for his or her own destiny.

The Mahayana developed about five hundred years after the death of the Lord Buddha. Whilst it denied nothing in the Hinayana, it stressed the compassion of the Lord Buddha, and the way in which his teachings benefitted all sentient beings. The ideal of the Mahayana is the Boddhisatva, the Enlightened One who remains in the earthly realm to teach. He is still responsible only for his own enlightenment, but his vow is to help all others to achieve that enlightenment in whatever way he can, by teaching, by example, or what ever way is appropriate. It was this vow which caused Chenrezi's head to explode into a thousand fragments; it is this vow by which Tenzin Gyatso, the Fourteenth Dalai Lama, lives.

The Vajrayana is the least-known of the three schools. Outside Tibet, there is some awareness of it in Japan, and some Hindu sects have their own Vajrayana, but many Buddhists are unaware even of its existence. Even the translations of the word differ: 'Vajra' (*Dorje* in Tibetan) can be translated as 'Thunderbolt', 'Diamond' or 'Adamantine', so 'Vajrayana' is rendered as 'Thunderbolt Path', 'Diamond Vehicle', or 'Adamantine Way'. It is a secret path, involving the transmutation of everyday experience into mystical reality; there is much in it that can be described as 'magic'. Because of this, many scholars are all too willing to write it off as a 'corrupt' or 'degenerate' form of Buddhism – but those who study and practice it are aware of its virtues.

The greatest Tibetan Lamas (the word *Lama* means 'teacher') have almost always been masters of all three schools, and the Dalai Lama is regarded as the greatest of all Lamas. He is quick to point out, though, that there are many Lamas who know more than he does about certain rites. For example, there are the Tantric rites involving sexual union, which his monastic vows necessarily exclude. It is said, however, that the Sixth Dalai Lama, who never took his final vows, was well versed in this aspect of the Tantrayana.

Consequently, it is easy to see the complex pressures which bear upon the Dalai Lama. Heir to a highly intellectual but also compassionate system of ethics two and a half thousand years old, he embodies a religious tradition. His knowledge alone, as a result of the years of study, meditation and initiations, is worth libraries. This is all the more important in view of the two great waves of destruction that have been visited upon Buddhist libraries; first a thousand years ago by the Moguls and secondly, since 1950, by the Chinese communists. There were, in Lhasa, books written on palm leaves, perhaps one and a half thousand years old, brought from India by the sages who brought Buddhism to Tibet. No one knows whether they still exist – but it is known that the Chinese used sacred texts to line shoes, light fires, and as lavatory paper. The oral tradition to which the Dalai Lama is heir is invaluable in the wake of this destruction.

As well as bearing this immense academic and spiritual burden, His Holiness is also a head of state, and one who feels keenly both for the hundred thousand who have followed him into exile and for the six million or so who have remained in Tibet. Consequently, he describes his work as being on two levels; first, his work for the Tibetan people, and secondly, his work for the good of all beings. Quoting Buddhist teachings, he says, "May I remember that all sentient beings were, in countless past lives, my mother and my father; and may I never forget what I owe to them." In the light of all this, it would not be surprising if he were an other-worldly and unapproachable man, absorbed by turns in abstractions and affairs of state; but he is not. Instead, he is the most human and immediate of men, and herein lies our second paradox – a paradox which, upon examination, leads to the dissolution of paradoxes. It is precisely by reducing things to an immediate, human level that he makes apparently vast and insoluble problems approachable.

It is a well-known ploy of religious leaders to blame the evil state of the world for everything, without making much attempt to improve matters apart from issuing a few rules and dogmas. This is not the Dalai Lama's way. Instead, he works with what is already there. He does not ask you to make leaps of faith, or to accept preposterous dogmas. Instead, he points out what you want... what you already know... what other people want and know... and brings it all together in exactly the way, you feel, that the Lord Buddha would have done. He is not interested in conflict: rather, in common ground. Who would have expected, for example, that he would have been one of the main forces behind the creation of a Tibetan Communist Party in exile? But, as he says, the aims of the Lord Buddha and of Karl Marx are not incompatible. Both were concerned with bringing happiness to the masses, the Buddha with spiritual happiness and Marx with material happiness. Is it not reasonable, then, to see how the two might work together? Even if, after due consideration, it should appear that the two are incompatible, is not the understanding of each deepened and enriched by the understanding of the other?

Although this is, by any standards, a fairly major topic to consider, it illustrates very clearly the openness and the clarity of thought which characterise the present Dalai Lama. Not everyone is concerned with such intellectual matters though, and for those who are not he will bring that same penetrating insight and fearless questioning into play on less weighty matters. Often, this takes the form of humour. One of the adjectives which springs to mind when talking about his sense of humour is 'wicked', though somehow that seems inappropriate when referring to a Dalai Lama. For example, during the late 1970s a number of people were getting very worked up about a grand conjunction of the planets, when they were all going to be in a straight line. Astrologers were predicting everything from the Second Coming to World War Three, and at one public teaching, where there were many Western camp-followers present, someone asked what was going to happen.

His Holiness has a particular mannerism when asked a question which requires some thought. He will reply with a little "Hm!", after which you can see that he is thinking hard about the answer. The length of the silence varies; as a rule, the longer the silence, the better the answer. A really long silence means that it will not only be a superbly perceptive answer; it will also be extremely easy to understand and couched in the clearest and most precise language. On this occasion, the silence seemed as if it would never end. Several people found that they were holding their breath: the tension built to almost unbearable levels. Finally, he looked up and smiled. "Well," he said, "I think we'll just wait and see."

Of course, the whole idea of overthrowing preconceptions and of using 'crazy wisdom' is well established in many mystical traditions, including Sufism and Zen Buddhism, but when we asked His Holiness if this was a central part of his teaching he replied that it was not; there were many occasions when it was a good thing to overthrow preconceptions, but there were also many occasions when it was better to let preconceptions stand. You have to work with what is available; and with some people, it is easier to work via their preconceptions.

The matter of preconceptions, and of other people's ideas, naturally leads to the question which is asked again and again, concerning the Dalai Lama's supposed divinity. One of the standard descriptions in the press is that he is a 'God-King'. King he is, in a sense, but he parries the question about being a god with another question: "Well, look at me. I think I'm a man. What do you think?" It is not an evasive answer; as he points out, it really does not matter whether you think of him as a god or not, because he does not behave any differently. In fact, only a very few people think of him as a 'god' – as a Christian or Muslim or Jew might think of a god. A much more usual view among Tibetans would be that he is a Boddhisattva, one who has voluntarily remained on earth to teach after achieving enlightenment. Even this view can lead to some strange comments at times. One prominent Tibetan, well known for his dislike of the Chinese, said "It's all very well for His Holiness to talk about loving them – but he's a Bodhisattva. It's much more difficult for ordinary guys like us."

For those who press the point about his being an incarnation of Chenrezi, the Dalai Lama uses an analogy. He uses the word 'manifestation' rather than 'incarnation', and asks them to imagine the reflection of the moon in a pool. Do we imagine that the moon has left the heavens and taken up residence in the pool? Of course not. But do we deny that we can see the moon – just as clearly as if it were real – in the pool? Again, of course not. He says that he may be some sort of manifestation or reflection of Chenrezi, just as the moon in the pool is a manifestation of the moon; or alternatively, he may be especially blessed by Chenrezi.

To anyone unfamiliar with Buddhism, and especially with

Tibetan Buddhism, it is hard to see how a religion which appears to have no room for a supreme being or beings can have 'gods'. As the Lord Buddha himself said, he knew nothing about God, only about suffering, the causes of suffering, and the means of ending suffering. The answer is that the word 'God' does not mean the same in the Buddhist tradition as it does in the Judeo-Christian/ Islamic tradition (or indeed any other theistic tradition with 'supreme beings'). The Buddhist 'gods' represent aspects of our own consciousness, but by personifying them it is made easier to meditate upon them. For example, 'compassion' is an abstract concept, and very difficult to meditate upon; but Chenrezi is an embodiment of compassion, and by meditating upon his attributes we can begin to understand the abstract better. There is no need for religion to be made any more difficult than it is, and the Tibetan concept of the 'lam rim' or 'graded path' makes a lot of sense. We slowly work up, through levels of abstraction, until we come to the place where abstraction is unnecessary. Seen in this light, the concept of a Buddhist 'god' makes perfect sense. The word itself may not be too appropriate – a better term might be 'awareness-being', a term we have already used – but the concept is not complicated.

The reason that there are so many deities is that human beings are so complex, and different people will achieve different results from meditating upon different aspects of their characters. Even the most bizarre deities become comprehensible in this light; the fearsome Tam-Din (*Hayagriva* in Sanskrit) is a good example. He is the transmutation of Rudra, who lived in charnel-houses and on the mountain-tops where the bodies of the dead were offered to the birds. Rudra's meat was human flesh, and his drink was human blood; he was dressed in human skins, girded with human bones. He symbolised 'black-freedom' – the freedom to do whatever you wish, unconstrained by thoughts of good or evil. Rudra was subjugated by Chenrezi, and when he realised just what he had been, he offered his body as the symbol of transmuted 'black-freedom'.

There are countless other deities, both peaceful and wrathful, but few Tibetans will practice more than two or three of them. Because there are so many deities, the Lama or teacher is very important; he (or she) will suggest to a pupil the most appropriate deities to meditate upon, and give the requisite initiations. Again, 'initiation' has all kinds of unfortunate overtones in English, but it really only means learning a way of doing something. The reason that some initiations are secret is that they require certain preconditions; you would not expect someone who knew nothing about electronics to try to repair a television, because he would probably wreck the television and possibly kill himself. Buddhism has been described as a 'science of the mind' – and if you are working on your mind you are (to use the same analogy) both the television and the repair man. The often-stated possibility that madness awaits the inexperienced practitioner is not the main reason why some practices are secret; a much more serious problem in most cases is simply going off course, and having to do a great deal of work to get back on course again.

There is, admittedly, a strong flavour of magic and sorcery in Tibetan Buddhism. This is due partly to the influence of Bön, the native animist tradition of Tibet, and partly to the Buddhist traditions themselves. According to orthodox Tibetan beliefs, Buddhism was effectively introduced into Tibet by an Indian teacher called Padmasambhava, or 'The Lotus Born'. He is so important in Tibet that he is known as Guru Rinpoche, or 'Precious Teacher'. When a previous Buddhist missionary had failed to subdue the demons that opposed him in Tibet, Guru Rinpoche was sent. By spectacular displays of magical powers, as well as by his immense knowledge of the *Dharma* (the body of Buddhist teaching), he overcame all opposition and firmly established Buddhism. This was in AD 747.

Since that time, magic has played an important part in Tibetan life, and 'Ngakpa' or 'Sorcerer' is a recognised title. In Dharamsala there is a well respected teacher called Lama Yeshe Dorje Rinpoche, who is widely known as 'Ngakpa-la' or 'Ngakpa Rinpoche' ('-la' is the standard Tibetan honorific, and the word 'Rinpoche', meaning 'Precious', is the normal way of referring to an incarnate Lama). One of his special skills is weather control, and during the hard and drawn-out winter of 1981-2 there were many complaints about the fact that he had been called away to Nepal by Dudjom Rinpoche, the head of his Nyingma order. "If only Ngakpa-la were here," was the general opinion, "we should never have weather like this." Of course, all these tales of magic are normally only reported at second- or third- or fourth-hand. But, while we were writing this book, we had one experience which was, if not conclusive, then at least persuasive. It happened at Tso-Pema ('Lotus Lake') at Rewalsar in Northern India. It is said that Guru Rinpoche meditated there, and that a local king who was either frightened or jealous of his powers ordered that he should be burned alive. An immense pyre was constructed, with Guru Rinpoche in the middle. When the flames were roaring, he magically transformed the pyre into the lake which is still there today. He, appropriately, was sitting on a lotus in the middle.

Every year, the Nyingma monastery at Tso-Pema holds *Cham* or Lama-dances at a Guru Rinpoche festival. During the festival, a little floating reed-island at the side of the lake detaches itself and circumnavigates the lake, moving in the same direction as the pilgrims on the shore. When it touches the side, the pilgrims throw *kata* onto it – the white presentation scarves called 'robes of the gods'. There is a good deal of pushing and shoving, and some people fall in. It does not look as if there is any way that the island could be propelled by a hidden swimmer or any other means. This alone is remarkable, but the weather was still more so. The morning of the *Cham* dances dawned cold and grey and wet. We expressed some alarm to the Lama who was with us. He said that there was no need to worry, because it would not rain during the dances.

And it did not. It rained before the dances, and it rained between the dances, and it rained after the dances, very convincingly and wetly. But it did not rain during the dances. Nor was it a question of the dancers coming out between showers. The dance cycle lasts for some hours, and each dance has a distinct beginning, middle and end. If there was a change from a simple costume to an elaborate one, taking several minutes, it would rain during the change and then stop when the dancers reappeared. If it was a quick change, the shower was correspondingly short.

This is one of those things which is so extraordinary that after a while we began to wonder whether memory was at fault – perhaps it rained a little bit during the dances, and we did not notice. But no. We were taking pictures all the way through, and neither Nikons nor Hasselblads take very kindly to getting wet. Besides, although the ground is wet, there is no rain in the pictures.

When questioned about magic the Dalai Lama seems curiously uninterested. "Yes", he says, "there are things which appear to be magical, but they are not very important". He has himself done things which appear to be magical, but he does not consider that important either. At first, this in infuriating, but after a while what he says begins to make sense. If the world is a fabrication of perception, an illusion, as Buddhism teaches, then why should it not be possibe to see things differently? Why should we not see things that are strange, or magical? And for a tale of magic, it is hard to surpass the story of the discovery of the present Dalai Lama, at the age of two, in Eastern Tibet.

2

The Discovery of the Dalai Lama

On the thirtieth day of the tenth month of the Water Bird year, 1933 in the Western reckoning, His Holiness the Great Thirteenth Dalai Lama passed to the Honourable Fields. He was nearly sixty years old, and under his rule Tibet had become a united and independent country.

When ordinary people die, they spend some time in the *Bardo* or between-life state, before their inability to free themselves from the wheel of existence causes them to take rebirth. They may do this in a human form, or in an animal form, or in one of the many other spirit forms, according to the lessons they need to learn and as a result of their *karma*. A Bodhisattva, on the other hand, is free of that wheel; he returns only to help others. As a Bodhisattva, the Dalai Lama would choose the time and place of his rebirth; and unlike other people, it would be a reincarnation of his previous self rather than a rebirth of his ego.

During his lifetime, the Great Thirteenth had left signs indicating that he might take rebirth in the north-east, though these were far from conclusive. Besides, Tibet is a big country, and the majority of the population live in the provinces of Kham and Amdo, to the north-east of Lhasa. After his death, more omens came to light. When a great Lama dies, his body often remains in the posture of meditation which it had when he died, and corruption and decay do not seem to begin: this is known as the State of Clear Light. When the Great Thirteenth's body was in a State of Clear Light, the head twisted around overnight to face the north-east. There were also signs in the north-eastern sky: rainbows, and clouds resembling elephants. A dragon-flower appeared from the direction of the stairway on the north-east side of the main courtyard of the Potala, the courtyard that was used for monastic debate, and a star-shaped fungus appeared on a wooden pillar in the chamber housing the *chörten* built to honour the memory of the Great Thirteenth. It was on the north-east side of the chamber and it could still be seen when the Fourteenth Dalai Lama left Tibet in 1959.

In the nature of things it would take time before the new incarnation could be found, and even then there would be long years of study and growing up before he was ready to rule the Land of Snows. At the death of the Great Thirteenth, a regent was appointed, and it was he who took responsibility for the search for the Fourteenth Dalai Lama. After he had carefully noted all the signs that had already been given, the Regent went to the lake of Lhamo Namtso in the Wood Pig year (1935). It is about ninety miles to the south-east of Lhasa, in the Chokhorgyal area, and it was recognised by the Second Dalai Lama as a place of great importance for Tibet because it is associated with Palden Lhamo Remati, a great protective deity. In the waters, adepts could see visions of what was to come. Sir Charles Bell gives an account of how such visions appear in his superb (but now almost unobtainable) book about the Great Thirteenth, *Portrait of the Dalai Lama,* as recounted by a Tibetan who had been there:

"The water of the lake is blue. You watch it from the hillside. A wind arises, and turns the blue water into white. A hole forms in this white water; the hole is blue-black. Clouds form above this hole, and below the clouds you see images showing future events."

The idea of going to such a place with the express purpose of seeing a vision was typical of Tibet, where magic was regarded as one of the natural sciences. First, the Regent saw the Tibetan letters *Ah, Ka* and *Ma.* Then he saw a vision of a monastery with roofs of gold and copper, with a twisting road leading to a mountain nearby. Where the road met the mountain, there was a small house with distinctive carved and blue-painted gable-ends. Nearby was a peach-tree in bloom, and a woman with a baby in her arms; the Regent knew that the baby was the Fourteenth Dalai Lama. The vision was recorded, and a copy was placed under seal so that it could not subsequently be tampered with. Armed with the information from the vision, the Regent next consulted the oracle at Samye. Oracles were widespread in Tibet: they saw the future in a mirror, sometimes called a breast-plate. The oracle at Samye was in little doubt: he actually gave his mirror to the party that had been formed to search the north-east, under the leadership of Lama Keutsang Rinpoche. To be on the safe side, and perhaps with an eye to confusing the Chinese (who still occupied parts of Eastern Tibet), two other parties were also despatched, one to the east and one to the south-east.

Each of the search parties took with them possessions of the Great Thirteenth, together with near-duplicates of these possessions that had not belonged to the previous body. Lama Keutsang Rinpoche's party had two rosaries, one yellow and one black; two walking-sticks, one with an iron handle and one with a bronze handle; and two *damarus,* or small ritual drums. One was a plain but beautiful ivory drum that had belonged to the Great Thirteenth, and the other was magnificently ornamented with a design of many kinds of flowers, and bound with variegated silks.

They set out in the Fire Rat year (1936). On the morning of their departure, they were confronted with knee-deep snow that had fallen during the night; but it all melted by nine in the morning. Both the snowfall and its swift disappearance were taken as good omens.

From Lhasa they passed through Bromh, and Kagritramo, and came to Nakchu Dzong where they spent ten days gathering supplies. A *dzong* is literally a fort, but it was the normal form of administrative centre for a region, a massive combination of fortress, city hall, monastery, and treasury. *Dzongs* dominated many hilltops in old Tibet, but as foci for the resistance they were prime targets for Chinese artillery. Most of those that were not destroyed in the fighting were destroyed later; some were a thousand and more years old. Continuing to the north-east, the searchers passed Sog Tseden monastery before crossing four passes in the Mala mountains. Heavy snowfalls slowed them down, but were regarded as good omens; after all, Tibet is the Land of Snows. On the twenty-ninth day of the twelfth month, over three years after the death of the Great Thirteenth, they arrived in Jye-kun-do, the home of the Panchen Lama. The Panchen Lama is regarded in many ways as the second most important lama in Tibet, after the Dalai Lama, and in several lifetimes they had been alternately teacher and pupil: the young Dalai Lama would be instructed by the Panchen Lama, and would then in his turn instruct the new Panchen Lama.

The Panchen Lama gave them an audience on the second day of the first month of the Fire Musk Deer year, which was early in 1937. He gave them the names of three young boys he had heard of who might possibly be the new incarnation, all of whom lived near Kumbum monastery with its distinctive roofs and cupolas of copper and gold. The first name on the list proved to belong to a child who had died; the second was still alive, but ran off crying as soon as he saw the search party; and the third lived in the remote village of Pari Takster, in a single-storied house with blue gable-ends at the end of a long and winding road beneath a mountain.

With mounting excitement, the search party realised that they might have found the new Dalai Lama. Accordingly, a detachment from the main party set out for the house. To improve secrecy, Lama Keutsang Rinpoche disguised himself as a servant, whilst a lesser official called Tsedrung Lobsang Tsewang took his place as leader. They found that the road was not an easy one, and that there was a choice between an upper path and a lower one. They chose the upper one, but a Chinese youth that they met just after they had set out told them that the lower one was better. It turned out to be much longer, but they arrived at the front of the house rather than at the back, which was of course more auspicious. Years later, when the official history of the search was being compiled, one of those who had been on it said, "We had a strange notion that the youth might have been a celestial being."

The house itself turned out to correspond perfectly to the Regent's description: square, one-storied, with distinctive blue eaves and a slate roof. Furthermore, there was a peach-tree in bloom nearby, although it was unseasonably early. As protocol required, the family itself received the leader of the group – the disguised Tsedrung Lobsang Tsewang. The 'servants', including Lama Keutsang Rinpoche, were taken into the kitchen to be fed with the other servants. As Keutsang Rinpoche walked into the kitchen a small boy was playing in there. As soon as the child saw the Lama, he ran to him shouting "Lama! Lama!", despite the fact that the Rinpoche was in disguise and the word 'Lama' is 'Aga' in the Amdo dialect, which was the language of the area and which was always spoken in the boy's house. Seating himself in the Lama's lap, he grabbed a rosary which had belonged to the Great Thirteenth before it had been given to Keutsang Rinpoche. "This is mine", he said, "please may I have it?" The Rinpoche told him that he could have it if he could guess who his visitor was, and the child replied, "Sera-aga". Sera, one of the three great monasteries near Lhasa, was indeed where Keutsang Rinpoche had come from.

When it was time to go, the little boy wanted to go with them. He had often told his parents that he was going to Lhasa, even at that tender age, and he used to straddle a window-sill and pretend that he was riding a horse to the capital. His parents had always thought that he was rather special, and they suspected that he might be an Incarnate Lama; they already had one son who had been Recognised and was installed at a nearby monastery. They thought, though, that he might be the reincarnation of a Tulku (Incarnate Lama) from Kumbum; they had no idea that he might even be the Dalai Lama himself.

The search party stayed nearby and sent for the others, as only a small party had originally gone to the house at Pari Takster. When they arrived, they began the tests. First, they presented him with both sets of rosaries, damarus, and walking-sticks, doggedly trying to conceal their excitement. The child did not hesitate over the rosaries or damarus, even though the 'wrong' damaru was much more brightly coloured and more likely to appeal to a child. With the walking sticks, though, he appeared less certain. He held one, and then the other; but eventually he chose the right one. It was only later that the search party found that *both* walking sticks had belonged to the Thirteenth Dalai Lama, and that the one over which the child had lingered before rejecting it in favour of the other had been used for a short time by the Great Thirteenth before he gave it to someone else, who had in turn passed it on before it came into Keutsang Rinpoche's hands.

Now the letters *Ah, Ka,* and *Ma* became clear. *Ah* was for Amdo, the province in which the village of Pari Takster lay. *Ka* and *Ma* could be taken to refer either to the monastery nearest the village, Karma Rolpai Dorje, or to the very much larger monasery of Kumbum nearby. To derive 'Kumbum' from 'Ka' and 'Ma' may seem a little far-fetched in the English transliteration, but in the original Tibetan orthography, with its silent letters and subscripted vowels, it is perfectly clear.

A physical examination revealed further signs traditionally associated with the Dalai Lama; a mark like a conch shell on the skin, for example, and two small bumps of flesh beneath the shoulder-blades which represent the two extra arms with which Chenrezi is often shown. He was just two years old, having been born in the Wood Pig year – the same year as the Regent had seen his vision in the lake at Chokhorgyal – so he was the right age. He was able to understand, and even to speak, the Lhasa dialect which would have been familiar to the Great Thirteenth, but which he would never have heard spoken at home. And he was already, at the age of two, beginning to show that extraordinary composure which everyone remarked upon during the long ceremonies which attended his arrival in Lhasa. It was not that he was particularly quiet or reserved; it was just that he was very self-possessed.

Despite all the evidence, the search party still hesitated to proclaim that he was the Fourteenth Dalai Lama. There were two good reasons for this. The first was that they were, after all, only a search party: they lacked the authority to make the official proclamation. The second was that parts of Amdo, including the village of Pari Takster, were still under Chinese influence. When the Chinese were driven out of Tibet in 1912, as will be recounted later, the far east of the country had not been completely freed. Representing as it did the western fringes of the Celestial Empire, it remained in a sort of no man's land, where the governors were warlords of a type who would not have been out of place a thousand years before. Ma Bu Feng, a Chinese Moslem, was the local warlord, and like most of his kind he was keenly alive to personal advantage. If he realised that he had the Dalai Lama in his power, there was no telling what he might do.

If you ask His Holiness about all this, and about the memories from his previous lives which were apparently carried over into his present life, he will say that quite honestly he does not remember very much even of his life as a child, much less events from his previous life. He explains that memories of the previous life are keenest when you are a child, but that they fade just as childhood memories do. When he was a child, there were several incidents which pointed to a memory of previous lives (especially as the Great Thirteenth); but like most people's childhood stories he now remembers these better from other people's telling than from his own memory. One amusing story concerns his insistence, when he got to Lhasa, that a certain box contained his teeth. When the box was opened, it contained a set of false teeth that had belonged to the

Great Thirteenth. Somehow, an example like that is much more convincing than a more obviously magical or mystical one.

The Dalai Lama says that it would theoretically be possible for him to trace his life backwards, meditating upon each breath, and thus to go back into previous lives; but he adds that it would be very difficult and time-consuming, and that there are more important things to do. This makes some Western investigators furious, but it illustrates again the paradoxes of his life. Although he is committed, like all Boddhisattvas, to the good of all sentient beings, he feels that there are better ways he can serve them than by conducting psychic experiments. Although the most public and open of teachers, he also has his own way of doing things.

Before describing how the Dalai Lama was taken from Amdo to Lhasa, how the Chinese governor was bribed to let him go, and how he was formally recognised as the Holder of the White Lotus, it is worthwhile tracing his spiritual ancestry, his previous thirteen lives, and the history of the nation of which he was to become head.

Great Ocean of Wisdom

Tibetans have a tremendous respect for the written word; it is all but sacred. In addition to Buddhist texts dating back to the first millenium AD, the great Tibetan libraries also had records of Tibetan history and of the Dalai Lamas. Now, many of the books they housed have been destroyed, looted, or lost by the Chinese invaders; but until 1959, it was perfectly easy to trace back the history of the Dalai Lamas to the first incarnation, in 1391. Enough information survives to reconstruct this history, but a great deal of it is now only available in modern books published outside Tibet in the eighteenth to twentieth centuries.

In order to understand the political structure of Tibet, one has to go back well beyond the time of the First Dalai Lama. A good starting point is the seventh century AD, when Tibet was a great military power. A succession of kings, the most famous of whom was Srongtsen Gampo, expanded Tibet far beyond her present borders, down into India in the south and into China in the east. The Chinese Emperor was then a tributary of Tibet, and on one occasion he was forced by a Tibetan punitive expedition to flee his own capital when China failed to pay Tibet the annual tribute of 10,000 rolls of silk. This incident puts an amusing twist on the Chinese claims for 'historical' dominance over Tibet.

King Srongtsen Gampo took several wives, among them a Nepalese princess and, in 641 AD, a Chinese princess. It was these two girls who introduced Buddhism to the Tibetan court. For the Chinese princess in particular, the familiar religion must have been a great comfort. She had been brought up with every luxury, and being sent as a political bride to a far Western kingdom must have been hard for her. Although there had probably been isolated Buddhist communities in Tibet for five hundred years or more, it was the adoption of Buddhism as the court religion which marked the real beginning of its spread. This culminated in the arrival of

Guru Rinpoche a hundred years later, in 747 AD, when he travelled throughout Tibet subduing demons and performing great feats of magic; by the end of the eighth century, the native Bön religion had to a great extent been supplanted by Buddhism. It was never replaced entirely, though, and there was very little of the bitter religious war which has marked the progress of so many other religions; in fact, Bön survives to this day, and the Bönpo have an equal say in Tibetan affairs with the heads of the four Buddhist religious schools.

With the spread of Buddhism, a wonderful thing happened. As the Tibetan saying has it, the previously warlike Tibetans 'laid their weapons at the foot of the Lotus Throne' – the throne of the Lord Buddha – and forswore the arts of war. It was not an immediate once and for all act by the whole of the country, but it gradually spread until by the end of the tenth century Tibet had withdrawn from its Chinese and Indian territories and remained within something like its present boundaries to practise the Way of the Buddha. They did not entirely forget their military past, and no one dared to invade them, but they were no longer an expansionist people. Even so, there was an annual pageant in Lhasa right up to the Chinese invasion, commemorating those days of military glory. The Tibetan army would dress in the military outfits of the past, including thousand-year-old armour stored in the Potala, and perform manoeuvres and feats of horsemanship.

The next two or three centuries were essentially isolationist, but because Tibetans have always been great travellers there was still considerable dealing between Tibet, Mongolia, and China. This was the age of Ghenghis Khan, the greatest of all the Mongol warlords; but, from the Tibetan records, a very different picture of him emerges from the conventional image. Most historical sources are either Persian or Chinese, both of whom scorned the Mongols as barbarians and were soundly beaten by them. Consequently, the innumerable stories of Mongol atrocities should be viewed with some suspicion. Tibetan sources show Genghis Khan as a harsh opponent, but just and indeed open-minded; they tell of how he summoned representatives of all the world's religions to his court, in a bid to determine which religion was best. There were Confucians, Taoists, Moslems, members of the various Buddhist schools and Christian orders, and so on, including magicians and shamans from both Tibet and Mongolia. He made no threats; it was simply a matter of inquiry. The story is that the Tibetan Buddhists won the day by telling the Khan to sit in his favourite chair, with a cup of his favourite brew beside him. Then they made the cup rise to his lips, without anyone touching it...

Regardless of what actually happened – though given the nature of Tibetan sorcery, the story really does not sound too unlikely – the Mongols and Tibetans thereafter enjoyed a unique priest–patron relationship, in which the Tibetans looked after the spiritual welfare of the Mongols, and the Mongols looked after the material well-being of the Tibetans. The Mongol lords made generous gifts to Tibetan monasteries and guaranteed the internal security of Tibet; and although there was a certain amount of jockeying for local secular power among Tibetan princelings, Tibet enjoyed a relatively stable religious climate in which the Dharma flourished. This priest–patron relationship was to crop up again and again throughout Tibetan history, sometimes to their advantage and sometimes to their detriment.

It was into this milieu that the First Dalai Lama was born, in the year 1391 of the Western calendar. From the day of his birth, miraculous things happened. He was born to very poor parents, in the bleak and inhospitable highlands of Western Tibet, and the very night after he was born robbers raided the poor hovel in which the family lived. His mother could not carry all her children, and so she hid the newest born between some rocks; she did not expect to see him alive again. The robbers found little enough to take, just a yak for a meal, and the parents were able to return the next day. Astonishingly, the child was still alive; and still more astonishingly, a great black crow stood guard over him. Anyone who knows the ways of crows will shudder at this story; it is no empty country tale that they peck the eyes from new-born lambs, and wait for them to die. But this was no ordinary crow. It was a manifestation of Palden Lhamo, the great protective deity of Tibet, also known as Maha Kali or the Great Black One. Her presence was echoed centuries later, when, just after the birth of the Fourteenth Dalai Lama, a pair of crows nested in the roof of his parents' house.

The child who so miraculously survived was given the name Pema Dorje, or Lotus Thunderbolt. He was a strong and healthy boy, but he was also very much interested in religion; when his father died he was still very young, but he composed a book of prayers to help his father's spirit in the Bardo state. Predictably, he became a monk; after many years of study, he visited Tsong-Khapa, the 'Great Reviver' of Tibetan Buddhism. It was Tsong-Khapa who founded the reformed 'Yellow Hat' school of Tibetan Buddhism, or Gelugpa: this was the fourth and last of the major schools extant today to be founded, after the Nyingma (Ancient Ones), Kagyud, and Sakya. Tsong-Khapa presented him with one of his own *shemtabs* or monastic skirts: then and now, giving a pupil an article of clothing was a mark of high regard.

Because of his immense energy, as well as his *Siddhis* or spiritual accomplishments, Pema Dorje became known as Gedun Drub. *Gedun* is a contraction of *Gyewa Dunpa,* and means 'one who desires virtuous ends' or 'one who performs virtuous acts', and corresponds to the Sanskrit words *Sangha,* the 'community of Buddhists'. *Drub* means 'brought to perfection' or 'completed', so the whole name might be read (in Bell's words) as 'The Perfecter of the Priesthood'.

It was during Gedun Drub's lifetime that many of the great monasteries of Tibet were founded, including perhaps the four greatest. He founded Tashi Lhunpo, the 'Mount of Good Auspices' himself in the early fifteenth century, and the three other great monasteries near Lhasa were contemporaneous. Ganden, 'The Joyous', was founded in 1409; Drepung, 'The Rice Heap', in 1416, and Sera, 'The Hailstorm', in 1419. Gedun Drub was the first High Lama of Drepung, which grew to become the biggest monastery in the world: at the time of the Chinese invasion, it housed over seven thousand seven hundred monks. It was a time of tremendous religious research and practice, and Gedun Drub was one of the leading figures of the time. After a long and noble life, "he showed the method of going beyond sorrow", as his biographers put it. He was recognised as having attained realisation, or Buddha-hood, and he was interred at his own Tashi Lhunpo.

In 1475 a child was born who seemed uncannily mature; he seemingly had memories of a past life, and was able to recognise things he had never seen before. Although the older sects – the Nyingma, Kagyud, and Sakya – had already accepted the possibility that a great teacher might reincarnate as a Tulku or Incarnate Lama, the Gelugpa had not until then done so. But the child seemed so

clearly to be a reincarnation of Gedun Drub that he was declared to
be his successor; under the name of Gedun Gyatso, he was installed
as the High Lama of Drepung. The name 'Gyatso', spelled in the
orthodox transliteration rGya–mtsho, means 'Ocean'; it has
subsequently been borne by all Dalai Lamas.

The choosing of successors by recognition of their reincarnation
is so alien to Western thought – and indeed to many schools of
Eastern thought – that it has been widely questioned and even
attacked. There have been two major objections; the first that
rebirth is simply impossible, and the second that the system is both
inherently uncertain, and open to abuse and exploitation.

The first objection is to a certain extent a matter of belief, but as
the story of the discovery of the present Dalai Lama shows, there is a
great deal of circumstantial evidence to support the idea of
reincarnation. Similar stories are told of the discovery of previous
Dalai Lamas, and of other high Lamas. A particularly interesting
story concerns the reincarnation of Ngari Rinpoche. In his previous
incarnation, he and the Great Thirteenth Dalai Lama were very
close, but they did not meet in the period immediately preceding
the death of the Great Thirteenth. In his last letter to his friend, the
Dalai Lama expressed his regrets that they would not meet again in
that lifetime, but added that in their next lives they would be very
close. The present Ngari Rinpoche is His Holiness's youngest
brother.

But there is more to it than this. The Great Mother (as His
Holiness's mother is known) lost many children in their infancy;
child mortality was high in Tibet. One who died, though, was
special; it was predicted by a Lama whom the family called in to
perform the funeral rites that he would be reborn again to the Great
Mother, and the body of the dead baby was marked with a smear of
butter. The next child was born with a streak which corresponded
exactly to that smear of butter – and it can still be seen today, though
Ngari Rinpoche is understandably modest about showing it.

The second objection to reincarnation is much stronger. Even the
Dalai Lama has said that perhaps fifty per cent of the incarnations
who were 'recognised' were not correctly identified, though he
adds quickly that no one knows, and it may be presumptuous of
him to make that judgement. His youngest brother, Ngari
Rinpoche, is one of the strongest critics of the system. He feels that

it is very convenient for the administrators of a monastery to choose as their leader a small child, whose education they can control, and whom they can influence in innumerable subtle and not so subtle ways. It was also the custom for an Incarnate Lama to have a 'business manager', as we have already seen, to administer his monasteries and estates; and the possibilities for self-enrichment there were immense. When he was twenty-five, Ngari Rinpoche put off his monk's robes and announced that henceforth he was to be known by his given name of Tendzin Choegyal; now he gets rather annoyed if people refer to him as Ngari Rinpoche. He neither admits nor denies being a Tulku, but he does say that he was not cut out to be a Lama.

Even Tendzin Choegyal agrees, though, that there is no doubt about the succession of His Holiness, or of certain other High Lamas; the only objection is that the whole system is – or at least, was – carried to extremes. A point to which the Dalai Lama and many other Tibetans repeatedly returned in interviews was that Tibetans are too bound by tradition. If something has worked in the past, or in one place, it is expected to work again, and in another place. A tradition rapidly becomes a custom, and a custom rapidly becomes an inflexible rule.

This is where the institution of Dalai Lama exhibits one of its most interesting paradoxes. As the supreme embodiment of the system, one might expect the Dalai Lama to be its strongest supporter but this is totally untrue of the present Dalai Lama, and of the Great Thirteenth, and of many of their predecessors. His Holiness freely states that there was a great deal that he was unhappy with in the old Tibet, and that there were many things that he wanted to change. The trouble was that he was caught between the tradition-bound monasteries on the one hand, and the Chinese on the other. He feels that he was kept too remote from his people, and he knows that the Chinese blocked many of his projected reforms because they would have been far more popular than the changes that the invaders were trying to enforce. Some, such as the scheme the Great Thirteenth had proposed for conscripting monks into the army, would have posed a direct threat; others, such as the land reforms which would have given the peasants tenure directly in fee of the Government instead of under great landlords, were simply too extreme for them. It would have been hard to rail against a 'reactionary clique' that actually gave the land to the peasants, and let them keep the produce.

To return to the days of the second Dalai Lama, though, the only unifying force in Tibet was religion. The Mongol Yuan dynasty had fallen in 1368, and the Ming dynasty ruled China. The status of Tibet was uncertain; it still had Mongol support, and the Chinese lacked the coordination to make any claims, but the internal political situation was fragmented. Inevitably, anyone with political ambitions on any scale allied himself with some Buddhist sect or prelate; then, as now, religion lent a tinge of respectability to the power struggles. This led to the unfortunate 'religious wars', which were conflicts between the nominal followers of the various schools rather than between the schools themselves – though there were, of course, some monks and others who became involved. At the fall of the Yuan dynasty, the Sakya sect came into the ascendancy for a while, but by the end of the fifteenth century the Kagyudpa were more to the fore. More than once there were clashes between those bearing the Kagyud and the Sakya banners, though the Nyingma and the Gelugpa mostly stayed out of politics. Nevertheless, there was a general decline in respect for the priesthood.

Gedun Gyatso was instrumental in keeping the Gelugpa above all this, working in the tradition of Gedun Drub and ultimately of Tsong-Khapa, enforcing strict monastic discipline, and consolidating the religious organisation that he headed. His life was totally dedicated to the priesthood, and when he went beyond sorrow at the age of fifty the Gelugpa were the spiritual vanguard of Tibetan Buddhism.

His successor, Sonam Gyatso, was born in 1543. Seeing the parlous state into which Tibet had sunk, he did his best to revive the priest-patron relationship which had existed between Tibet and Mongolia in the days of Genghis Khan. There were no Mongol leaders of that stature any more, but there were still some mighty warlords in Mongolia, and one of the greatest was Altan Khan. Furthermore, the Mongols still looked to the Tibetans for their spiritual mentors, and so it was that Sonam Gyatso arranged a meeting on the shores of the Kokonor lake in 1578.

It was an occasion of vivid and oriental splendour, the Tibetans in their yellow silk robes and Chinese embroideries, and the Khan surrounded by fierce and shaggy warriors, armed to the teeth and clad in strange armour. Swords stayed in their sheaths, though: it was a meeting of peace, and a moment of great historical importance. In the thin air, under the blue sky and beside the blue lake, the two great leaders, one spiritual and the other temporal, exchanged titles according to the custom of the time. Sonam Gyatso read the Khan's title first: *Chos-ki Gyalpo Ha'i Tshang-pa*, King of Religion, Majestic Purity. Then the Mongol bowed before the Tibetan, and called him the Dalai Lama, the Great Ocean Teacher. As a matter of interest, 'Dalai' is not the best rendition of the Mongol word. 'Talai', or even 'Tully', might be better, but 'Dalai' is so well established that it is more convenient to use this spelling. Rather confusingly, the new title was retrospectively applied to Gedun Drub and Gedun Gyatso, so Sonam Gyatso was the Third Dalai Lama. He was also the first Dalai Lama to involve himself in politics, even though he may have seen his actions as merely a way of stabilising Tibet and of reinforcing the old bonds with the Mongols. Certainly he did very little more in the secular field, and spent much of the rest of his life travelling and teaching among the Mongols.

Nevertheless, the consequences were far-reaching. Altan Khan and other Mongol leaders made rich and repeated gifts to Tibetan monasteries, and the Tibetans in return supplied many Lamas to the Mongols. The Ming dynasty had consolidated its position to such an extent that it might have been a threat to Tibet, but the re-emergence of Mongol allies made the Celestial Court wary of taking on the Land of Snows. Instead, Altan Khan acted as a mediator between the two nations, and even arranged for the Third Dalai Lama to meet the Son of Heaven (as the Chinese emperor was known) in 1588. Unfortunately, Sonam Gyatso passed to the Honourable Fields just before the meeting was due to take place, and so passed a chance which might have changed the course of Tibetan history.

His apparently untimely death is a great puzzle in the light of the Tibetan belief that the Dalai Lama can choose the length of his own life. On the other hand, the same reasoning says that a Bodhisattva will undoubtedly know things that are beyond the knowledge of ordinary men, and so will act accordingly. A particularly interesting example is the going beyond sorrow of the Great Thirteenth. Many say that he chose to pass to the Honourable Fields much earlier than he would otherwise have done, because he saw that his people's refusal to adopt the reforms that he advocated would result in a Chinese invasion, and he wanted the new incarnation to be young and strong in order to lead the Tibetan people through the years of tribulation that would follow. The Fourteenth Dalai Lama was fifteen when the Chinese invaded in 1950; had the Great Thirteenth lived instead, he would have been seventy-four years old.

Be that as it may, the Fourth Dalai Lama was born in 1589. Astonishingly, he was not Tibetan. Instead, the Inmost One took rebirth as a Mongol, the grandson of Altan Khan; he was known as Yon-tan Gyatso. Although some people have suggested that this was not a true reincarnation at all, but a blatant piece of political chicanery, there is no reason why that should have been so. As a result of the travels of the Third Dalai Lama, there were possibly more Mongol Buddhists than Tibetan; and there is no reason why the Dalai Lama should not take rebirth outside Tibet.

This raises the whole question of reincarnations outside Tibet, and it was a subject we were eager to ask the Dalai Lama about. There have been several reports of Tulkus taking rebirth in the West, and being recognised, and we wondered how genuine these reports were. Whilst His Holiness would neither confirm nor deny these incarnations, saying that the recognition was a matter for the sects and lineages concerned and that he had neither the time nor the opportunity to investigate them personally, he did say that there was no reason why such reincarnations should not occur and that they may in fact be necessary to the spread of Buddhism. Intriguingly, he added that he thinks that such reincarnations have already taken place, but he would not go into details.

The Fourth Dalai Lama was escorted to Lhasa in 1601 by a huge retinue of both Tibetans and Mongolians, and installed once more as the High Lama of Drepung. The massive Mongolian presence consolidated still further the temporal authority of the Dalai Lama, and by extension the authority of the political factions supporting the Gelugpa. Some of the supporters of the other schools were very unhappy about this, especially those who had thrown their weight behind the Karmapa, the head of the Karma Kagyud school.

Consequently, the beginning of the seventeenth century was marked by a great deal of squabbling and infighting between various powerful families and minor princes. The most dangerous of these disputes, and one which brought Tibet almost to civil war, was between the King of Tsang (in Western and Central Tibet) and the Phag-mo-gru family. The Phag-mo-gru had been staunch supporters of the Third Dalai Lama, and their allegiance went also to the Fourth, but the King of Tsang was worried about the growing Mongol influence. It may also have been that he had Bönpo supporters, for the old religion had always been strong in that area. He was ready to go to war to protect his own power and position, as well as to cut down the secular influence of the Dalai Lama. He was just one of the strongest princelings in a country in turmoil, and it was only the fact that no one trusted anyone else well enough to make any meaningful alliances that stopped the general free-for-all from turning into a full-fledged civil conflict.

Yontan Gyatso was still a very young man, in his late teens, when all this was brewing. Little is known about him outside the official biography, which like most of the official Tibetan biographies of Dalai Lamas concentrates almost exclusively on his religious practices; but it seems that he was either unable or unwilling to become involved in politics to the extent that was necessary. What is known is that he passed to the Honourable Fields in 1616, at the age of twenty-six. Some say that he was poisoned, but others say that he had decided that he had done all that he could. In order to understand this, and the short lives of some of the other Dalai Lamas who were to follow, it is essential to adjust one's mental framework considerably: here is a leader without political ambition, perhaps gifted with greater foresight than other people, who can reincarnate if that is the most suitable course of action. It does not matter whether outsiders believe all this; it is the framework within which the Dalai Lama operates.

The Fifth Dalai Lama, normally called the Great Fifth, was born at Chong-gyal in 1617 and took the name Ngawang Lobsang Gyatso. After his recognition, the Mongol warlords came to pay homage; but even though the new Holder of the White Lotus was Tibetan, there were factions in Tibet that were against him. The King of Tsang was one, and the political supporters of the Karma family Kagyud formed another; it may be that they hoped to install the Karmapa in the place of the Dalai Lama. This time, there was a clear-cut war: the Mongols simply invaded in support of the Dalai

Lama, and the King of Tsang and the supporters of the Karmapa were conclusively defeated. The Mongols then granted the Great Fifth Dalai Lama sovereignty over all the lands they had conquered, which made him King of Tibet as well as the most important spiritual leader in the country. Thus, under the Great Fifth, the secular and religious power came together and it has been the role of the Dalai Lama to control them both ever since.

This once again shows the Mongols in a completely different light from the Chinese and Persian sources. They exacted no tribute; they made no demands. Rather, they continued their tradition of supporting Tibetan monasteries, and they appeared to think that a unified Tibet under the leadership of the Dalai Lama was better than reducing the country to vassal status. Even if one takes the most cynical political view of their action, that a Tibet under the Dalai Lama was likely to be less of a military threat than a Tibet headed by the King of Tsang, for example, they still emerge with credit: they could so easily have installed their own puppet. It is worth pausing and thinking about this relationship, rather than trying to force it into some preconceived Western mould.

Under the Great Fifth, Tibet prospered as it had not done for three quarters of a millenium. Internal stability was guaranteed by the Mongol armies, but the Dalai Lama was still the head of state. Just how this worked is shown by the abortive invasion of Western Tibet by the young and unwary King of Ladakh. With Mongol help, the invasion was quickly beaten back, and Ladakh was made a semi-vassal state – but a vassal of Tibet, not Mongolia. They had to pay some tribute directly to Gushri Khan, the Mongol leader, but the greater part went to Lhasa. In fact, the tributes were not heavy, and seem to have been designed as much to teach Ladakh a lesson as anything else; trade continued to be a more important source of revenue than tribute.

Although Gushri Khan, the last of the great Mongol Khans, died in 1656, Tibet continued to prosper under the Great Fifth. He was a man of enormous energy, foresight, and practicality, and like the Thirteenth and Fourteenth Dalai Lamas he recognised what needed change in Tibet and enthusiastically applied himself to bringing about that change. It was he who set up the administrative structure of Tibet, with most offices filled by one monk and one layman; this made sure that partisan interests could never have too much effect, and ensured an excellent balance between practical administration and monastic ideals. It could be all too easy for a monk to forget that not all men are monks, forswearing comfort and possessions, and a secular official of too worldly an inclination might be tempted to line his own pockets and secure his own comforts at the expense of others. No one denies that there were individual cases of corruption and cruelty, but they were probably less widespread than in any other country with a similar standard of living, even today.

What the Great Fifth did not do was to impose Gelugpa sectarianism. The political supporters of the Karma Kagyud were treated firmly, and their estates confiscated, but the Kagyud sect was not suppressed in any way, and the other schools (including the Bönpo) remained completely free to continue in their old ways. As already mentioned, there are five places in the Tibetan Administration in Exile for the heads of the religious schools: one for the Nyingma, one for the Kagyud, one for the Sakya, one for the Gelugpa, and one for the Bön.

To this day, there is very little sectarianism in Tibetan Buddhism (though there can be some very heated debates on points of doctrine), and for this reason it is difficult to get a clear and concise definition of the way in which the schools differ from one another. The Dalai Lama was somewhat at a loss to explain this; he said that it was more a matter of feel, or perhaps flavour. As he expresses it, religion is like food for the mind, and just as no one food suits everyone, so does no one religion suit everyone. Some find Buddhism best; some find Christianity best; some prefer Islam; and so on. Even within one religion, there are many variations – Catholic, Quaker, Lutheran, Episcopalian, and so forth – and these variations help us to choose the path which is best for us. It would certainly be a great mistake to assume that the Tibetans of this period were fighting about differences of doctrine, because then as now people would take teachings from whichever different teacher suited them. Many Dalai Lamas, although prominent in the Gelugpa tradition, have had strong links with the Nyingma as well as having teachers from the other two schools.

What arose under the Great Fifth, therefore, was a most unusual state; a state where complete religious freedom was the norm, unlike Europe and America at the same period, and where the political apparatus of the state did no more than was strictly necessary. Politics, in fact, became (in the words of the Fourteenth Dalai Lama) what they should be, a necessary solution to problems and a matter of administration, rather than an end in themselves.

During the reign of the Great Fifth, many new monasteries and *dzongs* were built, and old ones refurbished. It was also at this time that the Peak Potala was begun, the magnificent building that stands on the Red Hill and dominates the Lhasa skyline. Part palace, part fortress, part treasure-house, part temple, part tomb, part administrative centre, it is a titanic building over nine hundred feet long, with countless rooms. Over the centuries, it became the repository for Tibetan culture. Store rooms were filled with priceless *thangkas* (religious paintings on silk), religious statues made of precious metals, and endless other things: it was here that the thousand-year-old armour from the days of Tibet's military greatness was stored. It became a symbol of Tibetan nation-hood.

Nor were the only advances material and visible. The Great Fifth himself is revered as a *Tertön*, or 'Discoverer of Hidden Treasure'. Guru Rinpoche hid many 'treasures' (*Terma*) which were both material, in the form of books, statues, and so forth, and *Gongter*, 'treasures in the heart', which might fairly be translated as 'revelations'. These teachings were prepared by Guru Rinpoche against the time when they would be needed, and the Great Fifth was one of the *Tertöns* who disclosed them. Incidentally, although the whole doctrine of *Terma* is regarded as Nyingma or 'Ancient Ones' tradition, the fact that a Dalai Lama could be a *Tertön* well illustrates the lack of sectarianism in Tibet.

Unfortunately, there were the inevitable external influences which would also affect Tibet's future. The Manchu or Ch'ing dynasty had toppled the Ming dynasty in 1644, and although the new Son of Heaven had a healthy respect for Mongol power at first, it became obvious after the passing of Gushri Khan in 1656 that Mongolia was on the wane. Consequently, despite friendly relations between the Great Fifth Dalai Lama and the Chinese Emperor, it was clear towards the end of the Tibetan ruler's life that the Chinese were casting covetous glances at their western neighbour. Tibet is, after all, a huge and sparsely populated country; and China is not big enough for its huge population. It is an interesting exercise to look at a Chinese-drawn map of China. After removing the minor Chinese claims, to parts of Russia for example, the fact remains that 60% of China's area consists of so-called 'Minority Nations' – for which read, 'Invaded Territories'. Take out Tibet, Mongolia and Turkestan, and China is very crowded indeed.

The Great Fifth passed to the Honourable Fields at the age of 65, in 1682. This posed immense political problems for the Tibetan government, as his advisers became on his death. If news of his death were made public, it could well have precipitated an invasion. Even if it did not, the newly unified Tibetan state was still fragile, and civil war was a real risk. Finally, the Potala was not yet completed; when it was, it would be a powerful symbol of unity. Consequently, the Regent decided to conceal the news of the Great Fifth's death, and to go on as if nothing had happened.

Accordingly, although a search was secretly instituted for the Sixth Dalai Lama, a monk was found who could pass for the Fifth Dalai Lama, and the Regent gave out that the Inmost One had embarked upon a retreat which might last for several years. This provided a good excuse for keeping public appearances to a minimum, and also helped to explain any differences in appearance and behaviour on the part of the impersonator. The deception was successful, for it was not until 1697, fifteen years after the death of the Great Fifth, that the Sixth Dalai Lama was publicly announced and enthroned. It might seem logical that the Tibetan people should be furious at having been duped, but any anger they felt was more than offset by the news that the Sixth was with them, and that the Inmost One would once more take a part in Tibetan affairs.

Tsanyang Gyatso, the Sixth Dalai Lama, was however a very different man from his predecessor. He was born in 1683 in Ögyen Ling, in what is now the Indian province of Arunachal Pradesh, and he was brought up in secret even though he was recognised as the new incarnation when still a child. He was fourteen when he was formally introduced to the people of Tibet, and by that time he had already formed tastes which were, to say the least, unconventional for a Dalai Lama. He was a self-confessed lover of women and wine by his late teens, and a great poet. His poetry survives to this day, and we can learn more about him from this than from any political analysis:

> Longing for the landlord's daughter
> Blossoming in youthful beauty
> Is pining for peaches
> Ripening on the high peach trees

The prolonged childhood which we accept as normal in the West did not exist in old Tibet. As in mediaeval and Elizabethan England, fourteen, thirteen, or even twelve was regarded as a reasonable marrying age for a girl, and a boy was considered a man when only a little older.

Other poems are more cryptic, such as:

> Pink clouds
> Hide frost and hailstorms
> He who is a half-monk
> Is an enemy of the Dharma

Although the Sixth took his preliminary vows, he repeatedly postponed the final ones. Eventually, when he was nineteen years old, he was formally summoned to take them by the Regent and the other ruling monks of Tibet. He kept the appointment, in 1702, but what he did astonished everyone: he handed back his robes, and announced that he was no longer a monk. It is by no means unusual for a monk to do this in Tibetan society, and absolutely no stigma is involved if he does so, but when the Dalai Lama did it the impact was tremendous. It did not mean, of course, that he was resigning as Dalai Lama; given the nature of the office, that would obviously be impossible. It did, however, mean that the Dalai Lama was not a monk. There is no particular reason why the Dalai Lama should be a monk; a Bodhisattva can work for the good of all sentient beings as easily as a layman as he can as a monk. Being a monk simplifies matters – the Fourteenth Dalai Lama quotes the old Tibetan proverb about a married man being a tree with branches and leaves, whilst a monk is a stick standing alone and falling alone – but it is not strictly necessary. Another of the songs of the Sixth Dalai Lama brings to mind the great Sufi poet, Omar Khayyam:

> People gossip about me
> I am sorry for what I have done
> I have taken three thin steps
> And landed myself in the tavern of my mistress

Because of his extraordinary behaviour, many people (including many contemporary Mongols) have denied that the Sixth was a true incarnation. The Fourteenth was in no doubt when we asked him, though: there were clear prophecies which covered the First to the Seventh Dalai Lamas.

This led inevitably to a question about the other prophecies concerning Dalai Lamas. His Holiness said that although the ones he had just referred to were clear, some of those dealing with later incarnations were unclear or perhaps even false. He was careful to point out that this does not mean the Dalai Lamas themselves were false, just that they were not clearly covered by prophecies. The Dalai Lama continues to reincarnate, he says, because the idea or office of the Dalai Lama is useful; and whether that usefulness is prophesied or not is not particularly relevant.

As for the often-quoted 'ancient prophecy' that the present Dalai Lama will be the last, this is simply a rumour circulated by the Chinese. The Dalai Lama himself says that he may or may not be the last Dalai Lama: there is certainly no prophecy that he will be the last of his lineage. He says this with a touch of asperity, though, as if such questions are not important, and repeatedly emphasises that the Dalai Lama is not essential to Tibet. Tibet, he says, was a powerful and independent nation long before the Dalai Lamas appeared on the scene, and it could be so again, with or without a Dalai Lama. He makes the interesting comment that he is neither the best Dalai Lama nor the worst, and adds that as long as he can serve the people of Tibet he will continue to take rebirth. Again and again he stresses this idea of usefulness: he says that if it were more useful to the Tibetan people that the Dalai Lama reincarnate as a bridge or an insect, then this is what he should do.

Incidentally, there are widely-respected prophecies that the Dalai Lama will return to Tibet, because there are events which are yet to happen and which can only happen in Tibet once His Holiness has returned; but on these, the Fourteenth Dalai Lama refuses to be drawn.

To return to the Sixth Dalai Lama, he is widely believed to have been a master of *Tantra*. This mystical or magical path uses the experiences of everyday life – work, food, drink, love, sex – and transmutes them into spiritual practices. It is an enormously difficult path, because of the concentration required: distraction, for obvious reasons, is all too easy. A few *Ngakpas* (sorcerers) follow the Tantrayana, but it is not widespread; the popular Tibetan view, which accurately reflects the philosophical theory behind this Path,

is that although you can climb further and faster you can also fall
further and harder, and that only a very skilful practitioner can
achieve the concentration required. One Western would-be
Tantrist who wanted to know about *yab-yum,* the sexual practices
symbolising the union of opposites, was told that when he could
blow a hole through a pile of barley-flour by mind-power alone,
then he might be qualified to start on the sexual Tantras. The Sixth
himself, when questioned about his exploits with the opposite sex,
replied to this effect: "Look. We all know about sex. You can do it,
and I can do it. But let's not pretend that we are doing the same
thing".

Despite his unusual lifestyle, very few Tibetans ever doubted that
the Sixth was the true Dalai Lama. The general belief was that when
he was out carousing in Lhasa, he was also simultaneously
meditating in the Potala, in another body. This belief is echoed in a
description of the Sixth by the Great Thirteenth, as quoted by Sir
Charles Bell in *Portrait of the Dalai Lama:*

He did not observe even the rules of a fully ordained priest. He drank wine
habitually. And he used to have his body in several places at the same time,
e.g. in Lhasa, in Kongpo, and elsewhere. Even the place where he retired
to the Honourable Fields is uncertain: one tomb of his is in Alasher in
Mongolia, whilst there is another in the Rice-Heap Monastery (Drepung).
Showing many bodies at the same time is disallowed in all the sects of our
religion, because it causes confusion in the work.

Surely, the Tibetan understatement easily surpasses the English!
The Great Thirteenth went on to say, "One of his bodies used to
appear in the crowd at the Reception Hall of the Seventh Dalai
Lama. One is said to appear also at my receptions, but I am unable
to say whether this is true or not."

Whatever his religious, mystical, and magical accomplishments,
there is no doubt that the Sixth was politically disastrous. There was
a plot to kill him in 1702, in which the Regent may have had a hand;
the plot misfired, and the Regent retired in 1703, though it may
simply have been that he felt that he could no longer rule in the
name of the Sixth. Lhazang Khan, one of the Mongol leaders, sent
repeated messages to the Chinese Emperor concerning the Sixth's
activities, and was prepared to go in himself in order to sort out
what he saw as the deplorable situation in Tibet. His forces clashed

with those of the deposed Regent in 1705; the Mongols won, and in 1706 the ex-Regent was beheaded. In the same year, Lhazang Khan declared the Dalai Lama deposed, and prepared to attack Lhasa.

This episode illustrates the divided nature of Tibetan politics perhaps better than any other. There have subsequently been frequent conflicts of interest between external 'protectors' and the Tibetan people, but this was the first since the institution of Dalai Lama had been founded. The Regent's position is curious, too, because he appears as an enemy of both the Dalai Lama and the Khan. Was he truly disloyal, or did he believe that Tibet's interests would have been better served without the embarrassing presence of the Dalai Lama? And then there was popular feeling. In circumstances which curiously paralleled the National Uprising in 1959, the people of Lhasa prepared to defend the Dalai Lama from the invaders, but he realised that the only outcome could be a massacre, and gave himself up to the Mongols. On November 14th, 1706, he died as he was being taken out of Tibet: he was twenty-six years old.

There is, however, another version of what became of him. According to a persistent legend, and to the 'Secret History of the Sixth Dalai Lama', he did not die at the hands of the Mongols – or if he did, it was only one of his several bodies. Instead, he made extensive pilgrimages in Central Tibet, India, Nepal, Mongolia, and even China. There are many places linked with his name in this 'Secret History', including the mountain which the Chinese call Wo-Tai-Shen and the Tibetans call Riwotsenga. This is the Five-Peaked Mountain where the Lord of Wisdom resides, who is called Jampalyang in Tibetan and Manjushri in Sanskrit, and the place where the Sixth Dalai Lama meditated is said still to exist today.

His removal from office was, however, the undoing of Lhazang Khan. In an attempt to regain the authority that he had lost by such a terrible action, he tried to declare that the Sixth Dalai Lama had been falsely chosen, and that another young monk (who was widely believed to be the Khan's own bastard son) was the true incarnation. But the Tibetans remembered the verse that the Sixth had written not long before he died:

> White crane
> Lend me your wings
> I shall not fly far
> From Lithang, I shall return

The search for the Seventh Dalai Lama centred upon Lithang, and the new incarnation was discovered in 1717. Shortly afterwards, Mongols loyal to the Dalai Lama fought and killed Lhazang Khan.

Although the reign of the Sixth seems with hindsight to be one of the turning-points in Tibetan history, and a turn for the worse, it could have been a much greater turning-point and the beginning of a Tibetan state that could have endured to the present day. Many of the poems of the Sixth are dedicated to a 'Sweetheart from Chonggyal' whom he apparently never met. According to Tibetan legend, if he had met this girl, he would have made the office of Dalai Lama hereditary, and a great deal would have been different.

The Seventh Dalai Lama, Kelsang Gyatso, was born in Lithang in 1708, recognised in 1717, and installed in 1720. Now that Tibet no longer enjoyed Mongol protection the Chinese made their presence unpleasantly obvious. The retinue that escorted Kelsang Gyatso to Lhasa contained many Chinese soldiers, and they did not withdraw once the Inmost One was enthroned. Instead, a 2000-strong Chinese garrison placed an intolerable strain on Lhasa's food supplies, and two Ambans or ambassador-administrators were appointed by the Chinese Emperor K'ang Hsi. In 1721 he also issued an imperial edict stating that Tibet was and always had been a vassal of China – a totally unfounded claim, and the principal opening shot in the campaign of Chinese opportunism which has continued ever since. Even history was distorted to support the claim: the proposed visit of the Great Fifth, some eighty years before, was re-interpreted as an act of homage and submission.

Apart from those in Lhasa who were immediately affected by the garrison no one took much notice of the Chinese edicts. There was simply no need to: Lhasa was so far from the Imperial capital, and communications across the vast empty country were so poor, that the impact of China was negligible. K'ang Hsi died in 1722, and his son Yung Chen withdrew the garrison but left the Ambans behind. Unfortunately, the Tibetan Regent Pho-la was far too ready to rely on the Chinese for advice, and the Seventh was not particularly interested in worldly affairs. As a result, Chinese influence steadily grew; and when it looked as if the Seventh might take a hand in the government of the country, the Regent persuaded him to make several extended journeys which kept him safely out of Lhasa for years at a time.

Many letters written by the Seventh Dalai Lama survive to this day, and in them he gives various friends and pupils spiritual advice in a very clear way and with a light touch, in a manner strongly reminiscent of the teachings of the present Dalai Lama. Reading them, it is impossible not to wonder what would have happened if that mind had been turned to the government of Tibet; but alas, it never was.

The Regent Pho-la died in 1747, and he was succeeded by his son. Both were ambitious, but the son lacked his father's sense of balance: he misused his power so grossly that the Ambans had him murdered. Although he was bad, at least he was Tibetan; the Tibetan crowd turned on the Ambans and killed them as soon as they found out what had happened.

During the reign of the Seventh Dalai Lama Chinese interference in Tibetan affairs became the norm. One of the worst and most divisive edicts was that which vested the rule of Tsang and Western Tibet in the Panchen Lama. Although the Tibetan people regarded it merely as a regional governorship, no one ever formally repudiated the edict and it was this sort of acceptance which allowed the Chinese to claim that Tibet was under the suzerainty of the Celestial Empire, so it was politically disastrous.

The Seventh Dalai Lama died in 1757, and the Eighth was born in 1758. He was recognised in 1762 and took the name Jampal Gyatso; he was given his majority in 1781, but although he lived until 1804 he took little part in the secular life of Tibet. Like the Seventh, he was more concerned with the practice of religion, and although he was a learned scholar his impact on Tibetan administration was not great. One thing that he did do, however, was to establish a constitutional cabinet, called the Kashag, which ensured that the Regents' power was at least tempered. The Regents, although nominally clerics, were often personally ambitious, and the Chinese played on this to increase their own influence. By the time the Eighth died, it would have taken a very remarkable man to break the power of the Chinese-backed regents and restore the importance of the Dalai Lama in secular matters.

The Ninth, Tenth, Eleventh, and Twelfth Dalai Lamas did not have the option of reasserting their influence. They all died very young; the Ninth lived from 1806–1816, the Tenth from 1816–1837, the Eleventh from 1838–1855, and the Twelfth from 1856–1876. It is quite likely that they were murdered as soon as there was any likelihood of their developing an interest in the secular (or indeed the religious) running of the country. The Chinese blamed their deaths on wicked Regents, but given that the Regents were frequently in the pocket of the Chinese this is a somewhat transparent protest. It was certainly the case that during the greater part of the nineteenth century the Chinese established tremendous influence in Tibet, and that it is from this period any claims they had over the country effectively arose. Even the Dalai Lamas were chosen with the intervention of the Chinese Emperor, who would have the Tibetans write the names of the three or four possible candidates and place them in a golden urn. He would then fish out the name of the new Dalai Lama with a pair of chopsticks. Although this might seem an impossibly aleatory approach, it is not necessarily so: after all, a fate which can ensure the recognition of the true Dalai Lama can also ensure that the correct name is picked from the urn; and besides, Chenrezi can manifest in different ways in different people, so all the candidates might be appropriate.

The four Dalai Lamas who died so young seem, from what little is known of them, to have been gentle and holy but not given to worldly affairs – even if they had been given the chance. The Thirteenth was also a good and holy man, but his impact on the Tibetan nation was to be immense.

The Asian Inheritance

The Great Thirteenth Dalai Lama, Thubten Gyatso, was born in 1876. The omens surrounding his birth were unmistakable: as his successor would do nearly sixty years later, the Regent went to the lake at Chokhorgyal, and although the lake was frozen over and covered with snow, a great wind arose and blew the snow away, so that the regent could see visions in the ice as if in a mirror. The child, when he was found, passed all the tests; he also described the whereabouts of an image of the Lord Buddha that the Twelfth Dalai Lama had given to a chief in Lithang, who had placed it inside a solid gold vase and hidden it in his rafters. The Nechung Oracle confirmed the correctness of the identification, and for the first time since 1762 the procedure with the Chinese Emperor and the golden urn was abandoned: no one doubted that this was the Dalai Lama. He was brought to Lhasa in 1878, and enthroned in 1879.

By the age of thirteen, he was well enough versed in Buddhism to deliver an authoritative teaching on the previous lives of the Lord Buddha, using insights he had gained in meditation. By the age of eighteen, he was sufficiently in control of the administration to be able to summon all the heads of the largest monasteries and instruct them to tighten up monastic discipline. At nineteen, he was given his majority; there is no fixed age for this, as it depends on the maturity of the young Dalai Lama, the needs of Tibet, and the predictions of the astrologers and soothsayers.

At around this time, in the mid-1890s, he faced the first major test of his ability and authority. He kept falling ill for no reason that his physicians could discover, and so the Nechung Oracle was consulted. In his trance, the oracle announced that there was a plot to kill the Dalai Lama, by magical means and (perhaps) by poison as well. The main conspirator was the Chief Minister, the Regent's brother, but several others were also involved – including, the Great Thirteenth suspected, the Regent himself. Nevertheless, he refused to allow the death penalty for anyone; after a flogging and other punishments, the conspirators were stripped of office and sent into exile. It was as a result of this episode that the monks of Tengye Ling were at odds with the Government and the Dalai Lama for many years afterwards: the Regent had been their Abbot, and they always believed that he had been unfairly treated.

It was a measure of the young Dalai Lama's personal strength that it was the Regent and Chief Minister who fell. It was a foretaste of things to come. Despite the fact that his upbringing had been exclusively religious, with no attempt to fit him to rule the country as King, he was to be the first Dalai Lama to resume that role for over three hundred years.

Afghanistan, Northern India, and to a lesser extent Tibet were of course the setting for the Great Game, the nineteenth century power struggle between the great Imperial powers. The British ruled India, and they were convinced that the Russians intended to invade Tibet through Mongolia in order to dominate Northern India and Afghanistan. The Russians, for their part, were understandably worried about the all-conquering British, and were determined to establish their 'spheres of influence' as a buffer. No one was very worried about the Chinese, because the Manchu dynasty was visibly on its last legs: cruel, corrupt, and capricious officials were lightly controlled by a lazy and selfish court.

The whole of the Northern Frontier of India was something of a shambles. The Indian Mutiny of 1857 had been put down, and the majority of the Indian sub-continent was as united as it would ever be, but it was still a motley collection of Principalities, Native States, and other political entities. At the very edges of British influence there were states which were British ruled in all but name; states which accepted British aid and guidance, especially with regard to foreign policy and defence, but which were otherwise independent; and states which had signed, more or less willingly, various treaties and agreements with the British which ranged from the comprehensive and meticulously observed to the deliberately vague and casual. The Tibetan/Indian border is a very long one, and states between the two countries included Lahaul and Spiti, Kashmir, Mustang, Ladakh, Bhutan, Nepal, Sikkim, Assam, the tribal North Eastern Frontier Area (NEFA), and even, although most people do not realise it, Burma.

In 1904 the British decided to consolidate their position in the far north of the sub-continent by invading Tibet and extracting some kind of treaty. They had already tried to obtain a treaty by diplomatic means, but their advances through the Chinese had proved entirely fruitless and communications to the Dalai Lama were returned unopened. Inside Tibet, the Dalai Lama was growing steadily more sure of his own power: he refused to accept even nominations to the Kashag from the Chinese, let alone Chinese members, and the Ambans had recognised their own power-lessness. They simply regaled the Emperor with regular false reports, so that the Son of Heaven became known in Tibet as the Bag of Lies. Encouraged by the success of his policy with the Chinese, the Great Thirteenth was also very wary of the British. First, he was afraid that they might turn out to be as bad as the Chinese – the guest who, after a few days' stay, declares that your house is now his – and second, he was under no illusions about how the British Empire had grown. A treaty was followed by trade, and once trade was established imperialism was not far behind: an army would be sent in to 'safeguard' trading interests.

The British, therefore, decided to send a military expedition. It was headed by Colonel Younghusband, who seems to have been the ideal man for the job. Far from being a gung-ho military type, he was concerned to prevent unnecessary bloodshed on either side; he realised that the chances of a successful mission would be very much higher that way. He was also fair and honest, two qualities which the Tibetans found refreshing after years of dealing with the Chinese. Finally, there was a streak of the mystic in his personality, which in his memoirs he confesses was brought to the fore by his experiences in Tibet. Years later, he was to found an inter-faith study centre in London where, still further in the future, the Fourteenth Dalai Lama would speak.

The Dalai Lama instructed his small army not to fight the British, but to resist them – a curious order. Although they did resist, and valiantly, there was little that they could do against the best-equipped, best-drilled, and best-organised military machine in the world. The British lost two hundred and two men, whilst the Tibetan casualties were several times that figure: Sir Charles Bell's estimate was eight to ten times, or perhaps more. When it became obvious that his army could no longer hold back the British, the twenty-eight year old Dalai Lama decided to withdraw to Mongolia. At that time Mongolia had not been partitioned between China and Russia; it was still an independent country, though its exact status was unclear.

He left his great seal with Lamo Shar Lobsang Gyaltsen, a trusted monk-official who was given all the powers of an Acting Regent, and it was he who concluded the treaty with Younghusband. The main terms were that Tibet would prevent other foreign powers from exercising any influence in her internal affairs; that the British protectorate over Sikkim was recognised by both Tibet and Britain; and that there should be three designated trade marts in Tibet, so that trade between these and British India should be encouraged. Once the treaty had been signed the British withdrew.

It was probably this withdrawal that laid the roots of friendship between Britain and Tibet. After centuries of dealing with the Chinese, the Tibetans were struck with the straightforwardness of the British, who simply left once they had concluded their treaty. This was something they could understand; this was a Tibetan way of doing things. The British would probably not have left so quickly or so completely if they had known that the Tibetans had little or no intention of sticking to the treaty, but the Tibetans saw it as a fine example of their own live and let live approach!

The Chinese, predictably, tried to turn all this to their advantage. First, they set up proclamations all over Tibet, saying that the Dalai Lama was deposed. The usual Tibetan reaction to these was to cover them with manure, but leave them posted: that was their opinion of the 'Bag of Lies'. The Tibetan Government continued to refer all important matters to His Holiness, at least as far as possible, and the Panchen Lama declined to accept the Emperor's appointment to the post of Regent.

In addition to these rather ineffectual gestures, the Chinese were also characteristically noisy. They said that His Holiness's departure into Mongolia was clear proof of Tibet's vassal status, in that he had run to the Celestial Empire for help and protection. They ignored both the fact that Mongolia was an independent state which was historically a second home for the Dalai Lama and other Lamas and the rather obvious point that they furnished no help or protection whatsoever. In fact, they were doing the very opposite: taking advantage of the absence of the Dalai Lama from his homeland, they seized their chance to invade. In order to make their task easier they took great pains to entertain His Holiness whenever possible, the better to control the information which reached him. They were evidently very successful in this, because he returned to Lhasa in December 1909, and in February 1910 Chinese troops entered Lhasa. He fled again, this time in a new direction: British India.

There is a Tibetan saying that once you have experienced the scorpion, the frog seems friendly. The frog is not much liked by Tibetans, to whom it is the symbol of sudden and violent action, but it is not really dangerous. The insidious scorpion is a far more deadly animal, and has the added distinction of being the lowest of all animal incarnations in popular Tibetan belief. The Chinese scorpion had driven the Dalai Lama to seek help from the British frog.

In mid-February 1910, after a very hard journey in the depths of the Tibetan winter, His Holiness and his party arrived at Gnatong. There was a small telegraph office there, set up by the British to link Tibet and India, which was manned by two ex-Sergeants of the British army. Sir Charles Bell talked to the two men in later years, and recounts their story in his *Portrait of the Dalai Lama*. They appear as likeable men, rough and ready, and there are some fine period pieces in their own account of the occasion. Sergeant Luff's original greeting to the advance party was "Which of you blighters is the Dalai Lama?", and he told Sir Charles how he and Sergeant Humphreys had guarded the Dalai Lama with rifles which had not a single round of ammunition:

Well, about those rifles. We had been given a transfer to Rungpo. You know Gnatong, sir, and how difficult it is to get any transport in summer, let alone in winter and snowing hard. So we had sent off our heavy boxes, and in them was our ammunition, and we had not a single round of ammunition for our rifles. However, His Holiness did not know, and slept soundly. He was absolutely worn out by fatigue and mental strain, which one could see was worrying him.

Sergeant Luff lent the Dalai Lama his own bed while he and Sergeant Humphreys stayed up on guard duty, and by the morning the Dalai Lama was ready to move on. He went via Kalimpong to Darjeeling, where he was well received and made welcome for as long as he wished to stay as a guest of the British government. The British were not, however, prepared to give any help at all in ridding Tibet of the Chinese, and in this respect His Holiness was sorely disappointed.

To counter this His Holiness met the man who was to become his most trusted adviser of any nationality, Sir Charles Bell. His biography of the Dalai Lama has already been mentioned many times, but it seems that until he became involved with Tibet he was no more than a moderately successful minor diplomat. His friendship with the Dalai Lama made him the most important single individual in the relationship between British India and Tibet, and in later years he was to become the British Resident in Lhasa. For the moment, he advised His Holiness as best he could on a vast range of topics, noting as he did so the Great Thirteenth's tremendous quickness of mind, acuteness, and wide-ranging interests – precisely those points which so many also discern in the Fourteenth Dalai Lama.

The lack of military help seems to have been based on two main arguments, one political and the other practical. The political argument was that China had over the years acquired some sort of suzerain rights over Tibet, and that Britain had no wish to interfere in Chinese internal affairs. At most this was an argument of convenience; the British Empire was not usually so finicky. The practical argument was that Tibet was simply too big and thinly populated to police effectively, especially if doing so meant opposing the Chinese from time to time.

On the other hand, both the strategic and economic importance of Tibet should have been obvious. The country is a natural fortress in the heart of Asia, and even a cursory inspection would have revealed the immense mineral wealth of the Land of Snows; in fact the British did once dispatch a surveyor to take a look at Tibet, but he seems to have been so preoccupied with his private hobby as an amateur naturalist that he paid no attention to the geology of Tibet at all.

But the Great Game was fading, and the British neglected to secure for themselves a loyal and friendly power at minimal expense, so it was left for the Tibetans themselves to free their country. Fortunately, they were aided in this by the fact that the Chinese Empire was rapidly disintegrating. The Manchu dynasty fell to the Nationalists, just as the Manchus had supplanted the Ming dynasty and the Ming had replaced the Yuan; and in the power struggle the remote wastes of Tibet were not important. Unaided, the Tibetans threw out the Chinese invaders in 1911, and in June 1912 the Dalai Lama was back in the Peak Potala, where he issued a proclamation formally reasserting Tibetan independence.

This expulsion of the Chinese is fundamental to any under-standing of the political status of Tibet. Regardless of whether the Chinese had acquired any rights, suzerain or otherwise, in the past, this marked the emergence of a nation which was by any of the definitions of international law free and independent. There are some analogies in the Scandinavian countries of Europe, but perhaps the most telling parallel is between the United States of America and Great Britain: once the rebellious colonists had thrown out the British, there was not much future in the British maintaining that they 'really' ruled the country. A re-invasion in 1850, for example, would have been naked aggression; and that is exactly what happened when China invaded Tibet in 1950.

As a result of his treatment at the hands of the British, and his friendship with Sir Charles Bell, the Dalai Lama was now far more willing to implement the terms of the 1904 treaty. Now, too, he was aware of the nature of the outside world; he could see clearly that Tibet was going to have to break with its mediaeval past and come to terms with the twentieth century if it was to survive. There would have to be an army; there would have to be secular education; and the whole administration, which had rumbled along substantially unchanged since the days of the Great Fifth, would have to be changed dramatically.

The trouble was that the Dalai Lama was almost alone in recognising this need for change. The great landowners were comfortable as they were: they wanted no change. The priesthood recognised that modernisation could only decrease their influence and privileges; they wanted no change. Even the secular middle class, which inevitably arose as a result of increased trade, was strongly xenophobic and reactionary; for the most part they were recruited from the ranks of the peasants, and their knowledge of the outside world was extremely limited. Because they came into contact only with the priests and landowners, rather than with the Dalai Lama himself, they too were opposed to change. The Fourteenth Dalai Lama has commented more than once on this Tibetan dislike of the new. As he says, no one objects to tradition;

but when tradition becomes blind and hide-bound, it becomes a problem. He sees this excessive devotion to tradition as the most serious potential flaw in the Tibetan national character; a cynic might see in it one of the major reasons why the Tibetans and the British have always got on so well.

As a result of these attitudes, His Holiness the Great Thirteenth Dalai Lama met with considerable opposition to almost all of the reforms that he tried to introduce. For example, a Western-style school in Lhasa was short-lived, and his plans for sending Tibetan children and young men abroad to school (in other words, to England) met with only very limited success: a very few young men did attend Rugby School, but for the most part parents found all sorts of excuses why their children should not go. Nevertheless, he did manage to make many changes. One story which beautifully illustrates his typically Tibetan mixture of practicality and tradition concerns the policing of Lhasa during Mönlam.

Mönlam is the prayer festival after the Tibetan New Year, or Losar, which usually falls in February. Traditionally, the secular magistrates were replaced during this period by monks; the Great Fifth had introduced this as a practical way of fusing religion and administration. Over the years, however, the monks had come to abuse their power: arbitrary fines and confiscations of property were commonplace. It was so bad that most wealthy people left Lhasa for the duration of the festival, and took their valuables with them. The Great Thirteenth summoned the monk-magistrates, and asked them by what authority they thought they were acting.

"By the authority of the Great Fifth Dalai Lama," came the cocky answer. With both tradition and the words of the Great Fifth behind them, they did not fear much for their own position. His Holiness replied coolly, "And *who* is the Greath Fifth Dalai Lama?" He also passed a law which made it illegal to leave Lhasa during Mönlam without good cause; several rich families who did not think that the new ruling would have much effect had an uncomfortable time explaining why they just happened to be riding out of Lhasa just after Losar, with all their valuables in their saddle-bags...

Another target for reform was the legal system. Formerly, petitions had been heard by lesser officials, who were not always above bribery. Now, any petition concerning the ownership of land automatically came to the attention of the Dalai Lama, and if the petitioner wrote the Dalai Lama's name on any petition, it had to be submitted to him. There was a safeguard built into the system, in that if the Dalai Lama decided that the case was trivial or vexatious, the petitioner not only lost his case but was also punished for wasting His Holiness's time.

In order to make sure that Government officials behaved as they were supposed to, he instituted a sort of reverse secret police. Unlike most secret police forces, who keep a watch on anyone opposed to the ruling regime, this one watched the officials on behalf of the people, in order to make sure that they were neither being unfair and harsh nor lining their own pockets. Any official who was caught misusing his power could expect to be reduced to the position of those he had abused.

The penalties for crime, too, were changed. Although many had wanted the death penalty for the conspirators who had plotted to kill him in the 1890s, he had not allowed it; and now, he made a determined effort to stamp out the mutilations that had sometimes been imposed as punishments, such as cutting off hands and pulling out eyes. Flogging was still allowed, but fines were encouraged and he also introduced one reform which would not be seen in the West for another fifty years or so, which was the idea of 'community service'. For instance, one offender was ordered to plant one thousand willow seedlings in the Norbulinka park, and another was sentenced to repair half a mile of road – though given the state of Tibetan roads, this is not as onerous as it might seem!

Imprisonment was only used rarely, and for the most serious crimes; the usual alternative was to allow the convict to beg in the streets, wearing fetters or a *cangue* or both. The *cangue,* known colloquially in Tibetan as 'the Chinese door', is a wooden neck-board or collar, very inconvenient and uncomfortable. Both *cangue* and fetters were removed at night, except in the case of serious crimes where a smaller and lighter *cangue* was worn constantly. Magistrates could impose sentences of up to three or four years; anything longer had to be referred to the Kashag.

From this it is clear that the appalling atrocities which are so lovingly described in Chinese propaganda are for the most part pure invention. It is true that even in the nineteenth century, murderers and those convicted of stealing from a temple could be sewn into a leather bag and thrown into a river – but it is significant that these cruel punishments flourished when the Chinese influence was at its height, and disappeared when the Great Thirteenth took control. There were, no doubt, isolated incidents of regional administrators who misused their authority, sometimes cruelly, but if any such atrocities came to the ears of His Holiness, the perpetrator could expect to lose land and position and to experience very unpleasant retribution.

Few of the Dalai Lama's officials were salaried; instead, they were expected to derive their income from grants of land. This was another target for reform, and obviously an unpopular one, but the Great Thirteenth tried to introduce a proper system of salaries. To list all of the reforms which he introduced would take a book in itself – from the reform of the coinage and the introduction of paper money to establishing a postal service – and the parallels between his life and that of the present Dalai Lama are plain. At every turn, though, he was resisted by Tibetan traditionalism and conservatism.

Perhaps his greatest failure, and the one that he felt most keenly, was his inability to establish a modern Tibetan army. Despite importing military experts from several countries, including an errant British bandsman who was responsible for *God Save The King* becoming a Tibetan national anthem, he was unable to persuade enough Tibetans to join the officer corps. His efforts were heroic, and in his Political Testament which he wrote shortly before he died he correctly predicted that Tibet would be invaded unless she modernised and prepared to defend herself; we have already come across the suggestion that when he failed to establish the army, he voluntarily withdrew to the Honourable Fields in order that the new incarnation should be young and vigorous when the invasion came.

At the time of his death, in the Water Bird year, Tibet was a country which was by any definition free and sovereign. There had been no Chinese interference, except in the far east of the country, since the Chinese were expelled in 1911, and although it was what would today be called a 'Third World' country, it was in a considerably better state than many, including some in the late twentieth century. The standard of living was low, but there was no famine, and although the country was still feudal and backward-looking, it was not an unpleasant place to live. This was the country which the two-year-old from Pari Takster inherited.

The Lion Throne

In the village of Takster, in the north-east of Tibet, Keutsang Rinpoche's search party was sure that they had found the Fourteenth Dalai Lama. Nevertheless, they lacked the authority to proclaim him themselves – that would need confirmation from Lhasa – and there was also the problem that the area was under Chinese control.

Consequently the first telegram to Lhasa was sent via the Chinese-controlled telegraph in code, but the message was clear enough to those on the other end. By mid-1938, the Regent had sent instructions to bring the child to Lhasa, and the Rinpoche was faced with the unpleasant task of negotiating with Ma Bu Feng.

He began by asking the governor for help in choosing the right child, a great compliment because this had in the past been the prerogative of the Emperor himself. The Moslems of Chinese Turkestan are a flexible breed, and the governor decided to make a test of his own to see which child might be the new incarnation. Twice he summoned all of the possible candidates, most of whom were makeweights introduced by the Tibetans, and questioned them. On the second occasion, he offered each of them a few sweets from a box, to see how they reacted. Some were too frightened to take any, and others greedily snatched a handful, but the child from Pari Takster alone politely took one sweet and ate it. This, combined with the answers to his questions, convinced the warlord. He sent all the other boys home, with a present of a roll of cloth each for their parents, and declared that he was satisfied that he had found the new incarnation.

Unfortunately, after this open-minded and open-handed display, events took a turn for the worse. To begin with, Ma Bu Feng would not allow the child to be taken to Lhasa unless he was declared then and there to be the new Dalai Lama. The Abbot of Kumbum Monastery supported him in this, but it is not hard to find the reason why. The previous Abbot, a much more straightforward man, had been shot on the orders of the Governor, who was afraid that he might tell the central government just how the province was being run. The negotiations dragged on and on. The Abbot made new demands: they were to receive a full set of the robes of the Great Thirteenth, plus a full set of the Kagyur and Tengur inscribed in letters of gold. This was no small request: there are 108 volumes of the Kagyur, or Teachings of the Buddha, and 225 volumes of the Tengur or Commentaries.

The governor in his turn insisted that the child should be escorted to Lhasa by a large body of Chinese troops 'for his own safety'. The Tibetans knew full well what would happen as soon as the Chinese reached Lhasa: they would be impossible to remove. Whether the governor seriously cared about all these demands, or whether he was simply laying the foundations for his eventual financial demands, he finally showed himself in his true colours. In return for a straightforward bribe of one hundred thousand Chinese dollars, the boy would be allowed to go. This was an enormous sum of money, equivalent at the time to about £7,500 or US $30,000, but at least it offered a solution to the dilemma and the Tibetans agreed. Part of the deal was that the Chinese escort would be reduced to a very few soldiers, and that no official proclamation would have to be made.

The Tibetans must have agreed too readily, however, because as soon as the money was paid Ma Bu Feng pulled the classic blackmailer's trick and demanded more. He wanted a hundred thousand Chinese dollars for the local military governor (he himself was the civil governor); a hundred thousand for his own staff and retinue, who might otherwise tell tales to the central government; a hundred thousand for Kumbum monasery; twenty thousand for the escort; and ten thousand for the expenses which he would incur in arranging all this. The total was Chinese $330,000, or about US $100,000 above the original bribe. The search party had, with difficulty, managed to obtain the original $100,000, but there was no way in which they could raise the additional cash. They repeated that there were other candidates (though this was not actually true), but the Governor was unimpressed: he just wanted the money.

More months passed, with the position effectively a stalemate, before it was resolved by chance. A party of Moslem pilgrims was passing through, and being merchants they were trading on the way. The Tibetans managed to borrow the money from them, to be repaid in rupees in Lhasa – a good deal from the merchants' point of view, as the rupee was worth more than the Chinese dollar at the time, and they were to be repaid coin for coin. The Dalai Lama's party would also be able to travel with the pilgrims, to their mutual advantage: the country through which they would be passing was dangerous and robber-infested, and a large party spelled increased safety. The Chinese escort was reduced to twenty soldiers.

Meanwhile, the young Dalai Lama had been kept safe at Kumbum monastery. He spent almost a year there, while the negotiations were going on and he remembers it as a lonely and miserable time. He was only four years old, and although he was treated with the respect that was due to his station he missed his family and his playmates. The only company of anyone near his own age came from his brother Lobsang Samten, who was two or three years older. The Dalai Lama remembers how he used to wait wistfully until his big brother had finished his lessons, sometimes peeking into the schoolroom, longing for the moment that they could play again.

The games they played were the same as all young Tibetan children play: dice, hide-and-seek, races. Lobsang Samten also recalls that they used to fight a lot: "One of us would poke the other, or say something, and it would go on from there…" At that time, they were both unaware that the younger of them was the Dalai Lama, and they used to fight incessantly. It was not their fighting, though, which used to cause the most problems: quite regularly the pair of them would find somewhere new to hide, and disappear for hours on end. There would then be a wholesale panic while Incarnate Lamas and venerable monks tried to find the two children, which they thought was tremendous fun. Their uncle, in whose charge they were, thought differently: he was a short-tempered man at the best of times, rather vain about his appearance and dignity, and the children's escapades used to drive him to distraction.

They finally set out on the first day of the sixth month of the Earth Hare year, a time that was astrologically auspicious for travelling. His Holiness had just celebrated his fourth birthday, and it was towards the end of the summer of 1939. The caravan consisted of the Moslem pilgrims, the Chinese escort, and a Tibetan contingent consisting of His Holiness, Lobsang Samten, their parents, and another older brother called Gyalo Thondup, who was nine. Most of the party walked or rode – the Dalai Lama's father was a keen horseman – but the two smaller boys rode in a *treljam,* which is a sort of sedan-chair carried between two mules. On particularly rough or dangerous parts of the track, man-power replaced mule-power, and on more than one occasion the stronger Lamas took it in turn to carry the young Presence on their backs. He much preferred this to travelling in the *treljam,* where he recalls being mostly bored. One of the attendants on the journey adds that he seemed very fretful, and occasionally cried; but his brother, who shared the transport, says that they used to pass the time by fighting in there as well! When the noise level rose too high, their parents would stop the *treljam* and ask what the trouble was: a little piece of rock candy, or some fruit, would take their minds off what they had been fighting about.

The journey was hard and slow, its pace limited by the members of the party who walked and the ungainly *treljams;* the Great Mother also rode in one of these. In the usual Tibetan way, they travelled from dawn to noon, and then made camp under the clear Tibetan sky. They were free, though, from the problems which normally afflicted such expeditions: they met no robbers, nor did their yaks and horses run off with their wild counterparts, and the Tibetan chronicler of the journey also records that they were free from bees. This may sound like a curious statement, but deaths from bee stings were not at all unusual in the summer months. Frequently days on end would pass without sight of another human being. For weeks, the only new faces were those of nomadic cattle-herders who came to ask blessings of the Lamas in the group. Once they were out of the Chinese-controlled area, spirits became very much lighter; but it was a long, long march.

They had been on the road for two and a half months before they drew close enough to Lhasa for an official welcoming party to be sent out: it was in September, during the eighth month of the Tibetan year, that the Government delegation was sent. They were still ten days' march from Lhasa when the party arrived. It included the Nechung oracle, who had presented his mirror to the search party; a *Geshé* (Doctor of Metaphysics) from Drepung monastery;

and a Cabinet Minister from the *Kashag*. It had already been decided in Lhasa that the child was the true incarnation, but it was up to the welcoming party to make the official proclamation. When he was brought into the presence of the Dalai Lama, the Cabinet Minister prostrated himself three times, and made the threefold offering of *Mendel Tensum*. This pledges the speech, body, and mind, and is the most profound offering that can be made. Then, he formally handed the child a letter from the Regent. It was read aloud to the crowd: it proclaimed that this was the Fourteenth Dalai Lama.

Incredible as it may seem, this was the first time that his parents realised who their son was. They had understood that he must be a very high incarnation, but the possibility that he might be the Dalai Lama had simply not occurred to them. Automatically they were elevated to the ranks of the most important in the land. Their son was the absolute spiritual and temporal ruler of Tibet; they joined in paying homage to him.

Everyone who remembers that occasion remarks on the way in which the little boy behaved. He received everyone as if it was the most natural thing in the world, dispensing blessings with perfect calm and equanimity, despite the fact that he was only just over four years old and had never had any experience of court life. On that day, he was dressed in the robes of a Buddhist *bhikksu* or monk, which he considers his most important title. After this ceremony, which took place at Nagchuka, he rode in the *phebjam,* a gilded palanquin. Willing hands bore him; ropes extending in front of and behind the palanquin itself allowed more people to have the honour of acting as bearers, which accounts for the story that he had forty-six people to carry him. The procession swelled every day, growing in both size and magnificence.

At Dum Uma Thang, he received the Regent and the Lord Chancellor and spent three days at Reting monastery. By now, it was time to hurry: official astrologers had determined that the whole of the ninth month would be an inauspicious time to arrive, and rather than wait until the tenth month the party decided to press on and arrive before the end of the eighth. Everyone wanted to get to Lhasa, because they had already been nearly three months on the road.

On the outskirts of Lhasa, at Dögu-thang, the last and greatest welcoming committee was assembled. The Prime Minister was there, with the rest of the cabinet, and the Abbots of Drepung, Ganden, and Sera. Hugh Richardson was also there, the head of the British Mission in Tibet. He was the first of the foreign national representatives to meet the Dalai Lama, but the Bhutanese, Nepalese, and Chinese were not far behind. The Tibetan army was on parade, ready to escort the Inmost One, and everyone in Lhasa who could walk was out to accompany the procession as it entered the Holy City.

This veneration of a four year old child may seem extraordinary, but it is important to remember that the Tibetans are a highly practical people, and gushing servility is not their way. Yes, the Dalai Lama is the most important person in the Tibetan nation. Yes, he is the focus both of that nation and of its religion. But that does not mean that everyone was permanently crawling in front of him, or singing his praises to his face. What the Tibetan people were doing was expressing their love and respect.

This is one of the most difficult things to convey to anyone who has not met the Dalai Lama. Respect seems natural when you meet him, but it is not awe. You can talk with him, and laugh with him, and discuss things with him, and although the underlying respect remains it is like being in the presence of a very old and warm friend. You feel too that there is nothing to hide; he will understand whatever you say. You know that you are in the presence of what the Indians call a *mahatma,* or Great Soul, and you cannot help liking him. He has the most beautiful smile, too, which will appear at the most unexpected moments – in the middle of a solemn *puja* in the Temple, or after a long explanation of some difficult point, when his brow has been furrowed with concentration. It is one of those smiles that is like the sun breaking through, and if it is directed at you, you never forget it.

Even as a child, these qualities were obvious. He radiated calm, which is very nearly unheard of in a four-year-old, and those who were there will tell how he sat through long ceremonies which would tax even an adult. They describe him as being at once restful and alert, which is a fair description to this day.

The actual entry into Lhasa took place in late 1939. The procession itself had been whittled down to a manageable size, with everyone accorded a position in keeping with his rank. The road he took was packed on both sides. Everyone was there: the aged, the infirm, and the sick were carried, so that they might at least have a glimpse of the Inmost One. There were thousands upon thousands of monks in their maroon robes, and the officials of the court wore their finest yellow ceremonial silks. The women wore beautiful dresses with vivid blouses and aprons; the riot of colour was dazzling. As the palanquin passed, a great cry went up: *"Kyi-pa nyima shar! Kyi-pa nyima shar!"* – "The sun of our happiness is risen!" As His Holiness said in *My Land and My People:* "I felt as if I were in a great park covered with beautiful flowers, whilst soft breezes blew across it and peacocks elegantly danced before me. There was an unforgettable scent of wild flowers, and a song of freedom and happiness in the air…"

In March 1940, just after the Tibetan new year, he was enthroned. It was an occasion of truly Oriental splendour. The Lion Throne of Tibet, which may be occupied only by the Dalai Lama, is a massive structure of gilded wood supported by eight carved and gilded lions – the Snow Lions of Tibet, which give the throne its name. There are five cushions in the Five Colours, and because no one may sit higher than the Inmost One, the whole structure towers some six or seven feet. Lesser Lamas and officials have proportionately lower seats, and in the highly formal days of old Tibet it was possible to ascertain anyone's status to the finest degree by the height of his seat. Small cushion-mattresses, rather similar to Japanese *tatame* cushions, would be stacked up and then covered with carpets; sometimes, two or even three carpets could be used to get the exact gradation of height.

The ceremonies were interminable. There were long, sonorous invocations, interspersed with the bass roar of the four-yard-long *dung-chen* or 'great horn'; the trilling and ringing of the *drilbu* or hand-bell; the cry, like an English hunting horn, of the *gyalings;* and the beating of many kinds of drum, from the rapid patter of the little hand-held *damaru* to the deep, dull, unearthly thump of drums that took two monks to carry. There were little ceremonial dances with music and mime, and debates on Buddhist topics – something of a spectator sport among Tibetans, and a subject to which we shall return later. All through this, the little boy sat with perfect composure, dispensing blessings in the appropriate way to the hundreds of people who came to pay homage, although no one had shown him how.

It was all a far cry from the way that things are organised now in Dharamsala. The *pujas* still go on for hours, but that is a mark of respect to the religion, not the man. Now, the Dalai Lama sits on a Western armchair at the same height as his guests when he is giving an audience, and laughingly pulls to their feet *Inji* (Westerners) who try to perform prostrations. There is, he admits, a good deal of reaction in his present attitude against the excessive ceremonial of the Tibet he knew. More than once, he said that all the protocol and etiquette that grew up around the Dalai Lama served no useful purpose: things that started out as a simple mark of respect became fossilised into ritual.

A good example of excessive etiquette is the convention that you should never turn your back on the Dalai Lama. As his brother Tendzin Choegyal pointed out, this is not very practical: Tibetan architecture, like the Tibetan landscape, is very uneven and given to sudden long drops, so too much backing away can lead to trouble. His sister, Mrs Pema Gyalpo, confirmed this with a story of an event she had once witnessed. A French nun was standing by the side of the road at Thekchen Choeling when the Dalai Lama was passing in his car. Head bowed, palms pressed firmly together, she kept on backing respectfully further and further out of the way until she disappeared backwards over the side of the road! Fortunately, although the hill slopes down for a thousand feet to the valley below, it is a gentle slope and well covered with trees and vegetation. The immediate drop was only a few feet, and she rolled for another few, but she was not hurt. The remarkable thing was that as she bounced and tumbled, her hands still remained firmly together.

Until His Holiness was six years old, he had little schooling. He presided at *pujas,* but his role was mostly passive: it was simply a matter of being there. He was assigned three monks to look after him, one to take care of his clothing and similar needs (the *Zimpon Khenpo*), one to look after his food (the *Supon Khenpo*), and one to look after his religious paraphernalia *(Choepon Khenpo)*. These three followed him everywhere he went.

Although at this age his time was his own, he had little to fill it. His only playmate was still his brother Lobsang Samten, whose time was increasingly taken up with his own schooling, and although the monks did their best to keep him amused, there were

no other children to play with. He and his parents could see one
another whenever they wanted, but there was now a barrier between
them: his role as Dalai Lama took precedence over his role as their
son, though they still remained as close as protocol would permit.
His father concerned himself mainly with his horses – he had always
been a great rider, even when he was a small farmer, and now he
supervised his stables himself – and the Great Mother had her
younger children to look after. Neither of his parents had their
heads turned by their sudden elevation to the nobility, and it was
only with difficulty that his mother could be persuaded to wear the
gorgeous silk coats that were expected of her: under them, she still
wore a simple *chuba*, and she retained her preference for simple
clothes to the end of her life. Rinchen Khando, Tendzin Choegyal's
wife, looked after her in her declining years. Looking after an
elderly mother-in-law is seldom easy, but Rinchen-la has only good
to say of her. In many ways, she seems to have been close to the
ancient Roman ideal, a capable woman who ruled the house well
and clung to the simple ways of the past.

Rinchen Khando-la tells a charming story of an audience she had
with the Dalai Lama when the Great Mother was still alive. He
asked her if she had any requests to make, but even though she is his
sister-in-law she still gets tongue-tied sometimes in his presence.
She stammered out a request to His Holiness to live as long as
possible, for the good of the Tibetan people. He laughed, and asked
her if there was anything more, something for herself. She asked
this time that he would say prayers for *Ama-la*, the usual Tibetan
word of respect for an older woman which means literally
'respected mother'. He laughed again. "Do you mean your Ama-la
or my Ama-la?" he said.

The little Dalai Lama, with or without his brother, roamed
through the endless rooms of the Potala and the Norbulingka or
Summer Palace. The buildings were every child's dream of a
magical attic, because there were store-rooms containing an
incredible variety of riches. Some contained conventional wealth –
statues made of gold and set with precious stones, or 'white gold', as
platinum was known in Tibet. Others contained treasures far more
valuable to a child – suits of armour, weapons, and mechanical
devices of all kinds.

The Dalai Lama's well-known interest in things mechanical dates from this time. He had only to play with some new mechanical toy, such as a music box or a clockwork animal, to be consumed with curiosity about how it worked; and in a very short time, he would have it to pieces. Some of the mechanical toys were very old and very valuable, because they were presents from the Tsars, who had employed some of the finest French craftsmen of the eighteenth and nineteenth centuries. The three guardians would wince when he dismembered yet another priceless antique; but then they would be wide-eyed in amazement when he reassembled it, and it ran like new.

He was not always successful, though. On one occasion, he found a particularly handsome music box which did not work; at some time in the past it had been over-wound, or perhaps even wound backwards. He was in the middle of dismantling it when suddenly the spring was freed, and it began to run backwards at many times the normal speed. The teeth of the musical 'comb', which were operated by lugs on a drum in the usual way, were weakened by rust: unable to stand the violent shock, they snapped and flew like shrapnel. The Dalai Lama just closed his eyes and ducked his head: "If even one of those pieces of metal had caught me in the eye, I would have been blinded". The crazy clattering jangling mechanism ran for perhaps ten seconds, but it seemed like an eternity to everyone who was present.

With increasing practice, though, he was able to perform the most remarkable feats. The first watch he ever took to pieces was his own, and it ran perfectly after he had put it back together again. Although he admits that there were a few failures after that, he rapidly became an expert watch repairer before his teens; Heinrich Harrer, author of *Seven Years in Tibet,* recounts how His Holiness repaired his watch, which ran perfectly ever afterwards. He was not afraid of new technology either: his brother Lobsang Samten says that he takes digital watches apart to this day, and has even mastered the microsoldering techniques needed to repair them. Nowadays, he has little time to take things apart just for the fun of it; but he would still rather repair something himself than have someone else do it.

As boys, he and Lobsang Samten also enjoyed more conventional pleasures. The Norbulingka was not just a summer palace; the name means 'Jewel Garden', and there were beautiful parks and ponds for running and even boating. The boat that the boys used was very small, and the three monk-guardians used to hover on the bank in an agony of concern, but nothing ever happened. The main lake was full of carp, and sometimes the two boys would catch them in a net, though they always let them go again. The fish were so tame that they would rise to the surface at the sound of oars, or even a football beside the lake, expecting to be fed. There were also hundreds of fruit trees in the Norbulingka, and they used to pick the fruit and eat it; His Holiness is not fond of fruit nowadays, and says that this might be a result of frequent over-indulgence as a child.

The surplus fruit, of which there was a tremendous amount, was given to the officials and others who lived between the Inner and Outer Walls of the Norbulingka; the Inner Wall, of course, marked the area reserved for His Holiness and his attendants. The Royal Family, as they were known, lived in this cordon between the Inner and Outer Walls, and there are several stories about them which are worth telling. One of particular interest concerns Tendzin Choegyal, the youngest child.

The Great Mother gave him a .22 rifle that had formerly belonged to Lobsang Samten. After a few days of regular target practice, he became bored; the windows of an unoccupied room in a Chinese house nearby were irresistible. The Chinese, understandably, were furious; they sent a servant around to complain. The Royal Family were not inclined to talk to Chinese servants; their gardener was left to explain matters. When the Chinese had stopped jumping up and down, he gravely explained that the Young Master had in fact been shooting at a target, but had missed. This only intensified the Chinaman's rage: he screamed "Shooting at a target? And missed? Six times? Six windows?" The gardener looked at him very coldly, with the air of one who is not accustomed to being questioned, and replied, "Yes".

Tendzin Choegyal also had a miniature pony, which as a foal he used to take up onto the roof of the house. Even after it had grown to full size, he persisted in this childish eccentricity; the cook, who was very traditionally minded, said that a horse on the roof was the strangest of all the strange things he had seen, and it bode ill for Tibet. He was to be proved right a thousand times over.

The behaviour of His Holiness's elder sister also shows that Tibetan ladies, from whatever class, were not inclined to be less adventurous than the men. In the 1950s, motor-cycling was a great fad in Lhasa, and even this young lady (she would have been about 19) got one. It was only a very low-powered machine, but she never quite mastered the art of stopping it (assuming, of course, that the brakes actually worked). As a result, she would career madly around the courtyard until she got tired, and then yell "OK – catch me!" Her brothers had a trying time, especially from being burnt by the hot exhaust pipe, but one of them recalls that when she was first learning to ride, their sister's leg was permanently marked with burns sustained when the machine fell over.

His Holiness was rather more decorous, but in addition to such innocent pursuits as foot-races on the lawn, he and Lobsang Samten used to fight. As Lobsang Samten explains, though, it was much harder to hit his little brother now that he was the Dalai Lama, "and so he used to beat me up!" He still swears that marks on his cheeks come from the merciless beatings His Holiness used to give him, but the way that he laughs when he tells the story gives the lie to what he says. It is obvious that the idea of being beaten up by the Dalai Lama still amuses him, four and a half decades after it happened.

Apparently, aged Lamas would also play the most undignified games with the young Presence. At the time, he says, he missed the company of other children; now, looking back on it, he is amazed at what wonderful playmates those old Lamas could be. Many of them had been administrators and officials since the previous century, and they might not have played games for fifty years, but they entered into the spirit of the thing with gusto.

Like his counterparts in an English boarding school, he was brought up entirely by men; in fact, the life of any young Tibetan monk is surprisingly similar to that of a young Englishman at boarding school, with the main difference being the uniform. To anyone who is not used to it, there is something very funny about the sight of diminuitive monks playing Frisbees or football. In His Holiness's case, there were of course no other pupils except his brother; and there was no feminine equivalent of the School Matron. Despite this, he is entirely at home in all sorts of company: any woman who has been fortunate enough to be granted an audience will tell you what a charming host he is. He greeted one, who had dressed in traditional Tibetan style, with a great smile and

"Ah, you look just like a Lhasa lady!". The stories, which are still widely believed, about his never speaking to women are sheer nonsense and he distributes blessings in the same way to both sexes, with a laying on of hands.

By the time he was six, the time had come for formal instruction. His first teacher was Ling Rinpoche, of whom both he and his elder brother were at firstly heartily frightened. The Rinpoche was not harsh, but he was very strict: the smallest error in a lesson that was supposed to have been learned by heart brought nothing worse than a stern stare, but it was not a stare that anyone would want repeated. Ling Rinpoche accompanied His Holiness when he fled Tibet in 1959, and remained his teacher and adviser until his death in December 1983.

The curriculum was obviously heavily biased towards the study of religion, but even acquiring the basic skills of reading and writing Tibetan is demanding. This is because most words contain one or (more often) several 'silent' letters. They are not strictly silent, in that they influence the tone of the letters following them, but they do result in some frightening-looking spellings. For example, the word 'Dorje' (thunderbolt) would be correctly transliterated as 'rDorje', and the wrathful deity *Tam-din* is spelled *rTa.mgrin*. This reaches truly spectacular proportions in such constructions as *Jam.dpal.dByangs* (Jampalyang, or Manjushri, Lord of Wisdom) and *Ri.bo.rtse.lnga* (Riwotsenga, the Five-Peaked Mountain where Jampalyang resides). The rules are hard to learn but they are consistent, though it is not hard to see why Tibetan words are rendered in different ways by different authors.

Once he had mastered reading and writing, it was time to embark upon the whole vast structure of Tibetan Buddhist learning. To begin with, there are the Five Major and Five Minor subjects. The Five Minor subjects are drama, dance and music, astrology, poetry and composition; His Holiness was particularly fond of drama and music. The Five Major subjects are Sanskrit, dialectics, arts and crafts, metaphysics and the philosophy of religion.

Because of the immense reverence which Tibetans feel for the Indian masters who introduced Buddhism to Tibet, the further sub-divisions are characterised both by Sanskrit names and by the infinitely fine parsing and categorisation which defeat so many would-be scholars from the West. For example, the study of dialectics together with metaphysics and the philosophy of religion is again divided into five branches: *Prajnaparamita,* the Transcendence of Wisdom; *Madhyamika,* the Middle Path; *Vinaya,* the Canon of Monastic Discipline; *Abidharma,* Metaphysics; and *Pramana,* Logic and Dialectics. *Pramana* was not accorded this importance in most of the Indian schools, but it is highly revered in Tibet because of the part that logic plays in Tibetan (and especially Gelugpa) religious education.

It was upon this formidable structure that the young Dalai Lama entered when he was six. At first sight, the way that he was taught closely resembled Western techniques of the nineteenth century: painstaking copy-book work, lecture-type lessons, and learning long passages by heart. There are, however, two major differences. The first is that understanding is promoted by dialectical debate between pupil and teacher, or between pupil and pupil under the direction of the teacher. Success in debate depends both on how fast the debater can recall the relevant scriptures, and on how well he can apply them to the subject in question. Neither a good memory nor intellectual ability is enough on its own.

The second is that meditation is a regular part of the curriculum. In one sense, meditation is the internal continuation of the debate, but there is much more to it than that. By visualising the various awareness-beings and imagining himself with their qualities, the student gains a deeper understanding of himself, of his religion, of the world, and of his relationships with religion and the world.

As the Dalai Lama explains there are two ways of approaching Buddhism: by faith, and by reason. The path of faith is good, in that it will lead the person who follows it to perform right actions which will help all beings, and to refrain from wrong actions which will harm them, but it is essentially limited. The path of reason, on the other hand, is limitless. By following the path of reason, one can understand everything and achieve realisation. Obviously, an education which demands so much (and offers so much) is not suited to everyone; it requires a high degree of stamina merely to complete the course, let alone master it. But His Holiness did not merely master his religious education: he even found time for outside interests.

As he grew older, he came into contact with more people – other monks, and the Austrian refugees from internment in British India,

Heinrich Harrer and Peter Aufschnaiter. Herr Harrer, a moun-
taineer who had had the misfortune to be in India when the Second
World War broke out, was to become a friend and unofficial teacher
of the Dalai Lama for some years; indeed, he remains a friend as His
Holiness approaches fifty and he is in his seventies.

When they met, in 1946, the Dalai Lama was eleven years old and
ravenous for news and information about the outside world.
Harrer, who had travelled a good deal and was something of an
extrovert, was a Godsend. He was able to give the boy first hand
information about the places he had visited, and also to help him
make sense of books he had in the Potala and Norbulingka; even
before he met Harrer, the Dalai Lama had begun to teach himself
English from books. The Austrian's English was more than adequate,
and he found himself surprisingly close to the theoretically unapproachable Dalai Lama.

At His Holiness's instigation, Harrer made several movie films of
Lhasa, which they watched on a projector in a private cinema in the
Potala. His Holiness had been fascinated by moving pictures from
the first time that he encountered them, and he had actually rebuilt a
broken projector himself in order to be able to see them. When you
consider that this also involved working out how the electrical
connections in the projector worked, without any theoretical
knowledge of the workings of electricity or practical experience of
even a lightswitch, the extent of his mechanical ability becomes
obvious. The films which Harrer made allowed the Dalai Lama, in a
way to visit Lhasa, something that he had always wanted to do but
which protocol forbade: the way in which he was prevented from
mixing with his people is one of the many things which he objected
to in the old Tibet. At first, there was a certain amount of resistance
from the monks when they saw Harrer with his movie camera, but
when it became known that he was working for the Inmost One
their complaints had to subside.

He would also sit with His Holiness as the boy pored over his
atlases, and tell him what he knew of the countries on the maps. His
Holiness says that this had always been something which fascinated
him: he used to read the books and magazines that had found their
way across from British India, and try to match the places they
illustrated and described with the places on the map. His head
would fill with the strange place-names of Europe and Africa and

America, and he would dream about what life might be like in those almost unimaginable lands.

Harrer tells some of the stories of the young Dalai Lama's mechanical ability, such as the way that he used to repair the ramshackle generator at the Norbulingka whenever it broke down, which was frequently, but there are many more. One of the most remarkable concerns the cars that His Holiness and another young man put together. At some time in the early 1930s, three cars had been brought over the Himalayas in pieces, on mule-back and men's backs, as a present for the Great Thirteenth. They had been reassembled in Lhasa, a big old Dodge and two baby Austins of 1927 vintage, but although he had given them a little use the Dalai Lama had died shortly afterwards, and the cars had languished in a store since. There was a driver-mechanic, but he was not allowed to touch them – until the Fourteenth Dalai Lama took an interest. The driver had carried out simple maintenance, but now His Holiness and another young monk enlisted his help in restoring them after fifteen years of neglect. The unsophisticated engineering of the old American car meant that they could get it running again, whilst they managed to build one good Austin by cannibalising the other for parts. This is not a remarkable feat for Westerners, perhaps, but when considering His Holiness's background and upbringing, it is extraordinary.

On the other hand, His Holiness's first attempts at driving were not marked by total success. The driver was a rather short-tempered man – apparently, when he was working on the cars, he would jerk back when he grazed his knuckles, bump his bald head, jerk forward, burn himself on the hot exhaust perhaps, jerk back again, bump his head, and perhaps repeat the performance half a dozen times to the accompaniment of colourful oaths in steadily growing volume – and he did not want His Holiness to drive. Consequently, the young Dalai Lama (who would have been in his late teens) decided to take the vehicle when the driver was away, and have a go at driving it. He had intended to go out of the Inner enclosure, drive around between the Inner and Outer Walls, and return. Unfortunately, he misjudged the steering and took down a gate-post on his way out. This was easy enough to conceal from the driver, but the smashed headlamp-glass was more of a problem. There was no possibility of glueing it back together, and frosted glass of the kind that he needed was nowhere to be found in Lhasa. His Holiness therefore set about a piece of plain glass with a brush, a toothpick, and a thick syrup of sugar solution, and exactly reproduced the pattern on the smashed glass. The driver never found out.

Perhaps the most poignant story of His Holiness's youth, however, concerns his telescope. In a high place on the Potala, he used to spend hours watching his people in the streets of Lhasa. He could not mix with them in person, but he desperately wanted to be a part of them. He believes that the hours he spent looking through that telescope may have affected his eyesight, which is why he now has to wear glasses. Whether or not that is the case, his determination to share the life of the Tibetan people may go some way towards explaining his behaviour in exile, and the way in which he now leads his people.

Soon, however, there was to be yet another strand to his life, outside both his education and his private interests. By 1949, the Chinese communists had gained supremacy in their struggle with the Nationalists; in 1950, as the Dalai Lama was approaching his fifteenth birthday, they were massing on the Tibetan border, poised to invade the Land of Snows.

Invasion

On October 7th, 1950, the Chinese armies invaded Tibet. They attacked on six fronts, and as the Great Thirteenth had foreseen, the tiny and ill-equipped Tibetan army was no match for them. The ironically-named People's Liberation Army of the People's Republic of China was soon deep inside Tibet, and it was obvious that they were going to capture Lhasa. In some places, the Tibetans surrendered immediately, hoping to avoid provoking the Chinese into the looting and destruction that had accompanied the invasion of 1909-10. In others, they fought heroically. Neither approach had much impact on the relentless Chinese advance.

The invasion was not entirely unexpected. The Great Thirteenth had all but spelled it out, and many people both inside and outside Tibet had realised that as soon as the communists felt that they were sufficiently in control of China, Mongolia, and Turkestan, they would invade Tibet. They had persistently claimed some sort of suzerainty over Tibet, amounting sometimes to sovereignty, but until the twentieth century it was substantially irrelevant because they lacked either the communication or the coordination to enforce their claims.

As we have already seen, the way in which the Tibetans threw the Chinese out during the death-throes of the Manchu empire had left the country independent from every point of view – foreign policy, legislature, army, independent postal system, coinage, and so forth – and this independence had been recognised *de jure* by many countries of the world and *de facto* by almost all of the others: to pretend that Tibet was a part of China would be like pretending that Turkey still ruled Greece, or that Mexico still owned Arizona.

It was, therefore, a blatantly opportunist invasion of a small and defenceless country by a larger one. It was made all the easier by the fact that the British had recently granted independence to India, which provided the edifying spectacle of a wicked imperialist power divesting itself of its empire whilst a freedom-loving socialist state expanded *its* empire. India was finding its own destiny by means of a bloody civil war, and it was still lost in a post-independence euphoria which blamed all the troubles of Asia on Western imperialism: they were not prepared to believe that an Asian power could be every bit as imperialist. Tibet could look for no help there.

Recognising their desperate position, and the ruthless nature of the opposition, the Tibetan government sent telegrams to a number of leading world powers asking for help. The silence was deafening: the two greatest disappointments were the British, who politely (but understandably) regretted that since the independence of India all British treaty obligations had devolved upon the Indian government, and the Americans, who declined even to receive a Tibetan delegation.

It is not difficult to see why the British should have reacted as they did; they had had enough problems dealing with Gandhi and his supporters, and they were recovering from a bitter and bloody world war. There was no great will to fight, and even if there had been, the Indian government would almost certainly have refused the British army permission to use India as a base. Again, America had traditionally had little interest in the area, and American foreign policy has always been uncertain to the point of non-existence, so it was no surprise that they did not intervene. But India must bear a heavy burden of blame, not only for doing nothing – which, given the internal condition of the country after partition, was perhaps understandable – but also for refusing to give even moral support to Tibet, largely because they believed first that imperialism was a Western phenomenon, and secondly that in any case the Chinese could be persuaded to leave Tibet in the same way that Britain had been persuaded to leave India. What they ignored, of course, was that the British were essentially civilised and humane; under the Chinese, any demonstration would have been met with gunfire, and a political dissident who went on hunger strike simply saved the army the trouble of putting a bullet in the back of his head.

Matters were not made any easier by the fragmented leadership in Tibet. A small progressive faction, carrying on in the tradition of the Great Thirteenth Dalai Lama, struggled with a much larger mélange of individual interests, power groups, and traditionalists both religious and secular. As the Fourteenth Dalai Lama approached his majority, the grosser power struggles were in abeyance – they were waiting to see which way the new leader would turn – but there was still a great deal of palace intrigue. In fact, there may have been an attempt at a *coup* only a few years earlier, in 1946: it is said that the untimely death of the Dalai Lama's father was a result of his taking poison intended for the Regent.

Very little is known about this, though allegations and counter-allegations are still being made, and it is possible that the Dalai Lama himself was another possible target. Several highly-placed Tibetans, who for obvious reasons would prefer not to have their names revealed, told us that Tibet (in the words of one of them) 'had it coming'.

Although His Holiness does not volunteer information on this topic, he does agree that Tibet had to change, and that because they had refused to change themselves they could hardly be surprised when someone else tried to do it for them. He feels that he was far too isolated from reality, and that many of the leaders of the old Tibet carried conservatism to absurd lengths. Since the death of the Great Thirteenth, corruption had begun to creep back into public life, and as he said, "You have to admit that our religion needed purifying".

Although these strong words come from the very highest sources in Tibet, there is also a counter-current. It may be, they say, that Tibet deserved to be invaded, and that the country's karma explains everything; but surely that karma has now been settled. What could anyone do that deserved mass murder, the impoverishment of the country, attempted genocide, and over thirty years of suffering for six million Tibetans?

The fragmented Tibetan government negotiated with the Chinese, much as the sparrow negotiates with the hawk, but they knew that they were impotent. It would take something greater to achieve anything, and one idea spread like wildfire: give the Dalai Lama his majority immediately. It would mean throwing the entire responsibility for the government of the country on a boy of fifteen, whose education had been almost exclusively religious, and who said himself that he did not feel ready for such an immense task. On the other hand, that same boy was not only of outstanding intelligence and ability: he was also the focus of devotion and national identity for six million people, the vast majority of whom would gladly die for him. Patriotism is a powerful emotion, and when it is coupled with religious fervour it is all but unstoppable.

Furthermore, although his training had been religious, it still suited him very well to be a leader. His long practice at religious debate meant that he could marshall facts and weigh them with impressive speed; and his position as Dalai Lama meant that there was no taint of personal ambition to affect his judgement. Even his own death was not of great importance to him. As far as ambition is concerned the Dalai Lama says that he would like to be remembered as a Gandhi figure, who secured Tibet's freedom and then turned the power over to younger men. With regard to the Chinese, he says "My enemy is my best friend and my best teacher, because he gives me the opportunity to learn in adversity. You do not learn much from your friends when you are comfortable: you learn much more from your enemies!"

From another man, this might sound like pious humbug. You have only to hear him say it to realise that he does not just believe it: he *knows* it.

A month after the attack, in November 1950, he was given his majority and invested with the temporal leadership of Tibet. He was just fifteen years old. Despite the fighting a few hundred miles to the east, nothing was spared to make it an occasion to be remembered by the people of Lhasa – the fondness of Lhasa-dwellers for party-going is a byword in Tibet. It was the enthronement all over again: a general amnesty was proclaimed, and prisons were emptied, and there were endless *pujas* and parties. There was a note of hysteria in some, though: there were still people who believed that everything would turn out all right now that the Dalai Lama was in control, but others realised just how short a time it might be before the Chinese were at their doors.

Late in 1950, His Holiness formulated an approach to the Chinese and the United Nations. Because Tibet was not a member of the United Nations – one of the biggest mistakes they ever made, in the Dalai Lama's eyes – they had to pursue a roundabout course of finding sponsors who would support their case, but as early as November 7th a letter was sent direct to the Secretary General of the United Nations drawing attention to what was going on in Tibet. In the letter, the obvious parallel with the Korean war was drawn – but nobody reacted. Tibet was just too isolated.

A letter sent at the same time to the Chinese government stated that although there had been some troubles of late, His Holiness was now the Head of State in Tibet, and wished to renew the friendly relations which had for so long existed between the two countries. In the same letter, he requested the return of Tibetan prisoners, and that the Chinese should withdraw from those parts of Tibet that they had already occupied. Predictably, this letter was completely ineffective.

Of all the people to whom the Tibetans appealed for help, the reaction of the United Nations was the least forgivable. This was precisely the situation which the United Nations had been set up to resist: unprovoked and opportunist aggression by a large and powerful state seeking *lebensraum* by invading a smaller and weaker one. They did not lift a finger. As we have seen, there was not even the excuse that Tibet was in any way a part of China, or that China exercised suzerainty: Tibet had made independent treaties with several major powers (including Britain) between 1912 and 1949, and during the Second World War even the United States had recognised Tibet's *de facto* independence when negotiating for the right to transport supplies through the country.

The Dalai Lama realised that his nation stood alone. As a young man of Eastern Tibetan extraction – a people to whom freedom comes above all else – he was prepared to stand his ground and tell the Chinese to get out; but his advisers, perhaps better schooled in Chinese political methods, told him that the only possibility was to leave Lhasa as long as there was any danger to him.

Their advice was based on two considerations. First, there was the paramount consideration of the safety of the Dalai Lama. Even today, after decades of Communist indoctrination, it is probably true that the majority of Tibetans would willingly die for the Dalai Lama: anything which placed him in the slightest danger would be unthinkable. Secondly, His Holiness is the symbol of Tibet: as long as he lives, so does a free Tibet live in the hearts of all Tibetans. Without him, the whole uphill struggle to resist the Chinese without assistance might just prove too much, and Tibet would cease to exist as a nation. He appointed two 'prime ministers' before leaving, with plenipotentiary powers to negotiate with the Chinese. As usual, one was a monk and the other a lay official; their names were Losang Tashi and Lukhangwa. Then, on December 19th, 1950, he left for Yatung, south of Lhasa and just on the Tibetan side of the border with Sikkim.

It was a huge caravan, with one and a half thousand pack animals, though the number of people was comparatively small: His Holiness and his immediate family, an escort of forty noblemen, and a personal guard of about two hundred picked soldiers armed with rifles, machine-guns, and field artillery. There were also several hundred servants and animal drivers. One of the main reasons for the huge number of pack animals relative to the number of people was that His Holiness was taking the opportunity of moving some of the treasure which had accumulated over the centuries to Sikkim. Nominally the personal property of the Dalai Lama, it was a small fraction of the gifts and tributes of centuries. His Holiness saw it as something which he held in trust for the people of Tibet, and he realised that if the worst came to the worst it would be essential to have some funds outside Tibet with which to continue the struggle against the Chinese. It consisted mostly of silver and gold bullion and when the Dalai Lama reached Yatung it continued on into Sikkim, where it was placed in safe keeping.

In Yatung, poised to flee into exile, the Dalai Lama went over the whole scenario again and again in his mind. He decided that the best thing to do, if it was at all possible, was to try and placate the Chinese and live with them as peacefully as possible. He had no illusions about this: he simply thought that it was the best chance for avoiding still more bloodshed and misery, on the Chinese side as well as the Tibetan.

We asked His Holiness what the possibility of resistance would have been if Tibet had followed the example of Switzerland and had a fully-equipped citizen army, or if they had had a 'well-regulated militia' with their own arms along the lines of that guaranteed by the Second Amendment to the Constitution of the United States. He shook his head. "At most," he said, "we would have had rifles, revolvers, perhaps a few machine-guns. We were fighting against aircraft, bombs, and heavy artillery. It would have made no difference." In fact, there was no gun control of any kind in Tibet, and more than one family had as their most prized possession a Bren gun; but against an opponent that had no compunction in shooting women and children hostages, or bombing a village or monastery because it might possibly be sheltering resistance fighters, bravery and small arms were hardly enough.

Meanwhile, in Eastern Tibet, the local Tibetan governor was

attempting to reason with the Chinese. The former governor, Lhalu, had just been replaced after his normal tour of duty by Ngabo Ngawang Jigme, who had only just been installed when the Chinese invaded. He believed that there was some possibility of negotiating and as he had on-the-spot experience he was appointed leader of a five-man delegation to Peking. He was told that he could treat with the Chinese on one very simple condition: that the Chinese army should advance no further during the negotiations. When he arrived in Peking, though, he found that the Chinese were as unable to imagine dealing with another state as an equal as they had ever been.

First, the delegation was refused all communication facilities with Lhasa. This meant that neither the two Prime Ministers nor the Dalai Lama had any idea of what was going on in Peking. Secondly, although the delegates were themselves initially well treated, they were soon shown the other side of their opponents' character. The Chinese presented them with a ready-drafted ten point agreement, and told them to sign it. It was drafted on the assumption that Tibet was a part of China, which raises the interesting question of why the Chinese found it necessary to negotiate: if they really were the sovereign power, what need was there to negotiate?

The Tibetans vigorously resisted this farcical 'agreement', but the only effect of this was that the Chinese reworded it so that there were seventeen points instead of ten, and then increased the pressure on them to sign Nor did this pressure stop at threats of personal violence, which recalls Chinese behaviour of nearly eight hundred years before. Genghis Khan sent ambassadors to the Chinese; the Chinese returned their mutilated bodies. He meditated at length on what to do, and came to the conclusion that any nation which could treat ambassadors like that was not civilised.

Thirdly, the Chinese armies were advancing all the time, though this was successfully concealed from the Tibetans. If the rate of their advance seems slow, it is worth remembering that they were encountering sporadic but violent resistance; that their supply lines were very long; that the army was in any case something of a rabble; and that they were fighting at very high altitudes. Violent exercise in the thin air of ten thousand feet or more can be dangerous, and the higher ranks were issued with oxygen bottles. Furthermore, the Tibetan winter was well under way, so conditions for the average

Chinese soldier were extremely harsh. Eventually, after prolonged physical and mental duress, the Tibetan delegation was prevailed upon to sign the 'agreement'. Even then, they refused to affix their seals, but this did not delay the Chinese for long: they forged duplicates forthwith.

The first that the Tibetan government heard of this 'agreement' was when it was broadcast over Peking radio. It was a farrago of nonsense, with no relation to reality and full of references to non-existent 'imperialist forces' in Tibet. In fact, it is worth quoting in its entirety, because it is the often-quoted 'Seventeen-Point Agreement', upon which China's subsequent actions were (nominally) based. It is also an agreement which the Chinese themselves repeatedly broke, which in the light of the circumstances under which it was dictated says little for Chinese integrity.

The Tibetan nationality is one of the nationalities with a long history within the boundaries of China and, like many other nationalities, it has done its glorious duty in the creation and development of the Motherland. But, over the last 100 years or more, imperialist forces penetrated into China and in consequence also penetrated into the Tibetan region and carried out all kinds of deceptions and provocations. Like previous reactionary Governments, the Kuomintang reactionary Government continued to carry out a policy of oppression and sowing dissention among the nationalities, causing division and disunity among the Tibetan people. The local government of Tibet did not oppose the imperialist deception and provocation, and adopted an unpatriotic attitude towards our great Motherland. Under such conditions, the Tibetan nationality and people were plunged into the depths of enslavement and suffering.

In 1949 basic victory was achieved on a nationwide scale in the Chinese people's war of liberation; the common domestic enemy of all nationalities – the Kuomintang reactionary Government – was overthrown, and the common foreign enemy of all nationalities – the aggressive imperialist forces – was driven out. On this basis, the founding of the People's Republic of China and of the Central People's Government was announced.

In accordance with the Common Programme passed by the Chinese People's Political Consultative Conference, the Central People's Government declared that all nationalities within the boundaries of the People's Republic of China are equal, and that they shall establish unity and mutual aid and oppose imperialism and their own public enemies, so that the People's Republic of China will become a big family of fraternity and co-operation, composed of all its nationalities. Within the big family of all nationalities of the People's Republic of China, national regional autonomy shall be exercised in areas where national minorities are concentrated, and all national minorities shall have freedom to develop their spoken and written languages and to preserve or reform their customs, habits, and religious beliefs, and the Central People's Government shall assist all national minorities to develop their political, economic, cultural, and educational construction work. Since then, all nationalities within the country – with the exception of Tibet and Taiwan – have gained liberation. Under the unified leadership of the Central People's Government and the direct leadership of higher levels of People's Governments, all national minorities have fully enjoyed the right of national equality and have established, or are establishing, national regional autonomy.

In order that the influence of aggressive imperialist forces in Tibet might be successfully eliminated, the unification of the territory and sovereignty of the People's Republic of China accomplished, and national defence safeguarded; in order that the Tibetan nationality and people might be freed and return to the big family of the People's Republic of China to enjoy the same rights of national equality as all other nationalities in the country and develop their political, economic, cultural and educational work, the Central People's Government, when it ordered the People's Liberation Army to march into Tibet, notified the local government of Tibet to send delegates to the central authorities to conduct talks for the conclusion of an agreement on measures for the peaceful liberation of Tibet.

In the latter part of April 1951, the delegates with full powers of the local government of Tibet arrived in Peking. The Central People's Government appointed representatives with full powers to conduct talks on a friendly basis with the delegates with full powers of the local government of Tibet. As a result of these talks, both parties agreed to establish this agreement and guarantee that it be carried into effect.

(1) The Tibetan people shall unite and drive out imperialist aggressive forces from Tibet; the Tibetan people shall return to the big family of the Motherland – the People's Republic of China.

(2) The local government of Tibet shall actively assist the People's Liberation Army to enter Tibet and consolidate the national defences.

(3) In accordance with the policy towards nationalities laid down in the Common Programme of the Chinese People's Political Consultative Committee, the Tibetan people have the right of exercising national regional autonomy under the unified leadership of the Central People's Government.

(4) The central authorities will not alter the existing political system in Tibet. The central authorities also will not alter the established status,

functions, and powers of the Dalai Lama. Officials of various ranks shall hold office as usual.

(5) The established status, functions, and powers of the Panchen Ngoerhtehni shall be maintained.

(6) By the established status, functions, and powers of the Dalai Lama and the Panchen Ngoerhtehni are meant the status and functions of the thirteenth Dalai Lama and of the ninth Panchen Ngoerhtehni when they were in friendly and amicable relations with each other.

(7) The policy of freedom of religious belief laid down in the Common Programme of the Chinese People's Political Consultative Committee shall be carried out. The religious beliefs, customs, and habits of the Tibetan people shall be respected and Lama monasteries shall be protected. The central authorities will not effect a change in the income of the monasteries.

(8) Tibetan troops shall be reorganised step by step into the People's Liberation Army and become a part of the national defence force of the People's Republic of China.

(9) The spoken and written language and school education of the Tibetan nationality shall be developed step by step in accordance with the actual conditions in Tibet.

(10) Tibetan agriculture, livestock-raising, industry, and commerce shall be developed step by step, and the people's livelihood shall be improved step by step, in accordance with the actual conditions in Tibet.

(11) In matters related to various reforms in Tibet, there will not be any compulsion on the part of the central authorities. The local government of Tibet shall carry out reforms of its own accord and, when the people raise demands for reform, they shall be settled by means of consultation with the leading personnel of Tibet.

(12) Insofar as former pro-imperialist and pro-Kuomintang officials resolutely sever relations with imperialism and the Kuomintang, and do not engage in sabotage or resistance, they may continue to hold office irrespective of their past.

(13) The People's Liberation Army entering Tibet shall abide by all the above-mentioned policies and shall also be fair in all buying and selling and shall not arbitrarily take a needle or thread from the people.

(14) The Central People's Government shall have centralised handling of all external affairs of the area of Tibet; and there will be peaceful co-existence with neighbouring countries and establishment and development of fair commercial and trading relations with them on the basis of equality, mutual benefit and mutual respect for territory and sovereignty.

(15) In order to ensure the implementation of this agreement, the Central People's Government shall set up a Military and Administrative Committee, and a Military Area Headquarters in Tibet, and apart from the personnel sent there by the Central People's Government, shall absorb as many local Tibetan personnel as possible to take part in the work. Local Tibetan personnel taking part in the Military and Administrative Committee may include patriotic elements from the local government of Tibet, various districts, and various principal monasteries; the name-list shall be drawn up after consultation between the representatives designated by the Central People's Government and various quarters concerned and shall be submitted to the Central People's Government for appointment.

(16) Funds needed by the Military and Administrative Committee, the Military Area Headquarters, and the People's Liberation Army shall be provided by the Central People's Government. The local government of Tibet should assist the People's Liberation Army in the purchase and transport of food, fodder, and other daily necessities.

(17) This agreement shall come into force immediately after signatures and seals are affixed to it.

Signed and sealed by the delegates of the Central People's Government with full powers:

Chief Delegate – Le Wei-Han (Chairman of the Commission of Nationalities Affairs)

Delegates – Chang Ching-wu, Chang Kuo-hua, Sun Chih-yuan

Delegates with full powers of the local government of Tibet:

Chief Delegate – Kalon Nagbou Nagabou Ngawang Jigme (Ngabo Shape)

Delegates – Dzasak Khemey Sonam Wangdi, Khentrung Thupten Tenthar, Khenchung Thupten Lekmuun, Rimshi Samposey Tenzin Thundup

Peking, 23rd May, 1951.

Such treaties seldom make edifying reading, but it is worth studying this one in detail, as the way in which the Chinese broke every clause that they could in their favour will become apparent in later chapters.

At the time, though, the Dalai Lama and the Kashag did not know just how cynically the Chinese were going to behave. Apart from the fantasies about 'imperialist aggressors' and the completely unacceptable assertions that Tibet was a part of China, there was some ground for hope in the document. The Chinese had made many guarantees of non-interference, and it looked as if it might be possible to come to some sort of working arrangement within the

1. The Great Thirteenth Dalai Lama, Lhasa, c. 1930.

2. After signing the treaty; the Younghusband expedition of 1904.

3. Mixed British, Tibetan and Chinese influences in a portrait of Sir Charles Bell *(back row, fourth from right)* with a Tibetan delegation and an unknown senior officer.

4. The Great Thirteenth Dalai Lama, with Sir Charles Bell seated on his right, probably about 1920.

5. Chenrezi, God of Compassion, in thousand-armed, eleven-headed form.

6. The mother and father of the Fourteenth Dalai Lama, with *(left to right)* Tendzin Choegyal, Mrs Pema Gyalpo (as she now is), and Lobsang Samten.

7. His Holiness the Dalai Lama at a very early age, possibly on the way to Lhasa in 1939.

8. The parents of the Fourteenth Dalai Lama with their two youngest children, about 1947.

9. The Fourteenth Dalai Lama, aged about 15.

10. The Peak Potala in Lhasa.

11. The flight to Tezpur after the Chinese invasion in 1950. His Holiness is in the palanquin; the smoke is pine-incense.

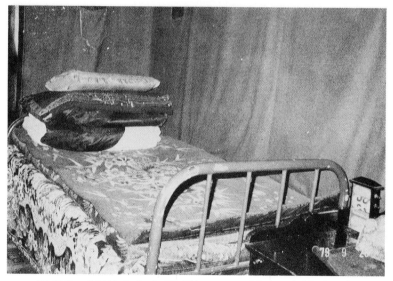

12. His Holiness's bed in the Potala. The Chinese preserve it 'as a symbol that he is always welcome to return'.

13. Soldiers in traditional dress. Parades in antique armour – some over a thousand years old – took place every year in Lhasa.

14. The Dalai Lama on a picnic, probably on the way back from China, 1955.

15. China, 1954. The Dalai Lama with Chou En-Lai.

16. The Buddha Jayanti, 1956: at Benares station.

17. During the Buddha Jayanti pilgrimage, 1956.

18. During the escape from Lhasa, March/April 1959.

19. At Tezpur in June 1959, immediately after the flight from Tibet.

20. The ruins of Kyigudo monastery, Kham, shelled and bombed by the Chinese.

21. The leader of a Tibetan guerilla band examining *thangkas* and religious books destroyed by the Chinese.

22. A Khamba guerilla with a *gau*, or portable shrine containing a photograph of His Holiness, worn as an amulet.

23. In Mongolia, 1979.

24. A *puja* in the Temple at Thekchen Choeling, about 1979.

25. Dharamsala, dawn, winter 1982.

26. His Holiness visiting Japan in 1980.

27. Their Holinesses the Pope and the Dalai Lama, Rome.

28. Speech commemorating the 25th anniversary of the Lhasa Uprising, 1959–1984. Dharamsala, March 10th 1984.

29. After the 1984 March 10th speech, Dharamsala.

30. His Holiness at his desk, Dharamsala 1984.

framework of the 'agreement'. There was even a certain amount that His Holiness agreed with concerning the need for reform in Tibet, and he hoped that by working with the Chinese there might be some genuine progress.

Accordingly, he agreed to meet the Chinese general who would be in command in Tibet. Astonishingly, in view of later Sino-Indian relations (and China's behaviour in attacking a peaceful border state), the Chinese general entered Tibet via India, so he passed through Yatung on the way. It was there that His Holiness met him, and he describes in his own words how he felt: "I do not know exactly what I had expected, but what I saw was three men in grey suits and peaked caps who looked extremely drab and insignificant among the splendid figures of my officials in their red and golden robes. Had I but known, the drabness was the state to which China was to reduce us all before the end, and the insignificance was certainly an illusion."

Living with the Chinese

In the summer of 1951, a garrison of about six thousand Chinese troops arrived to occupy Lhasa. They bought and rented some houses, but others they simply requisitioned despite Article 13 of the Seventeen-Point Agreement which said that they should not 'arbitrarily take a needle or thread from the people'. They also established a huge military camp near the Norbulingka. In order to feed this huge army, they then demanded a 'loan' of 2,000 tons of barley, which was far more than was available in government granaries. The Tibetan government had to buy or borrow the grain wherever it could, without any financial aid from the Chinese. Article 16 had already been broken.

Nor were these military and logistical problems the only ones. General Chang Chin-wu, one of the 'drab and insignificant' generals that His Holiness had seen in Yatung, threw a tantrum because he had not been received with the honours that he felt were due to him. The day he arrived, he was greeted by two ministers of the Kashag, and then he was the guest of honour at a dinner attended by both Prime Ministers, but he felt that he deserved better than this.

Among the soldiers of the occupying army, two attitudes prevailed. Some, mostly in the upper ranks, were out-and-out colonialists: like the worse imperialists of the nineteenth century, they expected the locals to jump to it and fulfil their every command. Others had genuinely believed that they were going to liberate the unfortunate peasants of Tibet – which, given the lot of the average peasant in China, was not an unreasonable assumption – and the contrast between the welcome they expected and the welcome they received was altogether too much for them. Some joined the ranks of the colonialists; some died at the hands of Tibetan freedom fighters; and a few made genuine efforts to help the Tibetans. These last suffered most, caught between Tibetan suspicion and the excesses of their own superiors.

In the face of all this, His Holiness was in a terrible dilemma. Above all else, he wanted to minimise the suffering of the Tibetan people, but in view of the complete disregard of the Chinese for even the agreement which they had imposed by force he had to accept that the prospects for a peaceful settlement were not good. As a young Amdowa, he could understand the urge that made his people fight. He was and is firmly committed to peace, but not to peace at any price; this was to become an increasing problem. He knew, though that if his people did fight, the Chinese would retaliate mercilessly: there would be no question about who would win.

He knew too that he was a pivot in the whole process. His people would do whatever he told them to, and if he had a better understanding of the situation than they, he could perhaps make more informed decisions. He did not want that responsibility, but he saw no alternative. It would have been easy for him to emulate many a deposed king, and go into exile, but he was driven by two things: the sense of duty which any honourable man would feel in his position, and his vow as a Bodhisattva to work for the good of all sentient beings.

Constantly, he tried to cool down the ever more heated tempers of both his own people and the Chinese. But at every turn there was a new problem. A few months after they had sent in the original garrison, the Chinese drafted in another eight or ten thousand men from China: precise figures are not available, least of all from the Chinese, but the net result was that for the first time in recorded history, well over a millenium, Lhasa was reduced to famine conditions. According to Article 10, 'the people's livelihood shall be improved step by step, in accordance with the actual conditions in Tibet'...

There were unforseeable results, too. There is an old custom in Lhasa, remarked upon by everyone who went there in pre-Invasion times, of singing pointed songs about topical incidents – a Tibetan equivalent of a West Indian calypso. Inevitably, the occupying Chinese troops were the butt of many such songs: even if they could not understand what the Tibetans were singing, the derision and laughter which accompanied the words injured their tender sensibilities. The net result was that Chang Chin-wu demanded a Tibetan government proclamation banning singing in the streets!

Others expressed their disapproval in more practical ways. Small children threw stones at Chinese soldiers, and their parents began to meet in small groups to discuss resistance. The country was very close to outright war.

The Dalai Lama did his best to discourage the nascent resistance movement, reminding people of their duties as Buddhists and making it known that he would not support any resistance group. On the other hand, he was also trying to persuade the Chinese that the state of unrest was only temporary, and that when things had settled down they would be all right. He and his ministers constantly tried to calm down the more hysterical overreactions of the Chinese, and to guide them along the paths which would lead to the least resistance from the Tibetans.

The Chinese did not appreciate this. They were utterly rude and intransigent, and regularly lost their tempers and screamed insults at the Tibetan officials with whom they were supposed to be negotiating over 'reforms', such as collectivisation, the integration of the Tibetan army into the Chinese, and the structure of local administration. In all fairness, the obstinacy of Tibetans is proverbial, and the Chinese cannot have made much headway.

At first, the Chinese dealt mainly with the two Prime Ministers and with other members of the Kashag, but they tried more and more to deal with His Holiness directly. Things came to a head when they fell out with both Prime Ministers in quick succession. First, General Chang Chin-wu lost his temper with the monastic Prime Minister, Losang Tashi, during an audience with His Holiness, who had to intervene to stop him attacking the monk. Next, during a long and angry discussion about amalgamating the armies, the lay Prime Minister Lukhangwa pointed out that the whole idea of friendly relations as expounded by the Chinese was absurd. "If you hit a man upon the head and break his skull," he said, "you can hardly expect him to be friendly". The Chinese stormed out, and made it known that they expected an apology. The next time they met with Lukhangwa, however, he expanded upon his theme.

Chinese anger against the pair of them was such that the Dalai Lama regretfully decided to accept their resignations. There would have been little point in their staying on, because the Chinese would have refused to deal with them, and His Holiness believes that if they had stayed on their personal safety would have been at risk. Thereafter, they dealt more and more with the Dalai Lama directly. As they saw it, there were three major advantages to this.

First, he was (and is) undoubtedly able to speak for all Tibet; such advice and advisers as he chooses to accept are his concern alone, and he need not refer his decisions to anyone. Secondly, he was (and is) less bound by tradition than any of his advisers. The Great Thirteenth had entertained few doubts about the need for change, and the Fourteenth had already voiced many similar ideas. The Chinese entertained hopes that they might be able to persuade him that their reforms were the right ones. Thirdly, and perhaps most importantly, he was only a teenager. The advisers were all politicians of many years' standing, and well experienced in the ways of the world; a teenager, standing on his own, must have looked like a much easier option.

What they did not realise was that this teenage boy was immune to promises of personal benefit, which made him very difficult to threaten or intimidate. Nor were they aware of his intelligence and quickness, which made him a formidable opponent in debate; there would be no question of slipping things past without his noticing. And finally, they completely underestimated his devotion to his land and his people. There were some Chinese who believed in the rightness of their cause as strongly as His Holiness believes in the rightness of his, but they were very much in the minority. Most had a very limited outlook, and could not comprehend the breadth of the Dalai Lama's vision, or appreciate the myriad factors he took into account before making any decision.

To the Chinese, his attitude looked like conciliation, if not actual weakness. As their confidence grew, their hysteria declined some-what, and the potentially explosive situation gradually calmed on both sides. They were still very insensitive, though: one example of their thoughtlessness was stationing armed guards outside the door when they were in audience with His Holiness. Not only was this a dire breach of diplomatic etiquette, it was also quite useless. If the Tibetan guards had thought that there was the slightest threat to the Inmost One, they would have killed every Chinaman in sight without compunction, no matter how many men they lost themselves.

What His Holiness was doing, apart from trying to cool down the immediate confrontation, was to buy time. He still had some hopes that one of the great powers, perhaps Britain, would come to his aid; and he knew that although there seemed to be no hope for the moment, things could change rapidly. If only he could keep the worst at bay for a while, the country might be in a fit state to take advantage of some future opportunity.

Contacts with other powers came to nothing, though. The British, as already stated, were having nothing to do with the area and the Indians were drunk with independence and the myth of the solidarity of Asian peoples. 'Hindi-Chini Bhai-Bhai' was the catch-phrase of the day (*bhai* means 'brother'), and the Indians were to go on advising the Tibetans to rely on Chinese goodwill until 1959. Shortly after that, they would find that the reason there had never been a war between China and India was that there had always been Tibet as a buffer state.

Faced with apparent cooperation, but little actual progress, the Chinese decided in the summer of 1952 to try a different tack. They suggested that a delegation of Tibetans – officials, and members of families who enjoyed some standing in Tibet – might care to tour China and see the advantages that Communism had brought to the country; they even suggested that this might allay Tibetan fears about freedom of religion, which they would see was practised freely throughout China.

The Tibetans were not deceived. They knew that the Chinese were past-masters at showing only what they wanted shown, and they also knew that a comparison between China old and new was irrelevant in Tibet. Tibet was not China, and did not share China's problems; their own problems were both smaller and different. Consequently, many sent servants instead of the family members that the Chinese wanted. This was made easier by the fact that accent does not indicate class in Tibet to anything like the extent that it does in most cultures; a servant is as likely as a nobleman to speak with the socially correct Lhasa accent.

The tour went through China proper, Inner Mongolia and north-east China. It was very heavily stage-managed, and at every stop the Tibetans were given long lectures about how the local people had benefitted from this or that innovation. The letters that they sent back were evidently written with an eye for the Chinese censor, and when they finally returned they were underwhelmed to a man.

Taking their cue from the Dalai Lama, they made polite noises whilst making absolutely no effort to cooperate any more than was strictly necessary, and this seems to have led the Chinese into thinking that they were making some progress. Later, other jaunts were organised for various sectors of Tibetan society, such as merchants, youth organisations, and monasteries.

Three years of this stalemate passed. Neither side felt that it was getting anywhere, but at least neither side felt that things were becoming intolerable: the Dalai Lama's waiting game seemed to be having some effect. In 1953, the Chinese invited His Holiness himself to go to China. By this time he was eighteen years old, and he had a practical training in diplomacy every bit as intense and demanding as his religious training. He felt that there might be a real chance of reaching some sort of understanding with the Chinese if he could speak to the central government himself; at the very least, he might be able to explain which reforms were suitable for Tibet, and which were not, and so change the course of the Chinese administrators in Tibet. Already, in addition to the known problems of famine, there were reports of Chinese atrocities and abuses of power, and he felt that there was some hope of heading off this sort of behaviour before it became widespread. Against strong advice from all sectors of Tibetan society, who feared that they would never see their Precious One again, he decided that he ought to go.

The journey was long and hard, but it was a matter of weeks now rather than months. The Chinese had built roads, with Tibetan forced labour, in order to be able to supply their military bases, so it was possible to use motor vehicles as the party neared China. The ride was slow and jolting, as the roads were no more than muddy and rutted dirt tracks, but it was better than walking.

On the way to China, at Sian, the Panchen Lama joined the party. They had already met briefly once, when the Panchen Lama (the Panchen Ngoerhtehni of the Agreement) had come to Lhasa to pay his respects to the Dalai Lama. He was even younger than the Dalai Lama, and had had one of the most peculiar upbringings imaginable. For centuries, the Chinese had tried to drive a wedge between the Dalai Lama and the Panchen Lama, the two most important Lamas in Tibet, and in the case of the Thirteenth Dalai Lama and the Ninth Panchen Lama, they had enjoyed a modest degree of success; the two were not on good terms when the Great Thirteenth died, though it was widely believed that the demise of the Panchen Lama shortly afterwards was a result of the remorse he felt over the quarrel.

The Tenth Panchen Lama had been brought up all his life in Chinese-controlled territory, and he had been subjected to a ceaseless stream of communist propaganda. He had only been recognised in 1951, and then as a part of a deal involving the Seventeen-Point Agreement: there had been two candidates put forward by the Tibetans, whilst he (although of Tibetan extraction) had been put forward by the Chinese. He was, apparently, a genuine incarnation and genuinely studied the Buddhist scriptures as would be expected. His Holiness says that he has no doubts that the Panchen Lama is a true Tibetan and has always worked for the good of Tibet – there was certainly a long period, from the 1960s to the 1970s, when he 'disappeared' under Chinese control – but the conflicts inherent in his upbringing must have been terrible.

The two Lamas continued on their way to Peking, where they were greeted handsomely. There were huge crowds, all waving and cheering; but they were all in uniform, all regimented, and His Holiness says that he had the uncomfortable feeling that they would as readily have been jeering and cat-calling if that was what they had been told to do. There was a feeling of unreality to everything, His Holiness says, but one tragic little glimpse emerges of how his youth was stolen from him. "Only a few years ago," he writes in *My Land and My People,* "flying or travelling by train would have seemed like a glorious dream. But now that I was doing them for the first time, my mind was much too full of our political misfortunes and my responsibilities for me to enjoy these new experiences".

Only two days after his arrival, he met Mao Tse-tung. Once again, the Tibetan understatement is employed to the full: "It was," the Dalai Lama says, "a memorable interview". The most difficult part was a point-blank question from Chairman Mao: was there anything which the Chinese representatives had done against his wishes? On the one hand, he could have reeled off a hundred or a thousand examples; on the other, he knew that to do so would probably have been rash to the point of suicide, for the Tibetan people if not for himself. With great diplomacy, he therefore indicated that because the Tibetan people had great hopes for the future under the leadership of Chairman Mao, they had always thought it best to express their opinions frankly and at the time when they differed from those of the Chinese representatives.

In a sequence of interviews, the Dalai Lama came to appreciate the extraordinary contradictions inherent in this very powerful man, who was effectively the dictator of the largest nation in the world. For example, at one meeting, Mao said, "I understand you very well. But of course, religion is poison. It has two great defects. It undermines the race, and secondly it retards the progress of the country. Tibet and Mongolia have both been poisoned by it". A few days later, he came to pay a social call; and in the course of it, he said that Buddhism was quite a good religion, that the Lord Buddha had given a lot of thought to improving the lot of the common people, and that the Goddess Tara (a very popular deity in Tibet) was a kind-hearted woman. Then he left.

On other occasions, His Holiness had the opportunity to see Mao at work. In general, he was not impressed with the Chinese method of government, in which old men sat in committees drinking endless cups of hot water (there was no tea, and His Holiness attributes his present liking for hot water to the amount of it he drank trying to ward off boredom) and listening to interminable speeches; four, five, six, and even seven hours were not unusual. Worst of all, at the end of their meanderings some senior official would stand up and state the party line, and everyone would agree with him: all their speeches were mere window-dressing.

When Mao was there, things were different. He was no lover of stereotyped party writing, and a long polemic against it appears in his own works. If empty words were being bandied about, he would angrily demand what was being *done*. On one occasion, when various high party officials were discussing the living standards of the people, he interrupted to say flatly that he was not satisfied, and quoted letters from his home village which criticised the behaviour of the local committee.

Although no one could object to such a 'grass roots' approach, it does lead one to wonder whether Mao did not spend so much time on detail that he lost sight of the bigger picture. There is no doubt that as a rhetorician, and possibly as a strategist, he was outstanding; but as the leader of a nation, it sometimes looks as if his charisma was greater than his ability, and he got out of his depth. There is nothing unusual in this; it is at least arguable that no Chinese leader who ever lived has succeeded in ruling more than some of the country, some of the time. Long before the communists came to power, China's administration was nominally centralised but in practice at the whim of far-flung administrators. Certainly the Dalai Lama, no mean judge of character, was impressed by Mao. At the time, he believed that China would not use any more force to impose her will on Tibet. When events proved him wrong, he could not reconcile the actions with the man and to this day, he finds it hard to believe that Mao was fully aware of what was happening in Tibet.

Chou-en Lai was another complex man. At first sight, he was the worst sort of career politician, a man who was most certainly not out of his depth. There is no doubt that he was instrumental in exercising strict control over Tibet, but he was in many ways an honourable man. Unlike many of those who surrounded him, he was not hysterical or destructive, and it is said that he did his best to reduce the carnage and destruction when the Tibetan uprising came in 1959. Many people owe their lives to him, lives which Mao was apparently prepared to sacrifice, and it was through his intercession that at least some of the great buildings of Lhasa, such as the Jokhang, were saved.

Apart from the Chinese leaders, the Dalai Lama also had the opportunity of meeting various other political figures, though the Chinese did their best to discourage anything more than the briefest social encounters at diplomatic parties and dinners. He particularly missed the opportunity to talk at any length with either the Russian Ambassador or Pandit Nehru, and although he met the Indian Ambassador the conversation was somewhat constrained by the fact that the Chinese would not let him use his own Tibetan-English translator, but insisted on a circuitous translation from Tibetan into Chinese, and then Chinese into English, so that they could keep control of what was being said.

It seemed, though, that there might yet be some hope for Tibet. The Chinese proposed a 'Preparatory Committee for the Tibet Autonomous Region', which was to consist of fifty-one members, only five of them Chinese, under the chairmanship of the Dalai Lama and the vice-chairmanship of the Panchen Lama. Briefly, his hopes were raised; but then, as he examined the proposed make-up of the committee, he realised that the odds were by no means as favourable as they seemed. In addition to the five Chinese members, twenty were to come from the Chinese-created 'Chamdo Liberation Committee' and 'Panchen Lama's Committee', so twenty-five of the fifty-one members were either Chinese or in the pocket of the Chinese. Of the remainder, fifteen came from the Tibetan government and eleven from various religious and public bodies, but both their appointment and their continuing tenure had to be approved by the Chinese. This meant that if they wanted to keep their seats it was better not to be too outspoken – and these seats were their only chance to do anything at all for Tibet, so keeping them was of the utmost importance.

With this rather dismal prospect before him, the Dalai Lama prepared for the return to Lhasa. He had been away for a little under a year, and as he returned he was able to see how things had deteriorated under the Chinese. Until then, anything he had heard had been at second hand; and the Chinese took good care that he heard as little as possible.

The picture their propaganda painted was one of Tibetan progress under the benevolent eye of the Chinese. One of their favourite themes was soldiers of the People's Liberation Army helping Tibetan peasants in the fields at harvest-time and so forth, and the pictures they showed of this happening were perfectly genuine. They were not, however, representative of what was going on in one tenth or even one hundredth part of Tibet. In most places, the Chinese commanding officers would not even let their soldiers out: the conflict between what they had been told and what could be seen all around them was too great for any Party theorist to resolve.

Collective farming was being imposed everywhere, in the teeth of opposition from every sector of Tibetan life: only a few collaborators, such as might be found anywhere, accepted even one iota of communist doctrine. Unsuitable crops and crop rotations were being enforced, either by men whose experience of farming was confined to the Chinese lowlands or by men with no experience of farming at all. If anything did grow, it was 'borrowed' or taken in taxes; hunger, even starvation, was widespread.

The Chinese civil and military administrators were, for the most part, unregenerate colonialists. In Peking, the Dalai Lama had seen that the Chinese retained at least some of the old courtesies: in Tibet, all pretence was abandoned. As one Chinese general told him, it did not matter what the Tibetan people wanted; the Chinese could draft in enough soldiers to make them do what they were told.

Many who have been to Tibet have commented on this attitude; those who had the opportunity to compare it with the British in India say that the Chinese behaved far worse. The British administrators may have regarded the Indians as ignorant natives, but at least they realised that they had their own culture and way of life. The Chinese, on the other hand, were determined to stamp out every vestige of Tibetan culture and to turn the Tibetans into Chinese. When they set up schools, the teaching medium was Chinese, and the Buddhist religion was mocked and reviled. The brightly-coloured materials traditionally used for Tibetan clothes suddenly became 'unavailable'; the well-known 'Mao jacket' was the only approved form of dress – except of course for servants, who did not appear to matter in the least. Stories abound of Chinese administrators who knew the Tibetan for 'hurry up' or 'get out', but had no idea of the words for 'please' and 'thank you'.

As the Dalai Lama travelled towards Lhasa, he talked with local Chinese administrators. He relayed what he had heard in Peking, and tried to point out the counter-productive nature of attempting to impose Chinese solutions on Tibetan problems. He could not make them listen; he would be gone soon, back to Lhasa, and Peking was far away. They were much more concerned with their own local empires and power struggles. One thing that he did notice was that virtually none of them was corrupt; this really was a new departure for Chinese local officials, and it reinforced his fears that the Chinese would be much harder to get rid of this time.

He also talked to his own people, who came to see him in droves. Despite his own misgivings, he pointed out that once the Preparatory Committee for the Tibet Autonomous Region was convened, Tibet would (in a sense) be reunited. They in turn told him of how the Chinese were behaving: learned Lamas being maltreated and harrassed by petty officials and soldiers, stories of casual brutality, and tales of Chinese soldiers who seemed to be outside the law. All the way to Lhasa he heard such stories, while he vainly tried to calm people's fears by telling them what he had heard in Peking.

When he arrived, it was not long before even his most modest hopes were dashed. When the Preparatory Committee for the Tibet Autonomous Region met, it was given an agenda prepared by the Party Work Group of the Chinese Communist Party in Tibet, which it was expected to rubber-stamp. It was obvious that the real power in Tibet was to be the Party Work Group, which was not elected and which consisted almost entirely of Chinese; the Preparatory Committee had been set up as a blind, to give some semblance of legality and continuity to what the Chinese were doing.

By the end of 1955, the situation was even worse than in 1951. The Chinese had taken advantage of the Dalai Lama's absence to make sweeping changes in many areas, and Tibet was on the point of rebellion. During Mönlam at the beginning of 1956, when huge numbers of Tibetans gathered in Lhasa for the prayer festival, a new phenomenon appeared. The crowds chose their own political leaders, men of no fixed political beliefs but who were able to put into words the discontent and anger all around them. Often articulate, often with a flair for action, they were the kind of 'popular leader' so often extolled in communist literature and so rarely found in real-life communism; the same phenomenon was to appear in Poland nearly a quarter of a century later, when Solidarity threw up leaders of its own.

The Chinese were not slow to react. They pinned the blame partly on the Tibetan cabinet, and partly on the popular new leaders. The three most prominent among them were thrown in jail by the Chinese, and to save them from probable torture and almost certain death, the Tibetan government had them arrested and transferred to a Tibetan prison. One died even there, but the other two were released when the three great monasteries – Drepung, Ganden, and Sera – gave surety for them.

These visible symptoms were not the only reaction against the Chinese. Everywhere, small groups were plotting against the invaders. Some, no longer caring that the Dalai Lama would not lend his name to a freedom movement, actually began to fight. At the beginning of 1956 there were sporadic outbreaks of fighting in Lithang, and in Chamdo the local Chinese general made a move which laid the foundations of the resistance there. He called together all the Tibetan leaders in his jurisdiction, and asked them to vote on whether communist reforms should be introduced at once (which he said was favoured by the Panchen Lama), or more gradually and not until they had been approved by the Tibetan people, which he alleged was the Dalai Lama's viewpoint. There were three hundred and fifty Tibetans there. Forty voted for immediate reforms – a surprisingly high number. One hundred voted that the reforms should be introduced gradually, when approved by the Dalai Lama and the people of Tibet. The rest voted that the reforms should never be introduced, and given that 'gradually, when approved' effectively meant 'never', this indicates the strength of feeling against the Chinese. The Chinese general told them all that the reforms would be introduced 'in due course'.

'In due course' turned out to be less than a month later. The two hundred or so who had proved so recalcitrant were summoned to Jomda Dzong, and held there for almost two weeks until they agreed to the introduction of the measures. Once they had obtained a verbal agreement from their captives, the Chinese relaxed their guard; and on the night before the prisoners were due to start their course of political indoctrination, every single one escaped. At a stroke, the Chinese general had managed to transform all those who could help the Chinese most into bitter and implacable enemies. The Tibetan resistance army was beginning to crystallise.

The year 1956 was, however, the anniversary of a much happier occasion. It was the 2500th anniversary of the enlightenment of the Lord Buddha, the 'Buddha Jayanti'. Quite unexpectedly, the Dalai Lama was personally invited to attend the ceremonies in India; the invitation was brought by the Maharaj Kumar of Sikkim himself, on behalf of the Maha Bodhi Society of India.

On a personal level, it was something that few Buddhists would want to turn down: an opportunity to make a pilgrimage to the holiest places of Buddhism. On the political level, it also offered a chance to stand back from a rapidly worsening situation and perhaps to enlist the help of some other democratic leaders, such as Pandit Nehru. There was a third reason; if his people were deprived of their figure-head, they might be a little less hot-headed – and if the worst came to the worst, he might be safer out of Tibet.

The Chinese were not in the least keen on the idea, and at first they tried to block it. They told him that he would be needed in Tibet; they told him that he would have to send a representative.

Just as if it was beginning to look as if he would not be allowed to go, the invitation was renewed, in the form of a telegram from the Government of India. This was much harder to decline, and so they finally agreed to let him go. Before he went, he was given a long lecture and a list of orders by General Chang Chin-wu. He was told point-blank that he must have nothing to do with any Nationalist Chinese (though from the Tibetan point of view the choice between the Nationalists and the communists was merely a choice of disasters); that all speeches had to be written beforehand, so that they could be vetted by the Chinese; and that any questions were to be met either with a noncommittal assurance that all was well after slight disturbances, or with the statement that this was a matter for Peking.

When he arrived in India, he was given an overwhelming welcome by the Indian Government and the Indian people; it was, he says, almost more like arriving home than arriving in a foreign country. Even at the beginning, though, there was an incident which showed how petty the Chinese could be. The interpreter of the Chinese Ambassador to India furtively removed the Tibetan flag which the Maharaj Kumar had affixed to the official car and replaced it with a Chinese one, an incident which would be amusing if it were not for its implications.

At first, his contacts were mainly in the religious sphere, but the separation was not always clear. Shortly after he arrived in Delhi he visited the Rajghat, where Gandhi was cremated, and a little afterwards he gave an address to the Buddha Jayanti symposium on the peace and freedom inherent in the teachings of the Lord Buddha. It was not the only time that the speech he delivered was different from the one that had been approved in Lhasa, and in it he stressed that Buddhist principles could lead not only to peace and happiness between individuals, but also to peace and happiness between nations. It was at this symposium that he affirmed something he has said many times since: the salvation of humanity lies in the religious instinct latent in all of us, and that it is the forcible repression of this instinct either by the individual or by society that is the enemy of peace.

Whenever he could, he also sought political contacts. As he says "We desperately wanted sympathetic wise advice". He spoke at length with Nehru, who was sympathetic but not wise, he seems to have been blinded by Gandhi worship, and still advised peaceful negotiation with the Chinese when that avenue was obviously worthless. He also had to be mindful of his own country's relationship with its giant neighbour, for India was still not a strong country, and it may also have been that the Dalai Lama was unable to stress sufficiently strongly how bad things were in Tibet; we have already seen how Tibetans are given to understatement, and he had to remember that the Chinese were watching his every move. Nehru did teach him a great deal about practical politics, but he offered no solutions to Tibet's problems.

He was, however, instrumental in arranging meetings between His Holiness and Chou-en Lai. The value of these might seem doubtful, as the Dalai Lama had already begun to suspect that the Chinese Prime Minister was quite capable of saying one thing and doing another, and that he was all too likely to value expediency and dogma to the exclusion of justice and truth. At initial talks with His Holiness however he conceded that 'local officials' might have made 'mistakes', and a little later he invited two of His Holiness's elder brothers to dinner at the Chinese embassy to discuss Tibetan problems further.

These two, Thubten Jigme Norbu and Gyalo Thondup, could afford to speak more freely than their brother; and they did so in no uncertain terms. Once more the Chinese remained unruffled. There had obviously been mistakes by local officials, they agreed, and promised that they would be rectified. They also reiterated their promise that they would withdraw as soon as Tibet could manage her own affairs – a point that Chairman Mao had made in Peking, but a curious offer in view of the fact that Tibet had been managing her own affairs perfectly well before they arrived, and would no doubt have done so even better under the unfettered leadership of the Fourteenth Dalai Lama.

It is difficult to say whether these assurances about local mistakes being rectified were sincere or not, but either way they paint a damning picture of Chinese politics. If they were sincere, it is a sorry indictment that the mistakes were not only left unrectified, but continued with varying degrees of severity to the present day. If they were simply soothing words, it is an even worse comment on China's leaders.

The Dalai Lama, meanwhile, continued his pilgrimage: Sanchi,

Ajanta, Benares, Bodh Gaya, Sarnath. At each stop, there were hundreds or even thousands of people waiting to greet him, many hoping for a blessing or at least a glimpse of the Inmost One. At every opportunity, he preached the doctrine of non-violence, and spoke of the path of peace which the Lord Buddha had clearly indicated.

When he reached Sarnath, there was a message waiting for him from the Chinese embassy. 'Spies and collaborators' were planning a huge revolt in Tibet, and it would be advisable for His Holiness to return as soon as possible. Matters were evidently serious, as Chou-en Lai was waiting to see him in Delhi.

When he saw Chou-en Lai, it was the same old story. There were no details of this impending revolution, but the Chinese were not prepared to tolerate Tibetan demands for self-determination; and all the while, he was still saying that no reforms would be introduced against the will of the people. The return to this intellectual Alice-in-Wonderland after his travels in a free and democratic India was an unwelcome reminder of what awaited His Holiness in Tibet, and when Chou-en Lai advised him not to visit Kalimpong 'for his own safety' but to return to Lhasa immediately, he rejected the advice. Kalimpong was a stronghold of Tibetans, many of them rich traders, and they were just the kind of people who could give practical support to any uprising against the Chinese. He would be safer there than anywhere else; the Chinese were simply afraid that he might learn how disaffected many Tibetans were with China.

He saw Nehru once more, and although the Indian statesman was still blind to the realities of Chinese imperialism he was able to give the Dalai Lama more useful and practical advice on the art of politics. He also undertook to make all the necessary arrangements for him to travel back to Tibet via Kalimpong; as he pointed out, India was a free country, and as their guest the Dalai Lama could go where he liked.

He actually returned via both Kalimpong and Gangtok, and in both places he was able to give religious teachings as well as re-assuring his people. He was distressed to see how many had been driven out of Tibet by Chinese cruelty; already, in late 1956, refugees were streaming out. Many had horrific tales to tell: although they would not dream of telling them directly to the Dalai Lama, they told them to his entourage and his entourage in turn passed them on to him.

Still hoping against hope that these stories were of isolated incidents, His Holiness pressed on into Tibet. The winter had already begun, and it was snowing hard on the high passes; it was almost a month before the Nathu-la pass was reopened, and progress after that was slow.

As he travelled, he heard of the extent of the fighting. Early in the year, as we have already seen, there had been some uprisings. Several had been very successful; Chinese garrisons had been wiped out in a number of places, and in the course of the year Ngapa (or Ngawa) and Gyalrong in Amdo, and Markham, Tawu, Lingka Shipa, Jupa, and Chartring in Kham had all come under Tibetan control. In June, the Chinese had bombed Lithang; the Tibetans retaliated with hit-and-run raids across the border, into China itself. The Chinese in turn drafted in another 40,000 soldiers. At this time, according to the resistance leader Gompo Tashi Andrugtsang, there were perhaps 6,000 Tibetan irregulars, so they were outnumbered seven to one by reinforcements alone.

Instead of learning from their reversals, the Chinese had simply forged ahead with their 'reforms'. Incredibly, they had hoisted huge red flags and portraits of Chairman Mao among the prayer flags which welcomed the Dalai Lama home; how they could imagine that this constituted a welcome is impossible to imagine.

On the way through Yatung, Gyantse, and Shigatse, he tried to reassure the people who flocked to see him by stating what was, after all, the official Chinese line. He told them that the Chinese were in Tibet to try to help the Tibetans; that Chou-en Lai had assured him that 'mistakes' would be rectified; and that no further reforms were to be introduced without the consent of the Tibetan people.

He could see as well as anyone that the Chinese were not living up to these assurances, but he reasoned that by following this approach he would at least avoid causing any worse trouble, including perhaps a rebellion which the Tibetans could only lose. Besides, if the Chinese Prime Minister had been sincere, the Tibetan people had everything to gain by calming down and giving Chinese administrators a chance.

He soon discovered that even so broad an analysis as this was of little use in dealing with the wildly capricious Chinese, who could veer from extreme friendliness to murderous hostility within the space of a few days, or even a few hours. So much depended on individual personalities, and whose political star was temporarily in the ascendant, that it was impossible to generalise.

Worse still, it became obvious that the stories he had heard in Kalimpong and Gangtok were not isolated incidents. At first he only received a few stories en route, but when he got to Lhasa they began to pour in. Torture and execution were commonplace, together with looting from and desecration of temples and holy places. Villages and monasteries were being bombed and shelled on the mere suspicion of harbouring guerillas.

The most horrifying stories are the ones that are told regarding individuals. Women were an easy target. A typical punishment for farmers who refused to accept collectivisation was to parade their teenage daughters naked in the street, with obscene gestures and yells from the Chinese soldiers. Rape, including multiple rape of nuns, was by no means unusual; when they tired of that, the Chinese soldiers would force monks and nuns to have intercourse at gun-point. These are not stories of what went on behind closed doors: these incidents happened in public. Tortures included flaying alive, and often the other villagers were made to watch as their friends were humiliated and killed. Husbands were killed in front of their wives; women and teenage girls were raped and killed in front of their families. Small children were handed guns and told to shoot their own parents; many had no idea of what they were doing.

Such stories are of course told against all invaders, but two independent reports may lend particular credence to these. One was the report of the Warren Committee in the United States, a committee set up by the Government not at a time when China was an enemy, but when every attempt was being made to woo them. They estimated that in China as a whole (in which they included Tibet), the number of people killed by the communist regime in the years 1949–1971 was between thirty-two million and sixty-three million. The other was the Geneva report of the International Commission of Jurists in 1959, who said:

"It is therefore the considered view of the International Commission of Jurists that the evidence points to:
  (a) a prima facie case of genocide contrary to Article 2(a) and (e) of the Genocide Convention of 1948:
  (b) a prima facie case of a systematic intention by such acts to destroy in

whole or in part the Tibetans as a separate nation and the Buddhist religion in Tibet."

The Chinese had by this time given up all attempt to impose their will other than by force. The result was predictable. A Tibetan will endure an incredible amount if he can continue to practice the teachings of the Lord Buddha, but if his religion is also attacked, his reaction will be implacable: there could be no more dangerous enemy. With so little to live for in the Chinese-dominated material realm, and faced with an attempt to destroy all the symbols of the spiritual realm, it was small wonder that the Tibetan people turned on their oppressors.

The chief hotbed of rebellion was the province of Kham, home of the Khamba people, where Chinese atrocities had been most widespread and horrible. A Khamba is a Tibetan writ large – often physically large, as they tend to be among the tallest of Tibetans – and you could not wish for a fiercer friend or a fiercer enemy. It has always been a matter of pride among Khambas to keep a gun hanging over the fireplace – formerly a Lee Metford or a Lee Enfield, nowadays an AK-47 'liberated' from the Chinese – and a good supply of ammunition for it. This was not for vendettas or petty wars: it was a symbolic reiteration of freedom. A rumour spread that the Chinese were going to try to confiscate all arms – a well-founded rumour, as it turned out – and when His Holiness heard this he knew that revolution was inevitable: "I knew without being told that a Khamba would never surrender his rifle – he would use it first."

Gompo Tashi Andrugtsang was a successful Khamba merchant. He was born in the year of the Fire Horse, so he was fifty-two years old in 1957. Despite his years and his success – he could easily have stayed in Kalimpong and grown rich – he was one of the moving spirits of the Tibetan resistance. Early in 1957, he was approached by the treasurer of Lithang monastery and others in Kham with a request that he ask the Government of Tibet for help in their struggle against the Chinese. His feelings on Tibetan self-determination were well known, and as a merchant he could still travel relatively freely inside Tibet. It was also known that he was a man who would not flinch from putting his words into action.

He approached His Holiness through Thupten Woyden Phala, the *Dronye Chenmo* or Lord Chamberlain; obviously, the contact had to be made in the strictest secrecy, or Chinese retaliation would be terrible. Thupten-la relayed the message to His Holiness.

The Dalai Lama was torn in two directions. On the one hand, as a Buddhist and a man of peace, he was unwilling to condone the use of armed force against the Chinese, the more so because as a statesman he realised that such an uprising was hopeless. It could only lead to reprisals and still more repressive measures. On the other hand, he knew that for some people, at least, things could not get much worse. He was a young man and a Tibetan, and as he says himself, he could not fail to be stirred by the courage and determination of the Tibetan freedom fighters.

To begin with, in 1957, he resisted requests for assistance. This was principally because he knew what the consequences of an uprising would be: he has since said that he believes that it is possible to fight, and indeed to kill, in a rightful cause. If you do choose such a course, you must do it with compassion and in full awareness of the consequences, which is not easy; but it may be the only course. He draws the parallel with smacking a naughty child: you do not do it in hate, but because you love the child.

With immense self-restraint, the would-be freedom fighters under Gompo Tashi Andrugtsang managed to hold back for still longer, but things were rapidly coming to a head. In 1957, he and other wealthy Tibetans sponsored a great offering of *Tensuk Shapten,* an affirmation of their faith in the Dalai Lama and a prayer for his long life; he was approaching twenty-two years of age. In addition to the offerings from the merchants, gold and precious stones to build a great throne were raised by popular subscription; the metal parts of the throne weighed 3164 *tolas* in gold alone, or over eighty pounds of the pure metal, and another eight *tolas* (3¼oz) went into gilding the wooden parts. Many of the gems were priceless.

The throne was offered to His Holiness on July 4th, 1957, and he ascended it among general rejoicing. It was decided that each year, at the same time, he would offer blessings from it; little did anyone realise that before the second year was out, the Precious Protector would be in exile.

Perhaps the Chinese welcomed such ceremonies as 'bread and circuses' to distract the Tibetan people, or perhaps they saw them as wasteful relics of a reactionary religion. What they did not see was the meetings between the prospective leaders of the resistance;

Gompo Tashi Andrugtsang and others used the ceremony as a cover to set up a complete network of resistance groups, which could be activated all over Tibet in a matter of a few days. If the Chinese had known about this, it might be that they would have let up in their attacks on Tibet, but in late 1957 and early 1958 they deported about 1,500 Chinese settlers who had come to Tibet as a sanctuary from the communists ten or fifteen years before. They were mostly small shopkeepers and restauranteurs, along with a few playhouse managers, and they flourished in a small way in business; they had been fully integrated into the old Tibet. The communists, perhaps understandably, suspected them of anti-communist activities, but the official reason given for their deportation was that they were passing information to the Tibetans. Most Tibetans who were in a position to know took this as a clear sign that more 'reforms' and 'improvements' were about to be introduced.

Gompo Tashi summoned a meeting of twenty-three leaders of resistance groups, who had adopted the name *Chushi Gangdrug;* the name means 'Four Rivers, Six Ranges'. They decided that it was time to organise resistance, and soon they were assured of the support of the Khambas, the Amdowas, a significant part of the Tibetan army, and several monasteries.

Resistance on such a scale is hard to disguise, and the Chinese got wind of it. They summoned the *Kashag,* the leaders of Ganden, Sera, and Drepung, and the Tibetan military command and warned them what would happen if there were any uprising. We do not know the exact words that they used, but this was the time that Chinese officials were touring the countryside telling the people that anyone in league with 'reactionaries' would be executed 'slowly and publicly'.

The Chinese also tried to insist that the Tibetan army be sent against the insurgents, which effectively forced the Tibetan government to refuse what amounted to a direct order. This was another major factor in inciting the freedom fighters to action: by mid-1958, full-scale fighting was under way.

It is quite amazing that virtually no news of this massive uprising appeared in the Western press, so effective was Chinese censorship. A lone voice was that of George Patterson, a brave and strange combination of missionary and journalist, but his reports were often accorded less space then Chinese denials.

Not all Chinese were against the Tibetans, though, and there were several cases of People's Liberation Army soldiers leaving the Chinese army and fighting with the Tibetans. One of the most remarkable stories is that of Chang Ho-ther, a Chinese artillery commander. Although he was treated with suspicion at first, the Tibetans learned that he really was on their side. He fought alongside them for nine months, dressed like a Khamba, and took the name Losang Tashi. When the fighting was over, he escaped to India with his fellow freedom fighters, and after a brief stay in Dharamsala he moved to the new Tibetan settlement of Bylakuppe in South India. Whenever His Holiness visits that settlement, he always has a few words with the old guerilla.

Even at this late stage, the resistance movement still had misgivings about fighting without the Dalai Lama's approval, and they sent repeated messages asking for his endorsement. By this time, His Holiness was no longer able to advise restraint in good conscience, but the Chinese monitored any official statements and he was unable to give them any encouragement. Fortunately, the Chinese censors were so heavy-handed, and the messages so clearly written for the benefit of the Chinese, that the freedom fighters could see behind the words. They knew that His Holiness might not approve of their actions, but they took comfort in the knowledge that he was not against them.

By the end of 1958, the revolt against the Chinese was in full flow. The battles were tremendous, but despite enormous Chinese superiority in numbers and equipment, the Chushi Gangdrug inflicted terrible damage: it was by no means unusual for five or ten Chinese to be killed for every one Tibetan, and the ratios were sometimes even more dramatic. The freedom fighters were using everything they could lay their hands on, from captured Chinese artillery and machine guns to swords, and their utter fearlessness terrified the Chinese. They also had to act as police, because the Chinese had armed and supported bands of robbers in order to blacken the name of the freedom fighters; these robbers were preying on ordinary Tibetan people. After a few robbers had been caught, tried in the field, sentenced to death, and shot, there was a marked reduction in the number of bandits.

Back in Lhasa, things were strained to breaking-point. The Chinese had plainly failed to impose their will, even by brute force,

Uprising and Escape

March 10th is commemorated by Tibetans in exile with the same sort of feeling that Americans have for the Fourth of July, or French for the Fourteenth. It was on March 10th, 1959, that the people of Lhasa rose against the Chinese.

Throughout the last part of 1958 and the beginning of 1959, life in Lhasa was characterised by the surreal mixture of normality and chaos that the Chinese had brought. For His Holiness, it was also a very important time personally: he submitted himself for his *Geshé* degree. Many people do not realise that he holds the highest academic degree which can be awarded in Tibet; it might be translated as 'Master of Metaphysics'. This degree is not awarded lightly, and no exceptions were made for the Dalai Lama. He had to present himself with twenty other candidates (not all of whom passed), each of whom was examined for a whole day by thirty opponents in succession – and not by fellow-candidates, but by examiners.

The examination was (and still is today) in the form of a public debate. It is conducted on a simple adversary basis. One contestant is seated, whilst the other roams around him asking questions, which are emphasised by dramatic formal gestures. Quite apart from their symbolism, which is an intrinsic part of the debate, these lend considerable theatrical effect to the questioning. The main gesture is a handclap, with the right arm moved in a great arc from above the head to waist level: the upturned right palm is slapped with the left, and then raised again. The action of the right hand symbolises the raising of all sentient beings from the hells in which they may find themselves, while that of the left symbolises the capping of the hells so that no more may enter. The seated contestant sits quietly and answers the questions. After a while, the two change places.

In this form, debates are a popular form of entertainment for both monks and laity. This may seem incredible to a Western reader, to whom the idea of watching two monks debating fine points of theology may seem at best to come a close second to watching paint dry. In practice, there is however a certain fascination; it is a little like one of those TV quiz shows, where the contestants are professional entertainers and celebrities, and the speed and range of the flow of talk is spectacular. Each contestant tries for a dialectical hold over the other. Trick questions are met with trick answers, or with replies that answer far more than was asked. Changing the ground of debate, or even the subject, is permitted if it is done skilfully and does not interrupt the flow of the argument. Humour is by no means out of place; sometimes it is the triumphant humour of a successful argument – "There, get out of *that* one!" – but mock dismay at an opponent's slow-wittedness is quite usual, and a particularly fine piece of logic-chopping will always draw an appreciative laugh from both the opponent and the audience.

To face thirty opponents in turn, in this sort of debate, with no choice of or control over the subjects, is an ordeal that few can face. Most *Geshé* candidates do not submit themselves until they are in their thirties, and some are in their forties. His Holiness was not quite twenty-four when he was awarded the degree.

It may seem amazing that such an examination could be held when the whole country was in ferment, but it is even more amazing that His Holiness should have been able to give his studies the attention they required. But as he has said, he is first a human being, and then a Buddhist monk, and it is to a large extent from his Buddhist studies that his serenity and wisdom flow – studies, it might be added, that he had made not only in his lifetime, but in many previous incarnations. In this light, it is perhaps less surprising that he should have taken his examinations. It was also true that no matter how bad things were in the provinces, Lhasa still attempted a semblance of normality; both the Chinese and the Tibetans needed it.

By one action, however, the Chinese were able to destroy that pretence; the bare facts are an extraordinary example of arrogance, insensitivity, and stupidity.

They invited the Dalai Lama to attend a theatrical performance in their military camp at some time in early March. They asked him to name a day which would be suitable, and he gave two or three;

Wednesday, March 10th, was one possibility. Less than forty-eight hours before the proposed performance on that day, the Chinese issued an invitation – which was very nearly a command – to attend the play.

Few Tibetans were enthusiastic about the Dalai Lama venturing into the heart of the Chinese military camp, but when the Chinese gave further instructions to the Commander of the Bodyguard it became clear that the risk was impossible. They stipulated that he should not be accompanied by his customary 25-strong armed bodyguard; that the armed guards who were customarily posted along any route which His Holiness travelled would not be permitted; that on the day of the performance the bridge between the military encampment and Lhasa would only be open to Chinese and Tibetans with permits; and that the whole visit should be kept secret. There were a hundred thousand Tibetans in Lhasa at the time, because many pilgrims had still not returned home after Losar and Mönlam, so the last condition would have been all but impossible to meet even if the others had been acceptable.

All of this was also done in the shadow of an official announcement from Peking that His Holiness would be attending the Chinese National Assembly at its next congress, despite its being common knowledge that he had so far carefully avoided accepting the invitation. Kidnapping looked like the least that could happen.

Nevertheless, the Dalai Lama decided to go. He knew that both sides only needed the slightest excuse to start shooting, and he hoped that he might exercise enough control over his own people to restrain them in the face of Chinese provocation, whereas he knew that there was nothing he could do to restrain the Chinese. Refusing to go to the play might be all the excuse they wanted; he felt that his duty was to go.

When he woke up next morning, he found that the matter had been taken out of his hands. The Norbulingka was surrounded by a crowd of perhaps thirty thousand Tibetans, who had come to their own conclusions: they were not going to allow their precious leader to fall into the hands of the Chinese.

Throughout the day, tempers ran higher. There were stonings: one official was mistaken for a Chinese and knocked unconscious, and a monastic official called Phakpa-la Kenchung was stoned to death by the crowd. He was known for his pro-Chinese sympathies, and for some unknown reason he risked his life by wearing Chinese clothing and carrying a Chinese pistol openly; it signed his death-warrant.

The crowd had at an early stage elected a sort of committee, whose leaders communicated to those inside the Norbulingka their simple message: if the Chinese insisted that His Holiness go to their camp, they would form a barricade to prevent it. If the Chinese fought, they would fight. Even unarmed, an angry crowd of tens of thousands is not to be trifled with, and many people had taken out of hiding whatever weapons they had, whether antique swords or modern machine pistols.

The Dalai Lama telephoned the Chinese general commanding the camp, explaining that he was unable to control what was happening and that he would be unable to attend the play. He also warned him that it would be extremely unwise for anyone from the Chinese camp to try to come to him, as the crowd might react violently. The same message was given to the *ad hoc* leaders of the crowd, and at about noon it was broadcast to the crowd with loudspeakers that His Holiness would not be going. The chants of 'Out with the Chinese' and 'Tibet for Tibetans' changed to cheers.

The underlying dilemma was however insoluble. The immediate problem was the matter of the visit to the Chinese camp, but this was plainly just the spark that had ignited the trouble. Unless the crowd dispersed, a massacre was virtually certain; the only hope was to try to disperse the crowd on the one hand, and placate the Chinese on the other.

The leaders of the crowd were adamant. Nothing would make them leave except an assurance from His Holiness that he would not only refrain from going this time, but that he would also refuse any future invitation to visit the Chinese camp. He was aware of the effect that such a promise might have on the Chinese, and also of the difficulty which he might have in keeping it, but still he agreed: he says that no price seemed too high to avert the disaster which was otherwise inevitable. Even then, the promise only placated some of the leaders and a few of the crowd, and hardly anyone left.

At about one o'clock, he sent his three closest advisers to the Chinese in order to explain what was going on, and what he was trying to do. At first, the crowd blocked the way even for the three ministers' cars, but after they had searched them thoroughly to make sure that His Holiness was not hidden in one of them, they allowed them to go.

The meeting with the Chinese was stormy. General Tan Kuan-sen no longer bothered to veil his threats, but lapsed into gutter obscenities. The Chinese would 'stamp out reactionaries', 'crush imperialist forces', and all the other hackneyed phrases of the communist vocabulary. He accused the Tibetan government of fomenting the revolution and supporting the Khambas, which as we have seen was the complete opposite of the truth, but he was no longer concerned with reason. The other two generals took their cue from him: one said, "Our government has been tolerant so far, but this is rebellion. This is the breaking point. We shall act now, so be prepared!" There was nothing the Tibetans could do; their suggestions that military intervention would be the worst possible reaction were scorned and abused. All they could do was listen to the tirade. After nearly four hours of this, they returned to the Norbulingka.

Nor was there any sign of improvement on the Tibetan side. Mass meetings were denouncing the Seventeen-Point Agreement and the way the Chinese had broken it; everywhere, there were demands for the Chinese to leave Tibet. At about six, a meeting *inside* the Norbulingka endorsed the declarations, adding that Tibet no longer recognised Chinese authority. Those present were mostly junior government officials, together with leaders of the crowd outside, but there were also members of the Kusang Regiment, the bodyguard of His Holiness. They announced that they would take no more orders from the Chinese high command; they put off the drab of the People's Liberation Army and dressed once more in the uniforms of the Tibetan army.

The Dalai Lama urged restraint, telling the leaders that it was their duty to try to calm the crowd rather than to inflame it, but feeling was now running so high that nothing could stop the revolt. Believing then as now that his highest duty was to avoid bloodshed on a massive scale, which was inevitable if Chinese forces clashed with the Tibetan crowd, His Holiness tried to play for time in the hope that feelings would calm down and the crowd disperse. In reply to a letter from the Chinese generals inviting him into the Chinese camp 'for his own protection', he unwittingly laid up trouble for himself by his conciliatory tone. His reply, and two subsequent letters, were held up by the Chinese as evidence that he had been prepared to accede to Chinese rule, but that he had been abducted against his will by 'reactionaries and imperialists'. Much as this distortion of the truth distressed him, he says that he would still write those letters if he had to relive the whole experience; they were the best way that he could see to avoid still worse trouble.

The impasse continued for almost a week, until the sixteenth of March. Suspicions were aroused when Chinese surveyors were seen aligning their instruments on the Norbulingka, and fears that they were preparing for an artillery bombardment were confirmed when a letter arrived from Ngabo, the former Governor of East Tibet who had first negotiated with the Chinese. He advised the Dalai Lama and the Kashag to take shelter in an inner part of the palace; the Chinese would take good care that he was not injured.

In an attempt to avoid what now seemed inevitable, the Kashag sent another placatory letter. This time it was addressed to Ngabo, and it said that the Cabinet recognised that the people were behaving foolishly and emotionally, but that there was still some chance of dispersing them. The first reply was a polite but noncommittal note reiterating what had been said before, and the second was two heavy mortar shells.

They landed harmlessly in a pond at four o'clock on the afternoon of the seventeenth, and it was clear that there was now no hope of a peaceful solution. Although His Holiness would undoubtedly have given himself up to the Chinese in order to avoid the forthcoming massacre, the Tibetan people denied him this option. As is by now clear, many Tibetans – perhaps the great majority – hold the person of the Precious One more valuable than their own. Even in a strictly practical sense, this is not an unrealistic viewpoint. As more than one Tibetan said to us in Dharamsala, "His Holiness is all that we have got". He is the figurehead; he is Tibet; he is Chenrezi. As long as he lives, the Tibetan people have a focus.

There was no choice but flight. This would not be easy. In addition to the Dalai Lama himself, there were three members of his immediate family: his mother, his elder sister Mrs Tsering Dolma, and his youngest brother Tendzin Choegyal. Fortunately, two of his brothers were in America, and his other brother and sister were already in India. There were also many other religious and political figures who would have to leave, either as advisers to His Holiness or for their own safety. A list of the people who accompanied him is given in Appendix II.

The difficulties surrounding the escape were immense. It was not merely a question of evading the Chinese: they would also have to run the gauntlet of the Tibetan crowd that still surrounded the Norbulingka; and then, on foot and horseback, they would have to escape detection by Chinese patrols with aircraft and motor vehicles. They could not get to the Potala, either to destroy state papers or to pick up even a fraction of the treasure that was housed there. Even if they had had the time, they would probably not have been able to carry anything. The harsh Tibetan winter was not yet over, and they would need to devote most of their energies to staying alive. His Holiness's younger brother recounts how a leather bag of diamonds worth hundreds of thousands of pounds was left behind in the rush; no one thought to pick it up, because it was not necessary for immediate survival.

The escape party was divided into three. The first to leave, just after nine o'clock in the evening, were His Holiness's mother, sister, and younger brother, with their small escort. The two women were disguised as Khamba men, both to avoid detection and to deter questions.

The second party left half an hour later. It consisted of the Dalai Lama, his Chamberlain, the Lord Chancellor, the Commander of the Bodyguard, and two ordinary soldiers. Before he left, His Holiness went to the *Gönkhang* (shrine or chapel) of the Mahakala who is one of the principal protectors of Tibet. He offered the deity a *katag* or silk scarf; giving katags is associated with arrivals and departures.

He was disguised as an ordinary soldier, wearing uniform and carrying his rifle. In order to improve the disguise, he removed his glasses; he says now, with a smile, that the idea of a soldier with eyesight like his was very unlikely, and in the poor light he could hardly see where he was going. The Chamberlain got them past the guards by saying that he was making a routine tour of inspection, and then the little party was outside the gates of the Jewel Park. It was the first time in nine years that he had been out through those gates without a ceremonial procession – the first time, in fact, since the flight to Yatung when the Chinese first invaded. As he left, he recalls in *My Land and My People*, "...I saw dimly in the darkness the groups of people who were still watching it, but none of them noticed the humble soldier, and I walked out unchallenged towards the dark road beyond".

On the way to the river, they had their first brush with outsiders. A Tibetan crowd was there, some of whom knew or at least suspected that the Dalai Lama would leave that night. The Chamberlain stopped to talk to their leaders, and gave them a few brief words of reassurance; no one thought to investigate the party further. When they reached the river, they crossed it in coracles, the faint splash of the paddles lost in the sounds of the river. The first stage of the journey had been accomplished: they had escaped from the Norbulingka.

On the other side of the river, they met up with the family party that had left earlier; a few minutes later, the third group arrived. This consisted of ministers, tutors, and advisers who had been smuggled out under a tarpaulin in the back of a truck. Protection was afforded by thirty Khamba guerillas, along with the few soldiers already in the party, and transport came in the form of ponies supplied by the monastery, though the steward had been unable to get good saddles for everyone. Everything had to be arranged in whispers, as they were still within earshot of Chinese sentries, let alone Chinese patrols. After a hurried conference, the whole party rode off: the first few miles, where they might run into Chinese patrols by sheer chance, and where the Chinese could get soldiers out fast and in force, were the most dangerous.

The night was dry and clear, which posed its own problems. Visibility was a mixed blessing, and although they could move fast the horses' hooves sounded frighteningly loud as they rode along. Fortunately, the wind was blowing from the north-west, the direction of the Chinese camp, so the sound was carried away. Tendzin Choegyal, His Holiness's youngest brother, was fourteen years old at the time; he remembers being struck by how fortunate they were with the wind and weather, and says that even now, a quarter of a century later, he has only to close his eyes and think of that night to relive every minute of it. He was still of an age when it was all an adventure, even though he was frightened, but the others in the party were all too aware of the dangers around them.

There was no road, but a typical Tibetan rock track – and such tracks can be very misleading unless you know tnem well. Once, His Holiness lost his way and had to turn his pony around to get back to the track, and a little later what they feared was a Chinese patrol turned out to be a detachment of Khambas guiding back some of th⸱ v that had wandered away and become completely lost. His Holiness knew that in the hills all around there were Khamba guerillas, though they never heard or saw anything. At one place, they came to a shallow stretch of river which Chinese trucks could easily ford; they left a Khamba rearguard there. If the Chinese had come, it would have been a suicide squad; but fortunately, the Chinese did not come.

At about three in the morning, after five hours of solid riding, they rested briefly at a peasant's house. Like many others on the route to India, the man was only too willing to give all that he had for the Dalai Lama's party. Such devotion hardly squares with Chinese accounts of the way in which the serfs were maltreated. There was little time for rest; taking as much care as they could to cover their tracks, both for their own sake and for their host's, they moved on.

During that interminable morning, when everyone was on the lookout for Chinese planes and Chinese patrols, there was one of those episodes from which legends spring. An old man joined the party as they were climbing, and seeing how His Holiness's pony was flagging, he made him a present of a pure white horse. The man's name was Tashi Norbu, or Auspicious Jewel, an old man who appeared from nowhere.....

The journey was hard. The weather varied from bright and clear but cold, to heavy snowfalls and rain. Some of the members of the party were no longer young, including the Great Mother, but there was no alternative to the relentless ride. By any standards, it was an epic journey through the beautiful but desolate Tibetan landscape, all the time looking out for a Chinese plane that might fly overhead and spot them. Often it was just a matter of putting one foot in front of another, of continuing for a few more yards...

Tendzin Choegyal had a camera with him, a 35mm Agfa, and from time to time he stopped to take pictures. In the whole course of the journey, he took five rolls of film, but when he reached India they were taken from him for safe keeping, and he has never seen them since. One or two pictures survive, but no one seems to know the whereabouts of the original films.

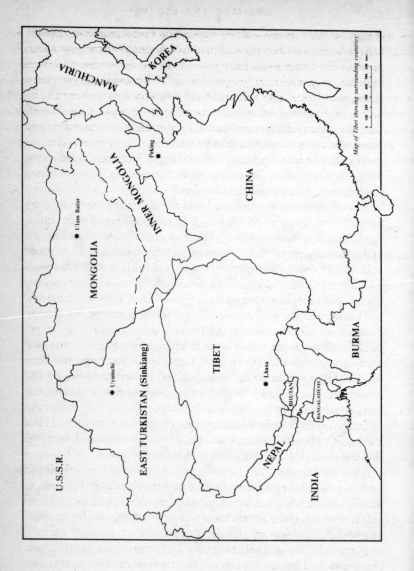

Map of Tibet showing surrounding countries

0 100 200 300 400 500 600 km.

U.S.S.R.

MONGOLIA

* Ulan Bator

* Uyumchi

EAST TURKISTAN (Sinkiang)

INNER MONGOLIA

MANCHURIA

KOREA

Peking *

CHINA

TIBET

* Lhasa

NEPAL

BHUTAN

BANGLADESH

INDIA

BURMA

For the first few days of the march, His Holiness and his advisers were still formulating plans. What they hoped to do was to get to Lhuntse Dzong, a great fortress near the Indian border, and from there to reopen negotiations with the Chinese. If the negotiations failed, the Indian border was near; if they succeeded, Lhasa might be saved. But on the seventh day of the journey, just after leaving Chenye, they received a message which made them realise that any hopes of a peaceful settlement were gone.

Among the Khamba guerillas who filled the hills all around the party, seldom in evidence but always watching their Precious Leader, there was a man called Tsepon Namseling. He had originally been sent out by the Kashag to try and persuade the Khambas to stop fighting, but when he saw what they were fighting against, he joined them. He had been with the freedom fighters for about seven months; and now he brought news that Lhasa had been bombarded.

He could only give an outline of what had happened, because he had not been there, but the next day a letter arrived from the Dalai Lama's private secretary which confirmed what Tsepon Namseling had said and added further details. Over the next few days, the story of what had happened became clear.

The shelling began at two in the morning on March 20th, just over forty-eight hours after His Holiness had left. The first target had been the Norbulingka, but after that they had turned their fire on the Potala, the Jokhang, the neighbouring monasteries, the Chakpori medical school, and the city of Lhasa and the village of Shol. Literally thousands were killed: the exact number will never be known, but the streets were littered with dead bodies. Many were women and children.

After the carnage, the Chinese had apparently inspected all the bodies, turning them over to see if they had killed the Dalai Lama. It was obvious that they did not care who else they had killed.

It is hard to appreciate just what this means, but a similar situation might be a crowd of thousands in front of some nationally important building, Parliament Square, perhaps, or the Capitol, being attacked by machine-guns, mortar shells and heavy artillery at short range. It is not merely a question of people being killed and buildings destroyed; nationhood is being assaulted. Long after they had blown any effective resistance to pieces, the Chinese went on with their wanton destruction.

When he received this news the Dalai Lama was forced to admit that it was inevitable he should leave his country; until then, like others in the party, he had harboured a secret hope that there might be some other way. He still had some ideas of setting up a regional government at Lhuntse Dzong, but in his heart he knew it would not work. He did not understand how the Chinese could behave as they did, and to this day he finds it hard to believe.

They marched on to Chongay, where His Holiness met more of the Khamba guerilla leaders. He knew what they had given up, and what they faced, and as he put it, "I could not honestly advise them to avoid violence."

The march continued. Winter was ending, and the snows were melting, so the paths were often slippery, or muddy morasses with icy puddles. On the high passes, there was still snow and ice; and every piece of fresh news brought more bad tidings. Just before they reached Lhuntse Dzong, they heard that the Chinese had dissolved the Tibetan Government, thereby destroying the last vestiges of the Seventeen-Point Agreement. From now on, there could be no pretence: the Chinese were simply an invading power.

Accordingly, the Dalai Lama proclaimed his Temporary Government at Lhuntse Dzong. Here, just ten days' march from Lhasa, he made a speech in which he stated that he was re-forming the Tibetan government with himself at its head, and that this was the legitimate government of Tibet. He made the speech on Tibetan soil to show that he would return, and to reaffirm the importance of Tibet as a nation. He knew that he would have to go into exile, and that there was no hope of a peaceful settlement in the near future once he had made that speech, but he also knew that it would provide a rallying-point for Tibetans and prove to them that although their Dalai Lama might not be among them, yet he had not left them. By his order, copies of the proclamation were sent to all the neighbouring *dzongs;* they were received with rejoicing.

From information that the Khambas had gathered, it looked as if the Chinese had some idea of where His Holiness might be; and as Lhuntse Dzong was an obvious target, they moved on to a smaller monastery a little closer to the Indian border. It was here that they faced the reality of not going back, and messengers were sent ahead to ask permission of the Government of India to cross the border, which was about sixty miles away as the crow flies or twice that on the rough, winding tracks and high passes that they would have to take. It represented about another week's journey for a party their size, and in their condition.

In many ways, this last part of the journey was the worst of all. The weather was terrible, and the party came close to frostbite. Ice formed on their eyebrows and even eyelashes, and they had to travel very slowly in order to spare the ponies, which were exhausted anyway and for which there was little or no fodder. Worse still, they were leaving Tibet and going into exile, something which was even more painful in reality than they had feared. Worst of all, it was on this leg of the journey that they were 'buzzed' by an aeroplane. It flew so low that they did not think it could have missed them, but so fast that they could not even see whether it had Chinese markings or not. Whatever it was, there were no consequences. Had the pilot not seen them? Had he not guessed who they were? Was he under orders to let them go? Did he decide for himself? We shall probably never know.

At Mangmang, the last Tibetan settlement before the border, they heard with mixed feelings that the Indian Government was prepared to grant His Holiness and the other Tibetan refugees asylum. They needed the encouragement, but that night they had to sleep in tents in torrential rain. His Holiness hardly slept at all, and by the morning he was too sick even to ride. Even after another day's rest, he was still in no state to travel, but there was no choice: if he stayed, he was endangering both the settlement and the Khambas who were protecting him. At his own request, he was helped onto the back of a *dzo,* the huge domestic cross between a yak and a cow. It was on this unlikely transport that the Holder of the White Lotus left his own land.

India

The Dalai Lama was too dazed and ill to notice much about the border crossing, but although the terrain changed little and it would still be a week before they reached the nearest railhead, there was now one major difference: they were in India, and therefore safe and free. Almost as soon as they had crossed, the Indian government sent a detachment of the Assam Rifles to protect them, and the soldiers were accompanied by officials and interpreters who had met His Holiness at the Buddha Jayanti. There was also a welcoming telegram from Nehru.

Even Nehru had realised by this time that the troubles of Asia had not all been the fault of European imperialists, and he had begun to see China for what it was. Although he was understandably nervous about what India's giant neighbour might do next, he made it clear that His Holiness was not merely given asylum, but welcomed as an honoured guest. He did not want to risk too much, though, and once the Dalai Lama was in the country Nehru did his best to ensure that he created as little international comment as possible. As *The Times* put it, "The Indian security cordon has... been as rigorously applied to exclude known friends as potential enemies."

From the moment when it was first known that the Dalai Lama was coming to India, and what route he was taking, there was a ban on commercial flights in the area – several journalists had tried to hire aircraft – and the wildness of the country through which he was passing meant that getting in by foot or motor-vehicle was next to impossible, even if permits were available; Assam and the North East Frontier Agency (NEFA) are tribal areas, and require special entry permits to this day.

The first stopping place where journalists might have been able to reach him was Bomdila, where he arrived in mid-April, but his whereabouts was masterfully concealed and the few reporters who did find out where he was were unable to get anywhere near him. From Bomdila, he went on by road to Tezpur; there, the Indian government had arranged a special narrow-gauge train to take him from the railhead to the main line, after which another special air-conditioned train would take him to his final destination.

At Tezpur, on Saturday 18th April, the Dalai Lama issued a long statement which recapitulated the events that led up to his flight, including the complete disregard by the Chinese of the Seventeen-Point Agreement, and then thanked the Indian people for the welcome he had received and for the promise of asylum. The statement was written in the third person, and read on his behalf; although there were a hundred or so journalists and photographers in Tezpur, none of them got much of a story other than the fact that he had arrived and was well.

It is not easy to get confirmation of why this excellent chance for publicity was so completely missed; but nor is it difficult to surmise – and this is confirmed by the answers you can get from Tibetans in a position to know.

The obvious inference is that Nehru was very frightened of Chinese reaction, and that he was doing everything in his power to avoid offending them short of actually refusing asylum.

Even if Nehru was excessively cautious, there were others in India who were not. Many Indian Members of Parliament were in favour of a more forceful stance, and one of their main spokesmen was Jai Prakash Narayan, who had the foresight to realise that India was already a great country in its own right. Since those days, more and more Indians have come to realise this, and Tibetans now enjoy very much more freedom of speech. Large Tibetan demonstrations outside the Chinese embassy in Delhi are now commonplace, and Tibetan spokesmen based in India plead their country's case with great force. But the Dalai Lama, as Head of State in exile, has always had to be more circumspect about what he says. His predilection for dwelling on the positive side of everything is well known, and there is no doubt that his thanks for the generosity of the Indian people are genuine, heartfelt, and wholly deserved by that nation.

The Chinese were quick to react to the Tezpur statement. The central propaganda agency immediately stated that the 'so-called' statement was full of lies and loopholes, and had plainly not been the work of the Dalai Lama. Their rather rambling denunciation predictably blamed 'spies and collaborators', and they suggested that the Dalai Lama was being held against his will. His Holiness said that their whole statement was such patent nonsense that it was not worth trying to refute. Later, when he arrived at Mussoorie, he issued a very short statement in the first person, confirming that he had made the Tezpur statement of his own free will, that he stood by everything on it, and that there had been no coercion at any time.

The journey to Mussoorie took four days; the party travelled by rail to Dehra Dun, and then by car to Mussoorie itself. At every stop, hundreds and sometimes thousands of Tibetans and Indians gathered to welcome him. It was one of the best things that could have happened: he was worn down by the journey, and particularly by the three hundred miles he had covered in just fifteen days between Lhasa and Bomdila, so the huge numbers of people who came to give their support cheered and encouraged him enormously. He knew that he was not alone, and that he still had a useful role as spokesman in the free world for his six million countrymen left behind in Tibet.

Mussoorie itself is a modest hill station at an altitude of some 6000 feet; like the other hill stations, it was a favourite resort for the British Raj during the hot weather, and although it is still hot by Tibetan standards the climate was much more agreeable than the dusty heat of the plains, where the hot season was just getting under way. A wealthy family of Indian industrialists, the Birlas, lent the Dalai Lama a bungalow there; the Indian Government surrounded it with armed guards. Although no one could decry the generosity of the Birlas, or deny the importance of security, it was fairly cramped; one of the correspondents writing for *The Times* expressed some doubt as to whether it was big enough for a normal healthy person to get any exercise at all. Certainly, the Dalai Lama could not take the brisk walks that he used to in the Norbulingka, but he did get some exercise: among other things, he played an energetic and successful game of table-tennis, at which he was rarely if ever beaten.

Meanwhile, in the Lok Sabha, Nehru had said that His Holiness would not be permitted to carry out any political activities. Jai Prakash Narayan was one of the leaders of the opposition to this stance: it could, he said, only be read as an act of self-interest bordering upon cowardice. As he was later to say, in 1964, "I am still of the opinion that I expressed in 1959 that India should support the cause of Tibet at the United Nations, and not remain neutral as in years before. It is both a case of cultural genocide and negation of the right of self determination..."He pointed out at the time that political exiles are normally permitted to muster all the support they can, and to make their case known to all and sundry; so long as they do not attempt to gather arms, or otherwise wage war from the country that has granted them asylum, they are normally permitted complete freedom of action. He was by no means alone in his views, but they did not prevail against Nehru and his majority in the government. Far from allowing the Dalai Lama freedom of action, the Indian government blocked even a press conference.

The reaction of the world's press was twofold. On the one hand, the story was was rapidly cooling; newspapers thrive on recent news, not old stories. On the other hand, there was still tremendous public interest in what some newspapers called 'the story of the century', and many papers were beginning to make acid comments about India's attitude. Eventually, the government gave way; but it made sure that the press conference would be as uncontroversial and indeed non-newsworthy as possible.

On June 10th it was announced that there would be a press conference on June 20th, but that only written questions would be answered and that these would have to be submitted by June 15th at the latest. The questions were, of course, carefully vetted by Indian security officials; 'censorship' is a hard word to use, but this came perilously close to it. Some indication of the interest that still existed comes from the number of newspaper correspondents present: 130, on a story that was two months old. Some indication of the Indian attitude comes from the number of questions: 92, from only 14 sources.

For the most part, the questions dealt only with matters of historical fact, such as the way in which the Seventeen-Point Agreement had been forced upon the Tibetans and then broken by the Chinese themselves. Others were of a general nature, mainly background questions about Tibet and the role of the Dalai Lama. At the end of the press conference, His Holiness read a statement which had been prepared beforehand, and thanked the press for presenting the Tibetan case to the world. Both he and they knew that if they had been allowed to put the questions they wanted, the

conference would have been explosive, and they also knew that this
abortive show had effectively killed the story just when it was most
important. Chinese atrocities alone would have guaranteed front
page coverage in the sensationalist press, and the more serious
papers could have devoted time and space to a political analysis; as it
was, there were a few one-column stories, and the reporters began
to drift away from Mussoorie.

Although there must have been a temptation to make much more
capital out of this conference, His Holiness was in no position to do
so. The Indian government made it perfectly clear that they would
not tolerate political statements, and his position was precarious; as
he said in a later interview in Mussoorie, he had received no
invitations from the governments of any other Buddhist countries
to visit them, though he had had many invitations from Buddhist
religious organisations. Not only was India the nearest country to
Tibet where he could hope to stay: it might well be the only country
anywhere. The blame for the lack of publicity which surrounded
the Tibetan cause must, therefore, rest squarely on the Indian
government in general and on Nehru in particular, for the voice of
Jai Prakash Narayan was far from the only one raised in the Lok
Sabha in support of the Tibetan cause.

The Indian government also refused to support Tibet's case at the
United Nations, again against the strident advice of Narayan and
others. His Holiness still had some hopes that the United Nations
might help them, but the difficulty lay in finding sponsors for a
United Nations motion: as Tibet had never joined, it had no direct
voice. Two countries agreed to sponsor the motion, the Federation
of Malaya and Ireland. Malaya, as a Buddhist country, might seem
a likely sponsor, but the way in which Catholic Ireland supported
Buddhist Tibet is surely a magnificent vindication of His Holiness's
assertion that the religious impulse represents what is noblest in
man. They requested that Tibet be discussed in the United Nations
in a letter dated September 28th, 1959, and a resolution was passed
by 45 votes to 9 with 26 abstentions (including India):

The General Assembly

Recalling the principles regarding fundamental human rights and freedoms
set out in the Charter of the United Nations and in the Universal
Declaration of Human Rights and adopted by the General Assembly on
December 10th, 1948,

Considering that the fundamental human rights and freedoms to which the Tibetan people, like all others, are entitled include the right to civil and religious liberty for all without distinction,

Mindful also of the distinctive cultural and religious heritage of the people of Tibet and of the autonomy which they have traditionally enjoyed,

Gravely concerned at reports, including the official statements of His Holiness the Dalai Lama to the effect that the fundamental rights and freedoms of the people of Tibet have been forcibly denied them,

Deploring the effect of these events in increasing international tensions and in embittering the relations between peoples at a time when earnest and positive efforts are being made by responsible leaders to reduce tension and improve international relations,

1. *Affirms* its belief that respect for the principles of the Charter of the United Nations is essential for the evolution of a peaceful world order based on the Rule of Law;

2. *Calls* for the respect of the fundamental human rights of the Tibetan people and for their distinctive cultural and religious life.

It was a milk-and-water resolution, but it was better than nothing; perhaps this was the sort of attitude that Nehru referred to in a letter written just before he died. In the letter, written to Dr Gopal Singh in 1964, he says that United Nations resolutions are useless anyway, and adds, "We are not indifferent to what has happened in Tibet. But we were unable to do anything EFFECTIVE about it."

He was quite right; the United Nations resolution was completely ineffective. In the face of such indifference, and with no prospect of an early return to Tibet, the Dalai Lama and the Administration in Exile (as it now became) realised that they would have to make long-term strategic plans.

The first problem which faced them was the ever-increasing flow of refugees out of Tibet. Literally hundreds of people were coming across the border every day, and the vast majority were destitute. A few of the richer people had managed to bring some gold or silver jewellery, or a little money, but the peasants had nothing to bring – and at that time, it was the ordinary peasants who were suffering worst, as many were starving and they were on the receiving end of the worst Chinese mistreatment. The brutal *thamzing* sessions, in which 'rich peasants' and 'reactionaries' were beaten and reviled as they 'confessed' how they had exploited the masses, had yet to reach their peak; they were mainly a phenomenon of the Cultural Revolution.

Although he had advisers and assistants to help him in raising money and negotiating with the Indian government for the settlement of these unfortunate people, a great deal of the work fell to the Dalai Lama. He had always been extremely conscientious, and now he worked non-stop. His advisers were also accustomed to deferring to him, so even when they did the work, the decisions were referred to him. His personal qualities – his breadth and depth of interest, his native intelligence, and the experience he had of diplomacy – meant that outsiders wanted to deal with him whenever possible, and his prestige and position meant that if it came to raising money or anything similar he was the natural spokesman: it is much harder to refuse a request from the Dalai Lama in person than to refuse one from some lesser official, or perhaps a committee, even though they might both ask for exactly the same thing.

Quite apart from this immediate and increasing problem, His Holiness also had to consider two other questions. One was publicising the Tibetan question and trying to regain freedom for Tibet, and the other was to make what plans were possible against the day that Tibet was once again free. As with the refugee problem, the Dalai Lama was the obvious person to publicise Tibet's cause, and as soon as the Indians relaxed the restrictions on interviews (which they did a few days after the June 20th press conference) he devoted as much time as he could to explaining his case to foreign journalists; to this day, this is a very high priority. When it came to planning the future of Tibet, he was not only the best qualified and most able candidate: he was the only one that the Tibetan people, whether in Tibet, or in exile, would consider.

With such a tremendous work-load, it was obvious that he would need something rather bigger than the bungalow in Mussoorie – and besides, it was only on loan. Mussoorie itself was also too small to accommodate the refugees who were streaming out of Tibet: as many as were able to do so came to Mussoorie in order to be as close as possible to their Precious Leader, and although there had as yet been no friction between Tibetans and Indians, the danger was there. There was also the question of climate. Although the climate of Mussorie is a considerable improvement on that of the Indian plains, it is still very hot and humid when compared with the clear thin air of Tibet. In fact, the air in Tibet is about as thin and dry as that in an aeroplane (though considerably cleaner), and anyone who has landed in a humid airport will be familiar with the feeling as of breathing underwater that comes when you step out of the plane. Furthermore, Tibetan hygiene left a lot to be desired: this was not important in Tibet, where it was dry and cold, but in India it meant that the Tibetans were prey to all sorts of diseases.

The Government of India was every bit as aware of the Tibetans' requirements as His Holiness was, and so they prepared a list of possible locations for what amounted to a Tibetan colony. After considering and investigating several possibilities, the Administration in Exile finally chose Dharamsala.

Dharamsala

Most people who go to Dharamsala nowadays do so in order to stay in the Tibetan community, and perhaps, if they are lucky, to see His Holiness. After a four-hour bus journey from Pathankot, the most convenient railway station, or twelve hours on the bus from Delhi, they arrive at the bus station in Kotwali Bazaar, just above Lower Dharamsala at an elevation of 4,000 feet.

Kotwali Bazaar is the main commercial centre for the Dharamsala group of settlements; a *kotwali* is a police station. At first sight, it is just another Indian village: crowded, full of small shops and beggars, perhaps slightly cleaner than average. Then, you see the occasional Tibetan face among the crowds, and the unmistakeable maroon robes of Tibetan monks and nuns. If you walk around, you will find that there are one or two Tibetan shops, and even a Tibetan hotel and restaurant, but the majority of the Tibetans live higher up on the mountain.

There are two roads from Kotwali Bazaar to McLeod Ganj, where the main Tibetan settlement is. One rises 2,000 feet in about two and a half miles; if you take this one, you will have to walk or hire a jeep, because few taxi drivers are prepared to force their ageing Ambassador cars up the many one-in-three hills. About half-way between the bazaar and McLeod Ganj, you will pass Gangchen Kyishong, the Library of Tibetan Works and Archives and Nechung Monastery; a little higher, you will find the Delek Hospital and the Tibetan Medical Centre, which deal with Western-style medicine and traditional Tibetan medicine respectively.

The other road is longer, with a gentler gradient and endless hairpin bends. This is the road that the taxis take, and the bus, which takes about three quarters of an hour to travel the seven miles, stopping a dozen times on the way. Before you reach Forsyth Ganj and the big Indian military base, you will see golden pinnacles on top of the mountain spur that dominates the valley. It is a sight that is not easily forgotten; it is Thekchen Choeling, the Great-Path Dharma-Place or Place of Mahayana Teaching, and among the buildings are the Temple, Namgyal monastery, some of the offices of the Administration in Exile, and the residence of His Holiness the Dalai Lama.

The bus continues. Forsyth Ganj is a one-street village, Indian in appearance but with many Tibetan residents, and a little further on you pass the Church of Saint John in the Wilderness, where Lord Elgin, sometime Viceroy of India, was buried in 1863. It is a strange sight: an English parish church among Himalayan pines.

At last, you come to McLeod Ganj, pronounced Mack-loud with equal emphasis on the two syllables. By the area where the bus stops is Nowrojee's Store, Established 1860; but that is the only reminder that you are still in India. There are Tibetans everywhere, running stalls and shops and buying and selling; monks and nuns in maroon and saffron robes; Tibetan children, irresistibly attractive despite the invariably runny noses; Apso terriers; a tree that serves as a sign-post, with a dozen metal signs in Tibetan and English nailed to it; a jumble of liveliness without that curious combination of frenzy and inactivity that always seems to characterise India. You are in a different country.

There are many other Tibetan settlements in India now, but this one is special: it is the 'Little Lhasa' of the state in exile. People come here to be near the Dalai Lama, for both spiritual and practical reasons; those who can, stay, but for the others it is the staging-post after the flight from Tibet, before they go on to the other settlements. The Administration has offices devoted to finding homes for these people, though increasing numbers are sent to other parts of India rather than kept in Dharamsala. If His Holiness is in residence, there may be a chance for the new arrivals to see him before they leave. After as much as thirty-five years of Communist domination, during which they may have been told that His Holiness is dead, this will be the greatest moment of their lives.

In 1960 McLeod Ganj was a ghost town. Although it had been a very fashionable hill station in the nineteenth century, as witness the presence of the Viceroy in the church's graveyard, it was devastated by an earthquake in 1903. Even now, crazily split and sloping remains of the well-made paths laid out in the time of the Raj bear witness to the havoc. Many buildings were destroyed. A few were rebuilt, and even a few new ones constructed, but the town never recovered. Few British went there in the hot season any more; when the British Raj left in 1947, the decline was almost complete. For over a decade, there was next to nothing there. Even Kotwali Bazaar was not the thriving commercial centre that it is now: one of the first Tibetans to settle there recalls that even lavatory paper had to be specially ordered from Delhi.

From the Tibetans' point of view, it was almost ideal. The elevation of 6,000 feet was not high by Tibetan standards – in fact, it was about the same as Mussoorie – but the terrain was reasonably Tibetan, and the climate was a great improvement over the sticky dusty heat of the plains. The mountains, which retain their snowy caps (albeit patchily) for the whole year, were a reminder of home, and the fact that the place was all but deserted meant that it was ideal for setting up a colony without coming into conflict with a local population. An Edwardian bungalow just above McLeod Ganj could easily be surrounded with barbed wire and guarded; this would be a residence for the Dalai Lama.

The Indian Government bought the bungalow, known as Swarg Ashram, for the Dalai Lama, and he lived there for some years. The current residence, colloquially if grandly referred to as 'The Palace', is on the other side of McLeod Ganj at the very end of the mountain spur; this makes it easier to guard than the 'Old Palace', which was set on the side of the mountain. Those who see either building are often surprised at what a modest home the Dalai Lama has; the present palace would not be out of place in one of the better suburbs of Los Angeles, and the Old Palace is so un-palatial that it is now used as a climbing centre and hostel.

The guards were provided by the Indian Government. They are police on special duty, and they are armed with rifles; in those early days, no one was sure what the Chinese might do, and as His Holiness became more and more known internationally there were obvious dangers from cranks and even terrorists.

From Swarg Ashram, the Dalai Lama began to set up all the machinery for running what would amount to a country-within-a-country. The most pressing problem was taking care of the refugees, especially the children, many of whom were orphans. To do this, he needed money, which he got from four main sources.

The first and greatest contribution came from the Indian

Government. They spent vast sums, not counting the value of the land that they made available, on establishing Dharamsala and then later settlements. Apart from the restrictions on the Dalai Lama's political comments, as already mentioned, they gave the money freely and without restriction. This could only be called a magnificent act of generosity in any country; given India's own internal needs and problems, it is all the more impressive.

The second source was foreign aid. Few governments were willing to recognise the Administration in Exile as the legitimate government of Tibet, but many were impressed by the work that the Administration did for the refugees. Some sent cash, and some sent donations in kind; contributions in the fields of medicine and education were particularly valuable. His Holiness unashamedly begged for the money; he has no false pride, and getting money for his people had to be the highest priority.

Thirdly, there was private aid, from India and from the rest of the world. Some money came from philanthropic foundations, some from individuals rich and poor, some from *ad hoc* organisations. Many people gave their time: doctors, nurses and teachers have all worked in Dharamsala on a voluntary basis, and this continues to this day.

Finally, there was a massive contribution from the Dalai Lama himself. The treasure that he had transferred to Sikkim in 1950, when the Chinese first invaded, was sold; it realised about £600,000, or one and a half million dollars at the then exchange rate. Although this money was the personal property of the Dalai Lama, he used it to set up a trust known as His Holiness the Dalai Lama's Charitable Trust. From the very start, the idea was that this money should be used for self-help, and in addition to income from investments, capital is furnished for the establishment of Tibetan handicraft centres, carpet factories, and the like. Unfortunately, a great deal of money was lost in the early days, when the Tibetans were not skilled at investment: several rogues took a share of the money, including an Indian who floated a company to manufacture cast-iron pipe, which turned out to be little more than a confidence trick. Losses amounted to over a quarter of a million pounds, a sickening loss under the circumstances.

Many people are suspicious of charities and relief organisations, believing that the majority of the money never reaches where it would do the most good, but is spent instead in feathering the nests of administrators. Nothing could be further from the truth in the case of the Tibetans. The Dalai Lama, as a monk, set an example which everyone followed. There are ten ranks or grades within the Administration, with the Dalai Lama himself as the sole occupant of the first rank, and then a descending scale through various administrative levels to the tenth rank for 'peons, drivers, and so on', to quote the official definition. As an example of salaries, an official of the eighth rank, a senior clerk, earned about RS500/- *a month* in 1983 – about £33 or US $50. No one works for the administration to get rich: we met several people who could have been earning very good salaries in the West, but who preferred instead to stay with their leader and their people and work for a free Tibet.

On many occasions, His Holiness has had considerable trouble in restraining expenditure on his behalf. Many people give him presents, as is only to be expected, and these can be really valuable – video cassette recorders, for example. Although he keeps some of these presents himself, especially when it would be embarrassing or impolite to do otherwise, his usual policy is to divert them to where they are most useful. The video recorder which was was given in 1983, for example, went to the Tibetan Institute of Performing Arts. His most impressive gift is probably the yellow Range Rover which the Canadian-Tibetan community gave him – the ideal vehicle for the Himalayas and for journeys into Ladakh and other wild parts of India. He normally travels Business Class on airlines, and he had tremendous difficulty in persuading people that flying first-class was a waste of money which could be better spent elsewhere.

In the early days when Dharamsala was first established, the present differentiation into the various Government offices had not begun, and the administration amounted to a series of committees or individuals each responsible to the Dalai Lama. His private secretary was able to deal with a great deal of the routine work, but his was the final voice in many decisions, including a large number that could equally well have been taken at a lower level. As we have repeatedly stressed, this was due both to his position and his personal qualities, but it meant that the task of government was truly his.

There were concentrations of Tibetans in Mussoorie and

increasingly in Dharamsala, but the great majority of Tibetan refugees in 1959-60 were working as labourers on road building projects for the Indian government. This was not simply charity: the work was back-breaking, but Tibetan men and women worked together at a rate which startled the Indians. This was especially true at high altitudes, where the general reckoning was that one Tibetan could work as hard as three or four Indians. They worked for next to nothing, living in the utmost poverty, and their children fell victim to innumerable diseases: the old Victorian cliché about India's 'unhealthy climate' is no exaggeration, and to people brought up in the thin cold air of Tibet it was if anything, even worse than it was for the *memsahib* and her children under the British Raj. Respiratory diseases were rife, and tuberculosis was a major killer. Worm infestation was commonplace; when the first post-mortems were carried out by volunteer doctors in Dharamsala, even they would sometimes vomit at the state of a child's stomach and intestines. The Dalai Lama realised that as long as they had no base, there was little hope for the Tibetan people; and so he asked the Indian government for help in setting up camps for road-workers, where they could be treated medically and instructed in basic hygiene. This was the origin of the first major Tibetan settlement outside Dharamsala, at Bylakuppe in Southern India, 52 miles from Mysore city. There the Dalai Lama appointed two representatives, Thupten Nyima and Phala Wangchuk Dorje, who worked with a representative of the Indian government to set up a camp on 3000 acres of land, leased rent- and tax-free to the Tibetans; the government's generosity in making this land available was increased even further by the way that they paid the majority of the travel expenses of the refugees from the northern provinces where they had been working. The first party of 666 people arrived in Mysore in mid-December, 1960; they lived in tents. That was one of the first projects to get under way.

There were still many Tibetan road-workers who were not settled, and although travelling doctors and nurses who visited the road camps could offer some help, the next priority was to get their children into schools and looked after. There were also innumerable homeless orphans, whose parents had either died whilst trying to escape from Tibet or succumbed to disease while working on the road gangs. There were non-residential schools in Mussoorie in early 1960, but the Dalai Lama wanted a residential school in Dharamsala. Many parents wanted their children to be there, where they would be near His Holiness, but at first the priority was strictly for orphans and the children of itinerant road-workers.

When Dharamsala was established, there were fifty-one orphaned and destitute children brought from the temporary refugee camp at Jammu. The Dalai Lama's elder sister, Mrs Tsering Dolma, volunteered to look after them; and on May 17th, 1960, the Nursery for Tibetan Refugee Children was founded. It was based in a tumbledown bungalow just above McLeod Ganj, with virtually no facilities and little accommodation: in the beginning, there were so few beds that the small children were laid crossways on a single bed, so that one bed might hold half a dozen children. By the end of 1960, nearly 500 orphans and other homeless children had joined the Nursery, and at one point over 120 children were sleeping in a room 20 feet by 30 feet.

Like her brother, Mrs Tsering Dolma worked incredibly hard. She arranged accommodation and food for volunteer workers, raised money, and personally supervised everything that she could. It was probably her endless efforts which contributed to her death at the end of 1964, but her work was taken over by Mrs Pema Gyalpo, their younger sister, almost immediately. Neither sister was ever prepared to suffer fools gladly, unless it was for the good of the children, but they had the satisfaction of seeing the Nursery grow into a full-fledged School. In Mrs Tsering Dolma's time it had already outgrown its former premises, and the Indian Government (which was already responsible for the existing premises) generously rented two bigger buildings still further up the hill, at Forsyth Bazaar. In 1966, with funds from the Norwegian Refugee Council, Swiss Aid to Tibetans and the Dalai Lama, these two buildings and 43 acres of land were bought as a permanent site for what has now become the Tibetan Children's Village. At the time of writing, Mrs Pema Gyalpo was still in charge and the school housed some twelve hundred children, though a thousand would have been a more comfortable figure, and there were almost two thousand day pupils.

The principal medium of instruction is English, because all schools in India must use either Hindi or English, and English is obviously of more use. On the other hand, the children will also need Hindi for their daily lives, so this is taught as well. To make sure that the Tibetan language is properly preserved, they also learn that. As a result, they grow up tri-lingual – and in three languages that use three different alphabets!

The third major project, after the settlements and the schools, was self-help. The Indian government was generous with its aid, but it was obviously undesirable that the Tibetans should continue to live on hand-outs as well as it being unreasonable to expect government aid indefinitely. The Great Thirteenth Dalai Lama had presided over a revival in Tibetan arts and crafts, to the extent that a master carpet weaver from Gyantse was employed at a government rank exceeding that of a district magistrate. He maintained a government-sponsored workshop called the *Dhonphel,* where master craftsmen worked on government projects; they were the best from their respective regions, and were highly paid, and they also took private commissions at steep fees. The Fourteenth Dalai Lama saw that the continuation of this tradition would be the best hope for Tibetan self-help apart from agriculture.

Of course, only a very few master craftsmen had escaped from Tibet, and few more were to follow in later years. Because of their relative prosperity, and because Buddhist motifs were inseparable from their work, they formed a special target for the Chinese. Those who were not killed were frequently beaten so badly during *thamzing* that they were blinded or crippled, and unable to work. *Thamzing,* for those unfamiliar with the term, is 'self-criticism'; the victim confesses his faults in public, and everyone else present is expected to join in, insulting him and physically assaulting him. Anyone who is insufficiently enthusiastic in condemning reactionary behaviour can expect to be the next victim.

Nevertheless, the best craftsmen in each field were found and employed as teachers. In the old Tibet, it had taken years to attain master craftsman status, just as in the guilds of mediaeval times in the west, but these few teachers did their best to transmit as much of their crafts as they could, as fast as possible. The most suitable craft was carpet-weaving, and the magnificent Tibetan carpets with their symbolic patterns became one of the staple products of the Tibetans in exile.

The very first handicraft centres were established even before Dharamsala, in 1959. The Tibetan Refugee Self-Help Centre in

Darjeeling was set up in October 1959, under the administration of a ten-member committee of Tibetan exiles; the Handicraft Centre in Dalhousie was started by the Indian Government in November, at the instigation of the Dalai Lama. It was not until 1963 that a similar body was set up in Dharamsala, under the title of the Tibetan Women's Co-operative Association; it is now known as the Tibetan Handicraft Production-cum-Sale Co-operative Industrial Society Limited, and it was initially funded jointly by a donation from His Holiness and a loan from the Council for Home Affairs. To show how basic conditions were in those days, the original eleven members received food but no salary: the aim was to provide work and subsistence for the old, the poor and the infirm.

Many more handicraft centres followed, and although the role of other donors increased as the Tibetan cause became better known, many owe their initial existence to a donation or interest-free loan from His Holiness's charitable trust and to his continued patronage. They are all a mixture of commercial enterprise and social institution; some that function as schools will only allow people to stay on until they are capable of working for a commercial enterprise, whilst others function as old people's homes, where the elderly are looked after in return for light work such as spinning wool and passing their knowledge on to the young. Some of the very old are among the few Tibetans who object to having their pictures taken; most love to see a photograph of themselves.

With the more basic self-help issues under way, His Holiness next turned his attention to preserving Tibetan culture. There was no great difficulty in preserving the fundamentals of the religion, because many of those who escaped were monks who re-founded their monasteries in Dharamsala and elsewhere. Little or no money was available from the Administration, so they worked in the traditional monastic fashion: self-help and begging. They built their own monasteries, and lived on what little charity the rest of Dharamsala could afford. As soon as a Tibetan has the bare minimum necessary for survival, he will begin to devote as much time and money as possible to the furtherance of the Dharma, so no monk or nun starved.

What was much more difficult was to preserve at least some of the trappings of the religion. The Dalai Lama says wryly that the Chinese did the Tibetans a favour by forcing them to purify their religion, which had in some cases become obsessed with form and splendour at the expense of content. To a great extent, though, Tibetan culture and religion are inseparable, and whilst it would have been inappropriate for master wood-carvers and image-makers to work for the few Tibetans who could afford their services, or for foreign collectors and aesthetes who could not understand or fully appreciate their work, it was entirely appropriate that they should work in monasteries and on a new temple. Intricate wood-carving is an integral part of Tibetan architecture, and the Dalai Lama commissioned the few skilled carvers who had escaped to teach others and to work on the new temple. Similarly, the metal workers who made the butter lamps and images for the shrines were pressed into service as both artisans and teachers; the Metalwork School in an out of the way part of Dharamsala is now administered by one of the major craftsmen from old Tibet, who teaches his young apprentices all that he learned in years of working for the most demanding customers.

The less obvious aspects of the culture were also supported. In 1960 the Tibetan Music, Dance and Drama Society was formed under the aegis of the Council for Tibetan Education; now it is known as the Tibetan Institute of Performing Arts, and each year it puts on a *Shoton* festival of *Lhamo,* the Tibetan folk operas which last all day.

Traditional Tibetan medicine exists (literally) alongside the modern Western variety; the Tibetan Medical Centre, which grew out of the Tibetan Dispensary founded in 1961 at the instigation of the Dalai Lama, is across the road from the Delek Welfare Hospital, built on land donated by the Dalai Lama. He also started the building fund for the Delek Hospital, though the great majority of the money came from the Norwegian Refugee Council and the Tibetan Friendship Group, New York. Confusingly, the Tibetan Medical Centre makes no charge for consultation, but does charge (very modestly) for the traditional Tibetan medicines, whilst the Delek Hospital makes a nominal charge for examinations but none for the drugs. Anyone who cannot afford even these modest fees is treated free, including Western hippies.

Hippies are one of the less agreeable aspects of life in Dharamsala. The great days of the overland treks in the 1960s corresponded with the expansion of the Tibetan colony, and Dharamsala became a favoured place for the hot season, when Goa was unbearable. It was cheap, it was friendly, and the livelier or more intelligent hippies could take a genuine interest in Tibetan culture and religion; one modern guide book aimed at neo-hippies refers to "the technicolour Tibetan outlook on life" and calls Dharamsala "a real little freak centre". At times, it is as if the 1960s had never ended: clouds of marijuana smoke roll across the little square at the bus stop from the hippies sitting on the steps outside the shops at the end of Bhagsunath Road, and the conversation consists of "Wow, man... far out". At one time, the hippies were so thick on the ground that His Holiness appointed an incarnate Lama to fulfil the endless demands they were making for Tibetan teachings; among the Tibetans, though not among the Westerners, he was known as 'Hippie Rinpoche'.

Nowadays, the few that take their Buddhism seriously will go along to the regular classes at the Library of Tibetan Works and Archives at Gangchen Kyishong. There, Tibetan teachers patiently expound the Greater Vehicle to a crowd that is constantly changing, but from which a few will become devout Buddhists. Some become monks or nuns, but not all who do so earn the respect of the Tibetans. One scandal involved a dance held at the Tibetan Institute of Performing Arts; Western monks and nuns were dancing as if it were a party in the West. It was not that they were specifically prohibited from doing so; it was just, as one *Tulku* said, that Western dancing is very provocative, and it can hardly have helped them to consider the Dharma. Tibetans generally have more respect for either sincere practitioners, who follow the traditional Tibetan ways, or for those Westerners who make no great show of their religion.

The LTWA, or Library as it is commonly called, is yet another brainchild of the Dalai Lama. With 44,000 Tibetan books, over 20,000 Tibetan manuscripts, and several thousand Western books on all aspects of Tibet and Tibetan society it is not merely a library; it is also a museum, containing many artefacts donated from the Dalai Lama's private collection, a centre for lectures and seminars, and a place where traditional Tibetan skills such as wood-carving and thangka–painting are taught. The building is an interesting blend of Tibetan architecture and modern materials, and it was opened in 1971. The Library publishes books in its own right, as well as reprinting many Tibetan works from the past. Most of its funding comes in the form of a Grant-in-Aid from the Indian government, which recognises the importance of the museum in a world-wide context.

As each of these institutions was founded, the Dalai Lama did his best to make it self-governing and self-sufficient. This was not only for the sake of efficiency and to reduce the amount of work referred to him; it was because he simply did not have time to be involved in every project at an everyday personal level. Quite apart from anything else, he was still doing his best to make sure that the Tibetan question was aired as often as possible.

An obvious forum was the United Nations, and His Holiness continued to seek sponsors there. Thailand and the Federation of Malaya submitted a Question in 1960, but it was not considered for lack of time. In 1961, Thailand and the Federation were joined by Ireland and El Salvador, and this time a draft resolution was adopted by 56 votes to 11 with 29 abstentions – again including India. It was basically a reaffirmation of the previous resolution, but it also took note of the huge numbers of refugees:

"Noting with deep anxiety the severe hardships which these events have inflicted on the Tibetan people as evidenced by the large scale exodus of Tibetan refugees to the neighbouring countries,"

The third and (at the time of writing) last draft resolution was submitted in 1965 by El Salvador, Ireland, Malaysia, Malta, Nicaragua, the Philippines and Thailand. The vote was 43 to 26 in favour, with 22 abstentions, but the significant thing was that India now voted for Tibet. This resolution was in the strongest terms yet, and the reaffirmation of the conviction about the Principles of the Charter and the Universal Declaration of Human Rights was pushed into second place: the first of the four points was

The General Assembly... (1) *Deplores* the continued violation of the fundamental rights and freedoms of the people of Tibet.

These Resolutions were not introduced by the various states with any thought of gain, nor was it particularly a question of solidarity among Buddhist states; it would be hard to find two countries more staunchly Catholic than Ireland and Malta, and there is a strong Catholic interest in the other supporters of the 1965 Resolution. They were simply calling for justice – a justice which the United Nations was unable or unwilling to grant.

The change in India's attitude was influenced by the border incidents which arose almost as soon as the Dalai Lama had left Tibet; China's expansionism became abundantly clear. Nehru's death also eased the restrictions that had been placed on the Dalai Lama, and after 1965 he began increasingly to make his case known directly.

In addition to his immediate work for the Tibetan people – the founding of settlements, schools, and self-help associations, the preservation of the culture, and the continued presentation of their case in world forums – the Dalai Lama had another scheme in mind. It was breathtaking in its audacity: nothing less than a complete reconstruction of the government of Tibet, against the day that the country was free again.

This may sound like an absurdly grandiose plan, but when the details are examined it becomes remarkably logical, almost inevitable. As the Dalai Lama freely admits, there was a lot wrong with the old Tibet. The innate conservatism of Tibetans, combined with a reaction against the dramatic events of the early years of the century, meant that they had tried to resist almost all of the changes which were inevitable if Tibet was to survive into the twentieth and twenty-first centuries. Powerful pressure groups, especially in the big monasteries, fought successfully against any attempt at modernisation. The administration, despite the great improvements made by the Great Thirteenth Dalai Lama, was frankly ramshackle. As His Holiness the Fourteenth Dalai Lama put it, "We cannot go back to the old Tibet – and even if we could, we do not want to."

Inside Tibet, in the 1950s, His Holiness had already tried to introduce some reforms. He wanted his own position to be more constitutional, so that ordinary Tibetans could share in government, but that was obviously unacceptable to the Chinese: the last thing they wanted was Tibetans to have any say in the running of their own country. His attempts at land reform were also unsuccessful: he had tried to continue the work of the Great Thirteenth, giving government officials salaries instead of grants of land, so that the peasants owned and worked their own land. This was a very much more acceptable plan than the Chinese ideas of collectivisation as far as most Tibetans were concerned, so the Chinese opposed the idea utterly.

What he wanted to do in Dharamsala, therefore, was to set up a Government in Exile that would serve as a model when Tibet was once more free. This model would be offered to the Tibetan people, and His Holiness hopes they will accept it; the main danger is that they will refuse to accept anything which limits his power, even if he expressly requests it.

He knew that he was the only person who would be acceptable to most Tibetans as Head of State, and so the plans were based on this. He also retained absolute discretion in his selection of advisers; the *Kashag* would continue as his cabinet.

The Government itself is made up of the Dalai Lama, the Kashag, representatives from each of the six main departments of the administration, and an elected chamber consisting of seventeen people: four each from Amdo, Kham, and U-Tsang, the three provinces of Tibet, and one from each of the five religious schools, Nyingma, Kagyud, Sakya, Gelug, and Bön. There is also a reserved seat which the Dalai Lama may fill directly, selecting a person of distinction in the fields of art, science, or literature.

The Dalai Lama does not usually preside over the body, though his opinion is often sought. The whole body functions as a committee, but only the votes of the elected deputies present are counted: decisions are made on a simple majority of those votes. The Chairman and Vice-Chairman of the Assembly are elected by the deputies from among their own number, and they are sworn in by the Dalai Lama.

As a transition from absolute monarchy to elected democracy, the system is surely masterful. The Dalai Lama retained enough status for himself to ensure continuity and acceptability to the majority of the Tibetan people, whilst ensuring that the real power is in the hands of the elected deputies. Because of the absence of sectarianism in Tibet, there is little danger of the religious representatives being voted in on a sectarian 'party ticket', whilst their inclusion means that religion is not too quickly stripped of secular power – to the approval of the monks and the populace alike. The fact that they are in a minority in the Assembly also means that they can be outvoted if necessary, though it is hard to imagine this happening.

Elections are held every three years, with universal suffrage at eighteen, though candidates must be twenty-five or older. The first

Commission of Tibetan People's Deputies met on September 2nd, 1960, and although it is now known as the Assembly of Tibetan People's Deputies it continues to meet in substantially the same form as it did then.

In order to safeguard the Tibetan system of democracy, the Dalai Lama also promulgated a constitution on March 10th, 1963, the fourth anniversary of the Lhasa uprising. He had announced the underlying principles in October 1961, but it took until 1963 to polish it to its final form. It is a long document, drawing heavily on the United Nations Declaration of Human Rights, and the whole text is given in Appendix 1, but it is worth quoting the Preamble here to show the premises on which it is based:

WHEREAS it has become increasingly evident that the system of government which has hitherto prevailed in Tibet has not proved sufficiently responsive to the present needs and future development of the people

AND WHEREAS it is deemed desirable and necessary that the principles of justice, equality and democracy laid down by the Lord Buddha should be reinforced and strengthened in the government of Tibet

AND WHEREAS it is deemed essential that the people of Tibet shall have a more effective voice in shaping their destiny

NOW, THEREFORE, His Holiness the Dalai Lama has been pleased to ordain, and it is hereby ordained as follows...

This would all be so much play-acting if there were not any real work to be done, and the Dalai Lama has tried to ensure that as many decisions as possible concerning the refugees and the future of Tibet are taken by the Assembly. They work through six main departments: the Council for Religious and Cultural Affairs, the Council for Home Affairs, the Council for Tibetan Education, the Paljor Office (Exchequer), the Information Office, and the Security Office.

The functions and scope of these departments are fairly self-explanatory, though it is worth noting that the Security Office also arranges audiences with His Holiness and acts as the Welfare Office for the Tibetan community in Dharamsala. One problem is that they continually encroach upon one another's territory, and there are many interdepartmental squabbles, but in general the dedication with which they work is most impressive. If this form of government can be continued when Tibet is free, then she will be one of the most fortunate countries in the world.

The whole Government in Exile (though the Indians prefer the term 'Administration', for obvious reasons) functions very much as a real government, running the state-within-a-state that Tibetan refugees in India comprise. They even exact taxes, which are neither high nor compulsory, but which (unlike most taxes) are gladly paid by most Tibetans. The Assembly is not, however, the only body that influences policy: there is also the General Meeting.

The Annual General Meeting is held early in the Tibetan year, March or May in the Western year; a meeting can also be summoned as an emergency body at any time. It is attended by the Kashag, by the elected deputies, by religious leaders, and by anyone in a responsible position in the Tibetan administration anywhere – the staff of the Central Tibetan Secretariat, the Tibetan Welfare Officers, representatives of Tibetan schools and other autonomous bodies, and locally elected representatives. It can be unwieldy, and most who attend agree that there are many tendentious and boring speeches, but it is one of the purest forms of democracy in the world. Besides, in among the speeches made for form's sake (and Tibetans can be traditionally Oriental in this respect), there are likely to be some really important contributions: anyone can have his or her say.

His Holiness views all this with some satisfaction, but he still feels that the Tibetan people are not as willing as they should be to express their own feelings. This sometimes leads to the rather amusing prospect of the Dalai Lama acting as his own opposition. For example, he believes that a synthesis of Marxism and Buddhism is not only possible, but desirable. The Lord Buddha wanted improvement in the spiritual realm, and Marx in the material; what alliance could be more fruitful? It was, therefore, at his instigation that a Tibetan Communist Party was formed, but it was never very successful. The few members it did attract generally found themselves with very divided loyalties, though its end in 1982 or so was apparently in the finest tradition of communist parties: as Gyari Rinpoche described it, "There were only four members left, and they all purged each other".

In the quarter century between the flight from Tibet and the writing of this book the Dalai Lama managed to lead his followers as a coherent, practical and organised body, proud of their history, their nationality, and their religion; and now it is time to consider the present.

11

A Day in the Life

Well before dawn, while it was still completely dark, a steady trickle of people walked the short road from McLeod Ganj to Thekchen Choeling. They were dressed warmly: February is cold in the Himalayas, especially at that hour of the morning. Most were carrying torches, and no one spoke very much; all except the monks and nuns were still half asleep. They were the first few on their way to the Losar Puja, the ritual to celebrate the arrival of the Tibetan New Year. We were among them. Later, most of Dharamsala would be outside the temple.

Butter lamps burned in the temple, and there were a few electric lamps. The monks of Namgyal monastery, beside the temple, were preparing for the *puja;* light shone from their windows. On the low verandah around the temple, an old woman and a small child were performing repeated prostrations. Others walked around the temple building, always clockwise, spinning the prayer wheels and telling their rosaries. One hundred and eight beads, one hundred and eight recitations of *Om Mani Padme Hum,* the words slurred together, *Om* ma-ni pay-may *hummm*. The old women have four tallies on their rosaries, each with ten beads: one million, eighty thousand recitations.

The first grey light was just turning to a deep blue as the monks began to file up onto the roof of the temple, their maroon shawls wrapped tightly around them to keep out the cold, their crested hats a brilliant yellow. They took up their places, facing each other in two blocks across an aisle between a throne that faced the east – and Tibet – and a smaller altar set with food and drink offerings. On the left of the throne was the monastic orchestra, with horns ranging from the shawm-like *gyalings* to the huge *dung-chen,* and drums mounted in frames; each monk also had his *dorje* and *drilbu,* thunderbolt and bell.

To the right, the monks sat in close-packed ranks. Behind them, there were two huge sculptures of dyed and kneaded butter. The ones on the roof were over six feet tall, but in the temple below there were others little more than a foot tall, incredibly intricate representations of various deities. These sculptures take many days to make, but when the Losar *pujas* are over, they are destroyed: the traditional use was to melt them down and use them as fuel for the butter lamps in the temple.

The Dalai Lama took his place on the throne. It was still an hour before dawn, and the sky was a deep clear blue. He began the rituals: chants, together with complex manipulations of ritual instruments such as the *dorje, drilbu* and *damaru* or hand-drum. As in a Catholic mass, some chants were reserved for the Dalai Lama as priest, whilst others came in the form of responses from the monks. As is usual, they were in a mixture of Sanskrit and Tibetan, following a rhythm which is at first incomprehensible but which, after a while, becomes a part of you so that you appreciate their unearthly beauty still more. The rhythms of the orchestra are also alien when you first hear them, but the instruments combine in a way that is fascinating to hear. They do not play together, as in a Western orchestra: rather, they fit together. It is an experience for all the senses.

A gentle but cold wind blew; the smell of Tibetan incense came in gusts. The *puja* went on, and on. An umbrella bearer moved to the centre of the aisle just before dawn; the moment of sunrise was pure magic, as the light changed from blue to gold and made all the colours glow and the metal of the horns and ritual implements sparkle. Part of the way through, there was a general distribution of hot buttered tea and rice with raisins; the first meal of the year, and very welcome when you have been sitting freezing in the same place for a couple of hours. The Dalai Lama continued to lead the chanting, sometimes loudly, sometimes softly, from time to time ringing the *drilbu* or twirling the *damaru,* which is a little drum made of two shallow cups placed back to back with skins stretched over the open sides. When the drum is twisted rapidly to and fro in the hand, the striker which is suspended on a long piece of thread hits the two sides alternately, making a rapid-fire sound that is unforgettable. A *damaru* was of course one of the possessions of the Great Thirteenth that the present Dalai Lama recognised when he was so young.

The *puja* lasted for almost four hours; the umbrella-bearer moved steadily to make sure that the Dalai Lama remained in the shade, and the sun was well up in the sky when the ritual procession moved downstairs inside the temple. It finished in there: the Dalai Lama was escorted surprisingly unobtrusively back through the guarded gates of the palace, and the crowd which had completely filled the large grassy forecourt between the palace and the temple slowly melted away.

This is the sort of thing which most people think of when they imagine the Dalai Lama's day, and it is an important part of his life. But as we have seen, he is more than just a leader of ritual. He has said himself that his typical day is the typical day of any monk, freedom fighter, politician and administrator. No two days are alike, but he does have a general pattern which he keeps to as far as is practicable.

He rises early, typically at about five, and spends an hour or more in meditation or spiritual practice. He does this on his own, and it plays a major part in preparing him for the pressures of the day. His practices are similar to those of any other monk, including meditation on the nature and attributes of the various awareness-beings and reflection upon the application of religion to daily life, as well as what the Japanese call 'no mind', a state symbolised in Tibetan practice by a mirror which sees all and reflects all, but retains no mark. It is a state of being in the here and now, yet transcending here and now; a state of timelessness and tranquillity. It is described in many Buddhist texts, but this is not the place for a dissertation: books have been filled describing this state.

When his meditation is finished, he listens to the radio. If the news begins before he has finished, he will break off and listen, returning to his religious practices when it is over. Only a highly skilled Lama could switch his concentration like this; 'one-pointed concentration' is one of the fundamentals of meditation, if not the fundamental, and losing it is all too easy.

Like many Tibetans, he has the greatest admiration for the BBC World Service and the Voice of America, because they provide the most comprehensive and least biased news service; he cannot understand the people who advocate that they should be cut back in the name of economy. The other two stations that he listens to are Radio Australia and All India Radio. Most of his background appreciation of world affairs comes from the radio, as he does not have time to read all the newspapers as thoroughly as he would like.

When questioned on his tastes in food, he says that the monastic ideal is to eat only what you can beg, but in his position this is hardly practical; instead, he eats whatever he is given. This even includes meat, much to the surprise of many, though this is to a great extent the result of advice from his doctors. A severe bout of hepatitis some years ago left him vulnerable to liverish reactions to some kinds of food, and they advised him that his hitherto vegetarian diet would not be the best for him. He does not drink milk, for the same reason. He did admit to a taste for *tsampa,* the classic Tibetan staple: it consists of parched barley pounded to a flour, and it is mixed with the liquid of your choice to make a dry crumbly dough that is eaten raw. The traditional liquid is black tea, made in the Tibetan fashion from tea-bricks, but broth, plain water, or even *chang* (barley-beer) can be used. The Dalai Lama said that although he used to eat *tsampa* when he was younger, there were several years when he did not like the stuff at all, and it was only as he was getting older that he was able to appreciate it again.

After breakfast, the main demands on his time for the rest of the morning come from Tibetan affairs of state. If the Tibetan National Working Committee is in session there will often be questions of policy referred to him. Otherwise, there are innumerable aspects of the day-to-day running of the Government in Exile which will occupy him. Some will be referred to him by his staff, and others he will enter into himself, as the final arbiter in any case.

An example of the latter occurred when his younger brother announced that he was going to hand back his robes and become a layman, and that he would be known by his given name of Tendzin Choegyal rather than his lineage name of Ngari Rinpoche. The reaction from the Rinpoche's monasteries was strong and plaintive, and Tendzin Choegyal argued in vain that he was no longer anyone's Lama, that the Lord Buddha himself had enjoined everyone to seek their own salvation because no one else could do it for them, and that the revenues which they were trying to give to him could be far better spent than in supporting him. They were adamant: he was their Lama, and their revenues were his. Why should he work? Just tell them what he wanted, and he should have it.

Eventually, His Holiness had to step in. His solution was straight-forward. His younger brother should visit the monasteries (which are in Ladakh) from time to time, and make sure that the money was well spent. He would go as a layman, but he would bear in mind the feeling that the local inhabitants had for him.

It is a small example, but it shows very clearly how the Dalai Lama has to work in order to change Tibetan society, from the roots, and often fighting a rearguard action from diehard traditionalists. His younger brother works in the Administration, at the customary minute salary, and there could not be a more devout or ardent supporter of the Dalai Lama. But he, like his brother, is a modernist, and he is one of the most outspoken critics of the faults of the old Tibet. The Great Thirteenth Dalai Lama said that in his next life he would have many brothers and sisters to help him with the work, and Tendzin Choegyal, Mrs Tsering Dolma and Mrs Pema Gyalpo, and Lobsang Samten (who runs the Tibetan Medical Centre) all bear this out. His two other brothers, one in the United States and one in Hong Kong, also do a great deal of unreported work for him, especially in the diplomatic sphere.

Although the description 'God-King' is, as we have seen, not a happy one, it is indisputable that the Dalai Lama does function as the King of Tibet, and in that role there are some very unexpected things for him to do. One is to review the Tibetan army, which paradoxically is stronger in exile than it ever was in Tibet. Now that the Indians have recognised the nature of the threat from the Chinese, they are prepared to accept Tibetan recruits in what is nominally a part of the Indian army. At the time of writing, there were ten thousand trained Tibetan paratroopers, and if those who have left the service, but remain available for active duty, are included the number rises to nearer fifteen thousand. Fifteen thousand paratroopers is a formidable army by any standards.

Again, although the Dalai Lama is spared having to read all that is written about Tibet in the world's newspapers, his staff do their best to keep abreast of it all. If there is anything which they feel should come to his attention, it filters up through his secretaries until (if it is important enough) he sees it. If statements are to be issued, they will be written for him – but he will cast a very close eye over them to make sure that they reflect his views, and show the Tibetan case in its clearest light.

A part of the morning is set aside for the study of Buddhist texts, because in another of his many roles the Dalai Lama is effectively the head of a great Buddhist university. The many monasteries all look to him as their leading scholar, and his scholarship is important to him: as we have seen, he gained his *Geshé* degree at an unusually early age. It might seem that there was little new to study, because Buddhism has already been around for two and a half thousand years, but this is not so. In the first place, the existing store of texts written over those two and a half millenia is so vast that no one could read them all, let alone master them all, in one lifetime. In the second place, the world is constantly changing, and so the relationship between Buddhism and the world changes. Buddhism is an intellectual path, not a dogmatic one, so there is always much to explore.

The Dalai Lama is himself the author of several books and one of the most accessible is *Universal Responsibility and the Good Heart*. It deals with day-to-day practicality, rather than with abstruse theology, and he explains that the good heart is the fundamental requirement for getting along with people. He reminds us again and again that all sentient beings desire happiness and the causes of happiness, freedom from suffering and the causes of suffering; the good heart is no more than the constant daily attempt to promote the general level of happiness in the world. By taking a little thought, we may be able to do something a different way, which involves no inconvenience to ourselves but which might make life very much easier for someone else; or, by making some very slight sacrifice, we may be able to gain for someone else a very much greater advantage.

If this sounds similar to the Christian doctrine of loving thy neighbour, it is precisely because it is. His Holiness points out how most of us have some experience of this sort of love, from our parents: most parents make sacrifices for their children. The difficult part is to extend this love so that it does not cover just our friends and family, but everyone else – even, eventually, our enemies. As the Christian teaching expresses it, "Love thine enemy as thyself".

This is the extension of the good heart into universal responsi-bility, when we no longer limit our attempts to help to those near and dear to us; we try to help everyone, because ultimately we are all part of one family. As the Dalai Lama says, "I do not react to you as another Tibetan, or as a German, or an Englishman, but simply as a man. We are all men: as long as we react to each other on this level, what is there to fight or argue about?"

It is very easy to ignore this sort of argument, or to dismiss it as platitudinous, but the Dalai Lama's great skill lies in showing how even a small step can make a very real difference. He emphasises that there is absolutely no need for religiosity in good-heartedness or universal responsibility. As he says, it is perfectly possible to exhibit the good heart without any reference to Christ, or the Lord Buddha, or the Prophet, or anyone else. Religion is an expression of the good heart, not its cause.

At noon, in accordance with monastic tradition, His Holiness eats the second and last meal of the day, usually Tibetan food. Tibetan *cuisine* is not the most exciting in the world, consisting mainly of variations on noodles and boiled meat and the ubiquitous *tsampa* or sometimes bread, but it is not as bad as it might appear from Tibetan restaurants in Dharamsala. The main problem there is poverty of ingredients: in the old Tibet, yak meat was the most prized, followed by beef, with pork and mutton a poor third and 'eater of fish and chicken' was a synonym for poverty. In Dharamsala, there is no yak-meat or beef, and the pork is unsafe; Indian mutton is not the ideal basis for anything. In pre-invasion times, most wealthy Tibetans employed Chinese chefs to provide variety, but as Tibet is too high and too cold to grow rice, the Chinese staple had to be imported.

Lunch is often eaten whilst reading state papers, or indeed anything else. The Dalai Lama is a voracious reader, and when he has time to read anything other than official papers and political reports he prefers non-fiction, on every topic under the sun. He also confesses with a grin to a weakness for war stories – as he says himself, an unlikely choice for a Dalai Lama. He likes the weightier magazines of the popular press, such as *Reader's Digest* and *Time,* and a good deal of his information on advances in science and technology comes from this source. He says that he wishes he could read English faster, then he could go deeper into things, but in conversation the range of his interests would be impressive in a leisured Westerner, let alone in someone of his background who works as hard as he does. For example, during one audience we talked about sub-atomic physics; he agreed that the non-dualist viewpoint typical of Buddhism was extremely useful in that strange world where a particle can simultaneously exhibit the qualities of both mass and energy and where the normal Western dualist either/or concepts broke down, but he also pointed out that this was by no means exclusively a Buddhist way of looking at things, and that it was quite possible for a non-Buddhist to adopt such a viewpoint.

After lunch there may be more state business, or he may devote some time to study and writing. He may even have some time to himself, but the afternoons are the main time for *darshans* or audiences. Innumerable people want to see the Dalai Lama, and there are various different types of *darshan* to enable as many different people as possible to do so.

Public audiences are for anyone, Tibetan or foreigner, who wants to seek His Holiness's blessing, and he tries to see as many people as he can. A typical afternoon's quota might consist of anything from one to three hundred people, who simply apply to the office for an audience. There is one office for Tibetans, and another for foreigners. After filling in a form, people are allocated a day and a time, and they have to bring their passports with them when they come to the palace.

The security check at the main gate is rigorous, and involves a body search for concealed weapons. Any gifts that are brought are examined. Then it is simply a question of waiting. There will be Tibetans, some freshly arrived from Tibet, dressed in their best *chubas* and bearing gifts of barley flour; there will be hippies, looking like something from the 1960s; there will be visitors from half a dozen countries, with English, Americans and Germans usually predominating but the occasional Japanese, Frenchman, Australian, or whatever as well. There are surprisingly few Indians. Everyone who is familiar with Tibetan etiquette will be carrying a *kata* or white silk scarf; originally a useful present, a bolt of cloth, *katas* became stylised over the centuries into a scarf eighteen inches to two feet wide and four to six feet long. They are first folded in half lengthwise, then concertina-fashion until only a foot or so is left to wrap around the folded scarf. The correct thing to do is to flick them to their full length, then present them held in the two hands.

The line of people is marshalled so that the Tibetans are at the front and the others at the rear, and the *darshan* starts. Each person is briefly presented to His Holiness, who usually makes some comment to them or asks a question: it is rather like a royal reception in Europe. He does not take the *katas* himself; a monk-official does that. After the *darshan*, Tibetans are given a 'protection cord', a piece of knotted coloured cord worn around the neck as an amulet-cum-souvenir. Foreigners are not given one unless they ask; this is because the symbolism of the cord might not be understood by everyone, and because Tibetans in general are slightly suspicious of foreigners who adopt Tibetan ways too readily. Protection cords are not only knotted by the Dalai Lama; most Lamas tie them, and lengths of cord like technicolour bootlaces are on sale in several shops in Dharamsala. If you give an appropriate length to a Lama, he will tie his own particular knot in it, bless it, blow on it, and give it back. The ones tied by the Dalai Lama are given out by another monk-official.

Anyone who applies sufficiently far in advance is likely to be granted a public audience, though every attempt will be made to fit people in at short notice if possible. On the other hand, some people have a very strange idea of their own importance: once, when we were talking with Tempa Tsering-la from His Holiness's Private Office, a hippy was arguing with great agitation that he had to see the Dalai Lama in the next twenty minutes, as his bus left in half an hour!

A public audience may not sound like much to non-Buddhists, though any Catholic who has had a Papal audience will immediately see the parallel. Most people, though, find them to be surprisingly moving experiences: His Holiness radiates calm and peace, and it is wonderful to have that beautiful smile directed at you.

Private audiences are rather more difficult to arrange, though again the Dalai Lama will make every effort to see as many people as possible. The candidates for private audiences may be divided into three kinds: Tibetans who want to discuss something with the Dalai Lama, foreigners who come to Dharamsala on a pilgrimage or to study Buddhism, and journalists.

There are some complaints from Tibetans living in Dharamsala that the officials there do not give them the same opportunities to see His Holiness that foreigners or visitors from other Tibetan settlements have, but it seems to be generally true that most Tibetans have a good chance of seeing His Holiness in a private audience if they seriously want one. This shows up yet another aspect of the Dalai Lama's role, which is akin to that of a parish priest. He is always ready to give advice wherever he can, to anyone who asks, and his people are his highest priority.

The pilgrims and students will be dealt with elsewhere if at all possible, but he still manages to see many of them himself. Few will get in without arranging it previously, but if they have already made contacts elsewhere, a letter in advance will often secure an audience.

The third category, the journalists, are a very mixed bag. The Dalai Lama is obviously alive to the value of coverage in the world's press, both in making known the Tibetans' case and in increasing knowledge of Buddhism, and so he is prepared to devote as much time as possible to journalists. On the other hand, there are three problems: fake journalists, repetitive questions, and questions that are downright stupid.

If you believed the people you met in Dharamsala, about half the foreigners there are journalists – especially photo-journalists, which is the claim made by almost everyone who owns a camera, especially when they are trying to beg film. Many of these people plead journalism in an attempt to get a private audience, but the Private Office has grown skilled at discriminating. Unless the would-be journalist has obviously done a fair amount of research beforehand, and preferably contacted the Office in advance of coming to Dharamsala, there is little chance of a private audience.

As for repetitive questions, a few hours' research in the Library of Tibetan Works and Archives would make the great majority of obvious questions unnecessary. The Dalai Lama has, as already mentioned, written several books, and the files of newspaper interviews lead one to wonder how he has time to do anything apart from giving audiences to journalists. He bears with these questions with inordinate good patience, though from time to time he cannot resist a joke. For example, he was asked for what must have seemed like the five millionth time what he missed most about Tibet, and replied with a perfectly straight face, "The yaks". A few minutes later, he apologised for that one: it was the first thing, he said, that had come into his head. But how do you pick out the one thing you miss most when you are exiled from your native land? On another occasion, when an English journalist was enthusing about the beautiful chanting at a multi-faith service where there were

Christians, Sikhs, Jews, Buddhists, and many others, he said, "Yes, that is what we all have in common – the chanting!"

He uses the same technique for the stupid questions. He will try to give straight answers as long as he can, but eventually he cannot contain himself. One of the best examples of this came in an interview with a journalist with remarkably naive views on government: she was a disciple of Beuys, the well-known painter and little-known politician. When she asked about the best way to get elected, he answered, "Invent a big slogan – make many promises – and after you get power you will find some point to excuse yourself". Because he seldom keeps a straight face for more than thirty seconds, a trait he shares with many Tibetans, it is often impossible to tell from his expression whether he is joking. His brothers are even worse: they will tell you something outrageous in exactly the same tone of voice that they use to impart some perfectly genuine piece of information. It is not malicious: it is just typical of the Tibetan sense of humour. Even when he said that ruthless exploitation was an excellent form of government, she seems to have been totally unaware that the Dalai Lama was no longer taking the interview entirely seriously. He has to be careful what he says in such cases, though, because the Chinese would love to quote him out of context.

Once the audiences are over, or if there are no audiences, he will return to prayer and meditation. Late in the afternoon he will rest, and drink a glass of hot water. His evenings can be very varied. There is often more work to do, but if there is not, he may spend time in prayer or meditation, or just relax. He is fond of television; his colour set at the Palace can receive both Indian and Pakistani programmes, because of the elevation. He has a weakness for natural history programmes and for action films, especially war stories. He is often too tired to do anything more than watch television, but if he has the energy in the evenings or if he has any spare time during the day, he has several other interests.

The best-known is probably his mechanical inclination, and he still loves to repair things himself. In addition to a modest collection of mechanical tools, he also has a small electronics workshop. He is prepared to attempt almost anything, and he is apparently almost always successful. His older brother Lobsang Samten said that this has always been characteristic of him: he was always just so *good* at everything he tried.

Surprisingly, he is a crack shot — another characteristic he shares with the Great Thirteenth – and he keeps a powerful air-pistol for target practice. Once, there was a wasps' nest outside his dining room; he saw a hornet repeatedly raiding it and killing the grubs. Next lunchtime, he brought his air-pistol and laid it down beside his plate. The hornet did not come that day. The next day, he had the air-pistol with him again. When the hornet flew in, he waited until it settled and began to drag one of the grubs out. Then he shot it; an impressive demonstration of accuracy, and of defending the defenceless.

He is also keen on gardening, and has a private garden at the palace. Much of the work is necessarily done by gardeners, but he prefers to do the potting and similar delicate tasks himself whenever he has the time. Again, the Great Thirteenth was an enthusiastic gardener; the English flowers he grew were known in Tibet as 'Indian flowers' because the British seeds were imported via India. According to the present Dalai Lama, gardening in India is much more difficult than in Tibet, because the monsoons invariably destroy so much of the work; but it is still worth it.

He used to be interested in photography, and he still owns several cameras. When he was in Tibet, he was presented by the manufacturers of the Leica with camera number 555 555, but it was left behind. He takes few photographs himself now.

One hobby which seems particularly appropriate is feeding birds. According to legend, at the time of the Religious Kings a thousand years ago, all charity was reserved for the birds, because the standard of living was so high that no one else needed it. One of the names for Mount Everest is Kang Cha Dzima Lung-pa (usually shortened to Kang Cha-ma-lung), which translates literally as snow/country/taken-care-of/birds, or 'the Snowy Mountain Bird Sanctuary'. The Dalai Lama prefers to feed the small birds, because they cooperate more than big ones: each takes his own morsel and retires, whereas the big birds fight and try to keep everything for themselves. He has rigged up a sort of shelter to keep the ravens away, and if a hawk hovers around in the hope of making a meal of one of the smaller birds he frightens it away with his air-pistol or an air-rifle. He shoots to miss; the noise is apparently quite sufficient.

12

A Lama to the World

There is no doubt that the Dalai Lama loves to travel. As a boy, he used to dream over the pages of atlases in the Potala: to him, the countries of the West are every bit as mysterious and magical as Tibet might seem to someone in London or New York. Nor is there any doubt that he is a very welcome visitor wherever he goes; huge audiences come to hear him speak. Sincere Buddhists and Tibetologists mingle with the casually interested and a good sprinkling of downright cranks, but they all want to hear what he has to say.

In some ways, his teaching may be likened to an enormous brocade, woven with many colours and depicting innumerable scenes. The silk of which it is woven is Buddhism, and every part is linked to every other part, but even a small part may be appreciated on its own. Some parts will seem like common-sense advice from an old and valued friend, whilst others reveal insights into esoteric Buddhist teachings which show the simplicity behind the complexity. He will set some goal which seems unattainable, and then tell you how to attain it; the clarity of his teaching is wonderful.

As an example, he points out the futility of worrying. If you can do something, do it; if you cannot, then stop worrying. Everyone agrees that this is good advice – but it is advice which may seem impossible to follow. Not so, he says. No one can stop worrying completely, but everyone can cut down the extent to which they worry by just a tiny bit. Once you have made that start, it is a little easier to stop worrying about something else; it is a self-stoking process, so the next time you try it is easier again, and the next time, until the amount of worry in your life is dramatically reduced.

Because of this clarity, many people from other religious traditions find that they begin to understand their own religion better. The Christian teaching that you should 'take no thought for the morrow' sounds very like His Holiness's advice to stop worrying. Winston Churchill expressed it another way: "When I look back on all these worries I remember the story of the old man who said on his deathbed that he had had a lot of trouble in his life, most of which never happened."

Together with the clarity, there is a great humility. This is said of many religious teachers, and of some it is patently untrue, but the Dalai Lama quotes the great Shantideva: "If the blessed Buddha cannot please all sentient beings, then how could I?" He has written, "If there is anything you like in what I said, fine. If not, no problem; all you have to do is reject it."

This refusal to lay down dogma, together with a clear attitude to right and wrong, is what makes him so much a Lama for his time. In the West, there are traditions of dogma which have turned into traditions of bigotry, and traditions of freedom which have turned into traditions of licence; both have proved unsuccessful. The Dalai Lama teaches another tradition, that of individual responsibility and awareness. If there is confusion about what is right and what is wrong it is a matter of ignorance. Overcome the ignorance, and you overcome the confusion. This is why his teachings so often have the flavour of a reminder, the re-awakening of something that we always knew.

It is a form of teaching which finds little favour with authoritarians: the thought-police of centralised religion and centralised government, nurtured on the idea that man is wicked and depraved and that they alone have the key to salvation, hate it. Regrettably, there are many sects in all religions which take this attitude: Christianity, Islam, Hinduism, even Buddhism are all tainted. But there are also sects in every religion that have always taught what the Dalai Lama teaches: in Christianity, the most obvious example is the Society of Friends, or Quakers. His Holiness speaks in the Catholic Cathedral Church of St Patrick in New York, and in the Methodist Central Hall in Westminster, in the heart of London. He not only believes in the underlying similarity of religions: he demonstrates it.

He is not, however, one of those ascetics who teaches that everyone should renounce the world. The West is materially rich, he says, and that is good: no one can doubt that it is better to be warm and well fed than to be cold, wet, and hungry. Rather than abandoning this material progress, the goal should be to find ways of incorporating it with spiritual progress. As he explains it, material progress is supposed to bring happiness, and it does, up to a point. But when we have all the material goods we could reasonably want, and we are still searching for something, we should realise that materialism is not everything: "One of the most important things is compassion. We cannot buy it in one of New York City's big shops. You cannot produce it by machine. But by inner development, yes. Without inner peace, it is impossible to have world peace." On the other hand, he specifically warns those who want to cut themselves off from materialism: "You new Buddhists in Western society also need to avoid the two extremes. One of these extremes would be complete isolation from the general way of life, and also from society... It is better to remain in society, and to lead a general way of life. That's my belief."

This is no more or less than the Lord Buddha's teaching of the 'middle path', but religion and everyday life are so clearly separated in some people's minds that they find it very difficult to accept. A recurring difficulty for many people is the Dalai Lama's dual role in politics and religion: they cannot see how politics can fail to contaminate religion, or at least lead to a conflict. The Dalai Lama settles this simply. Politics, he explains, is a means to an end, a way of solving human problems. If politicians approach these problems with the right motives, there can be no contamination: if they have the wrong motives, then it is they who are at fault, not politics *per se*. His most famous remark in this context is that although politicians can be 'dirty', politics are not.

These teachings and many others appear in his own writings, in transcripts of interviews, and in public speeches that he has made in his travels. Few have been fortunate enough to have a conversation with the Dalai Lama, but thousands or hundreds of thousands have been able to hear him on his travels, so it is worth spending some time considering these.

As a boy, poring over his atlases, the Dalai Lama feared that he might never travel: Tibetan protocol would have forbidden it. Then, when the Chinese came, things looked even worse. The journey to China was hardly one he would have chosen, and we have seen how the Chinese opposed his attending the Buddha Jayanti celebrations. Even in India, there was not much likelihood of travel: for those first few months in Mussoorie, he was a virtual prisoner.

By the early 1960s, when the first flood of refugees had been settled and the Government in Exile established, it was different. Nehru had died, and the Indian Government was much less worried about Chinese reactions: they had already fought a border war, and the actuality had proved less traumatic than the anticipation.

There were many reasons to travel. Apart from personal interest, he had received many invitations from universities and Buddhist associations throughout the world.

There were Tibetan refugees in several countries, and they wanted to see their Dalai Lama: they were prepared to meet a large part of his expenses. There were refugee organisations all over the world who had helped the Tibetans enormously, as well as several individuals, and the Dalai Lama wanted to thank them personally for their work.

There were also many problems. There was the question of financing the journey, though that was not so much a problem of raising the money as of apportioning who should pay what. There was the matter of security: in those days, there were still fears of a Chinese-backed assassination attempt, and His Holiness might also have presented an easy and very visible target to the urban guerillas and hijackers who were beginning to come into international prominence. The biggest difficulty was with the governments of the countries he wanted to visit. Some were directly afraid of Chinese military action, whilst others had or were hoping for trade links with China. Compared with the negotiations required on this level, finance and security were hardly problems at all.

Because of these considerations, the first two trips did not come about until 1967. In September of that year, the Dalai Lama went to Japan for four weeks at the invitation of several Buddhist groups including the Japanese Buddhist Missionary Association; most of the expenses were paid by the *Yomimuri Shimbun*, one of the largest daily papers in Japan. The visit was hardly reported at all in the West, but in Asia it was a major news story. In November, he went to Thailand for four days. The exact dates of these and subsequent trips are given in Appendix II.

On both visits, His Holiness was very well received by the various sponsoring groups, but he did not see many people who were not already interested either in Buddhism or in the Tibetan cause. The exception to this was the press: he spoke to many reporters, who were sometimes exasperated at his refusal to answer questions of a political nature but who nevertheless filed almost unanimously favourable stories.

The effect of this was twofold. First, it showed the Dalai Lama that there was considerable interest and popular support for his travels, which made him all the more determined to travel more widely. Secondly, it showed both the Indian government and other governments that the Dalai Lama was not going to provoke riots or acts of retribution from the Chinese. The Chinese had ranted that the visits were 'imperialist interference with internal Chinese affairs', but no one listened.

Negotiations were therefore renewed on many levels, both with governments and with the various individuals and organisations that had invited the Dalai Lama to speak. The governments were the greatest problem, but only two refused outright to allow him into their countries. One was France, which has never been famous for the courage of its governments, and the other was the biggest and most powerful country in the world, the United States of America.

Their extraordinary decision was a great disappointment to the Dalai Lama for three reasons. First, he had always wanted to see America for himself. Secondly, it meant turning down many invitations from all over the United States and Canada. Thirdly, and of most importance politically, he would not have the support of the American press. He has a high regard for the value of the press, and a strong belief in its influence, and he knew that the American press was likely to prove much more responsive than the European.

Nevertheless, he decided to make a European tour. There were many relief organisations to thank there, as well as Tibetans to visit in Switzerland (there were close to a thousand in 1970, and by the early 1980s there were over three thousand), and Buddhist organisations in England were particularly insistent that he should come.

The Chinese did their best to sabotage the visit, but they proved (in their own phrase of the period) to be a paper tiger. The most significant demonstration of their impotence was to come in Sweden, where they lodged a formal protest with the government when the Dalai Lama arrived: the Swedish response was to increase

security and make it more visible, with sirens and an official escort
for the Tibetan motorcade. For the most part, Chinese protests and
threats were informal, but they were made to many people.

They had good reason to fear the tour, of course. For many years,
their propaganda had gone substantially unopposed. As well as
official Peking propaganda, they had been able to rely on party
hacks like Han Suyin, who spouted Chinese propaganda and
embellished it with nonsense of their own: one classic report stated
that there were no vowels in Tibetan because it was too cold to
pronounce them! There were also the various Chinese Friendship
Societies and Leagues, which included among the curious and those
interested in promoting international understanding a good
number of fellow-travellers who could be relied upon to write
letters to newspapers stating the party line. And finally, there had
been several stage-managed tours of China for Western reporters,
some of whom believed what they were told.

In the event, the tour itself finally took place in 1973. His Holiness
visited Rome, where he met the Pope, and then went on through
Switzerland (which had been nervous about letting him in – and
indeed a Swiss paper alleged that previous plans for visits in 1968
and 1970-1 had been cancelled because the government would not
grant him a visa) and to the Netherlands, where he was received by
Prince Bernhard and Queen Juliana. From there he went on via
Belgium to Ireland, where the government not surprisingly
accorded him an official welcome, and then to Norway. There, the
Oslo paper *Morgenbladet* summed up the feelings of many when it
learned that the King had been dissuaded from receiving the Dalai
Lama. "Who in the world are we afraid of?" it asked. "Is it the
Chinese? And when did they become so dangerous that we had to
disregard all decency for their sake?"

After Norway came Sweden, where the newspapers proved
particularly receptive. It was in an interview with a Swedish paper
that His Holiness gave a very clear exposition of his views on
violence, in reply to a question about the Tibetan resistance. He
said, "If the motive is good, and there are no other possibilities, then
seen most deeply it (violence) is non-violence, because its aim is to
help others".

It was also in Sweden that the supporters of Peking made their
poor stand. Two or three members of the Swedish-Chinese

Friendship Society wrote to the *Sydsvenska Dagbladet,* trotting out hoary old lies about human sacrifices and the oppression of the peasants. They were demolished in the same correspondence columns by several people whose views were more representative of the average Swede. Jan Anderssen produced an unchallengeable argument: even if everything the supporters of the Chinese had said was true, why had every single Tibetan refugee left the country since 1950?

From Sweden he crossed into Denmark, where he met Prince Peter, a long-time supporter of the Tibetan cause. After that, he flew into the United Kingdom, where he spent ten days – the longest stay in any European country on that tour. There were several reasons for the extra time in the United Kingdom, including the long standing special relationship Tibet had had with Britain prior to Indian independence and the considerable interest that there had always been in Britain in Tibetan Buddhism. His Holiness also took the opportunity to rest for a while, because his schedule had been very demanding.

Although surprisingly little appeared in the papers, public interest was high. He was interviewed on television, and a question was asked in Parliament about why he had not been received as befitted a religious leader of his status; the government's reply was that it was a private visit, and so an official welcome would not have been appropriate. Far more people came to see him than had been expected, and security had to be increased considerably after an incident in London where a crowd surged forward out of control. There was no question of animosity: they just wanted to see the Dalai Lama.

In the light of this enthusiasm, the low level of press reporting is all the more puzzling. There was a major exhibition about China running in London at the time, and most papers had already reported favourably on that, so perhaps they were unwilling to contradict themselves. It is extraordinary, though, that the longest item in the popular press was John Gittings' disgraceful piece in the *Guardian*. Gems included "… we have a particularly good picture of what happened in Tibet from the records of the Red Guards" (which is like saying that the Goths could be relied upon for an account of the sack of Rome), the flat statement that the fighting in 1959 had been between different communist factions, and that the

Tibetan rebels had had little or no impact, and a statement so fatuous that it is astonishing that any paper would print it: "The Dalai Lama needs China more than China needs the Dalai Lama".

Germany was the next stop, and although the German government had (like all the other countries visited) placed restrictions on what he could say or do, Annemarie Ranger (then President of the Bundestag) made a point of attending a reception given in his honour. After two days in Austria, His Holiness returned to Dharamsala on the 6th of November, having spent about five weeks in Europe.

For the most part, His Holiness had met only people who were either interested in Buddhism and the Tibetan cause or fellow clerics: as well as His Holiness the Pope, he had seen several bishops and archbishops, and taken every opportunity to talk with them about resemblances and differences between his religion and theirs. He had been introduced (in private) to various politicians, and had doubtless sought their advice, but he had carefully refrained from making any political or inflammatory statements. He had made very few public appearances, and in most countries except England these had not been well attended: this was more a matter of deliberately poor publicity than a lack of interest, as the reactions of the newspapers showed. With only a very few exceptions, such as a predictably hostile reaction from the Swedish paper *Arbetet* (the title means 'The Worker'), press reports had been overwhelmingly favourable. Many people who read them joined in the papers' indignation about the restrictions that had been placed on His Holiness's freedom of speech, and others were annoyed that poor publicity had meant that they had missed hearing him speak or at least seeing him. There was no doubt that the trip had been a major success.

This meant that the chances of an American tour were greatly enhanced, and negotiations were renewed. This was the time of Nixon's *rapprochement* with the Chinese, though, and the State Department was not about to let a few minor things like genocide interfere with the prospect of trade. Even though the body of support for the Tibetan cause was steadily growing in the United States, it was 1977 before the necessary official permission was granted, and it would take two more years before the trip itself could go ahead.

Meanwhile, the Dalai Lama had plenty to do in India. As well as spending time in Dharamsala, he travelled extensively inside India. He visited many Tibetan settlements – more were being founded all the time – and gave religious teachings in Bodh Gaya and other Buddhist centres. He did go outside India twice, once to Switzerland in 1974 for a medical check-up, and once to attend the twelfth World Fellowship of Buddhists conference in Tokyo, but the first was a purely private visit and the second was very brief, involving only two nights' stay in Tokyo.

The 1979 tour was massive. It began with a visit to the Mongolian People's Republic on June 12th, and from there he flew on to Switzerland. From Switzerland he went to Greece, then returned to Switzerland; and on September 10th he flew to the United States.

Mongolia had been a satellite state of the USSR by treaty for a long time, and the Russians obviously hoped to make political capital out of the visit. The Dalai Lama was visiting a Soviet-bloc country before he went to America, and as far as they were concerned it was a useful slight to the Chinese. What the Russians were not prepared for was the tremendous depth of Buddhist feeling in Mongolia. The great Khans of the past were long dead, but the Mongolian people retained their loyalty to the man they had so long ago called the Great Ocean Teacher. Their Soviet masters had to go to all sorts of lengths to discourage people from seeing the Dalai Lama, resorting to such ingenious excuses as lack of accommodation for would-be pilgrims, an inability to provide adequate security (for whose benefit?), and the fact that too much working time would be lost.

Despite this, and despite the way that the Russians made it clear that they would prefer a distinctly cool reception, the welcome was as close to tumultuous as it could be in the Soviet Union. Those who could, presented *katas:* the Mongolian version is slate-blue instead of snowy or creamy white, but the symbolism and the sentiment are the same. Two vignettes in particular stand out. One is an old man who darted out of the crowd to shake the Dalai Lama's hand; His Holiness felt a concealed rosary that the man wanted to be blessed by his touch. The other took place in a department store: as he was being shown around, the girls who manned the counters silently left their posts and followed him, one by one, saying nothing, hardly daring to breathe. When he was about to leave, he turned to shake the hand of one of them. The result was a near-riot; once he had offered his hand, they all but fought to touch it.

He saw a few temples, and took part in religious ceremonies, but what impressed him most was the way that Buddhism had remained a living force in everyday life. He left Mongolia convinced more than ever of the indestructibility of the religious impulse, which had survived in young and old despite decades of communist repression.

In Switzerland, he noticed a marked change in the attitude of the younger Tibetans. They were much more aware of their heritage than they had been in 1973, or as Tenzin Geyche put it, "more Tibetan". Many Tibetans had done very well for themselves, and in the process they had both rediscovered their national pride and become more visible in the community. There were also more of them, including many children born in Switzerland and speaking Tibetan with a Swiss-German accent.

The Swiss government was as careful as before to make no official acknowledgement of his presence, but they did allow him considerably more freedom. As a result, and because more time was available, he was able to give many more public talks. These were well attended, each more so than the last. He avoided political topics, but talked about his favourite themes: universal responsibility and the good heart, the need for compassion, and the way in which religion could be used as a tool to achieve greater happiness. He answered questions from the audience, which ranged from the profound to the trivial – though no one asked the same question as an American lady was later to do, about whether her Lhasa Apso (which she did not have with her) was actually a Tibetan dog or not. Even questions like this received a serious answer: after a few questions about its size, and shape, and colour, and behaviour, His Holiness announced that he thought it probably was.

His complete openness was one of the things that endeared him to his audiences, as was the clarity with which he explained things. His ability to fill a hall was nowhere better shown than during his three-day visit to Greece in early August. The Centre for Tibetan Studies and Meditation was a small place in Athens, but they managed to borrow a conference hall in a smart hotel. On the first day, it was more than half empty: only the members of the Centre, and a few of their friends, were there to occupy the front rows of seats. On the second day, the seats at the back were filled; and on the third, the hall was packed to capacity.

The attitude of the Greek government was encouraging, too. They placed a vast official car at his disposal, which apparently looked quite incongruous in the modest area where His Holiness was staying, and the Minister of Culture received him officially.

Because of the increasing publicity, there were also a few people who were apparently opposed to him at one of the meetings in Greece; on the way into the conference hall, there was some sort of commotion. The organisers tried to hustle them out of the way, but the Dalai Lama intervened and asked that they be allowed to stay. The organisers would not permit it, but His Holiness explained afterwards that he would have liked to have answered any questions that they had: their attitude had surely been one of ignorance, and it would have been better to try to dispel their ignorance rather than pushing them to one side.

From Greece he went back to Switzerland, and continued to teach and talk there. He also had a thorough medical check-up, and spent as much time with the Tibetan community as he could. It is not unreasonable to suspect that he also made political overtures to a number of people, but it is impossible to obtain confirmation of this; obviously, he would not wish to embarrass the Swiss or any other government by doing so overtly. On September 10th he flew to New York.

From the moment that he landed, there was no doubt that he was attracting a lot of media coverage. The American people extended their traditional welcome to the Dalai Lama and his party, and press coverage was immense if often superficial and self-consciously jokey. Despite a weakness for headlines which said "Hello Dalai", the majority of newspapers managed to convey at least some idea of who he was and of what had happened in Tibet, and the overwhelming feeling was one of support.

From the first major public event, an inter-faith service in St Patrick's Cathedral, the public reaction was tremendous. There were public talks at many universities which were usually packed to capacity, and His Holiness also spoke to smaller gatherings of academics and Buddhists, often dealing with the finer points of doctrine in a way that transformed bafflement into an understanding that seemed as if it had always been there. He always talked in a way that suited his audience: for example, at his first press conference in New York, one reporter asked him if he had a message for the people of the United States. He replied with one word: "Compassion".

This visit was covered in some detail by Marcia Keegan in her book *The Dalai Lama's Historic Visit to North America* (it also deals with the Canadian tour in 1980), but it is worth recording some of the highlights here. His Holiness was not officially received by the government, but he did meet the Senate Foreign Relations Committee, whom he greatly impressed. Jacob K. Javits, Republican Senator for New York, said, "His Holiness is a fabulous man, a devoted patriot, and he gave us all the impression that he was the symbol of freedom". Congressman Charles Rose of North Carolina introduced a public talk by His Holiness at Constitution Hall; one of Marcia Keegan's most striking pictures shows the Dalai Lama in this most American of places, with the American Eagle high above his head.

In the universities, he did a great deal to promote the idea of Buddhism as an academic subject; since that visit, several universities have established new departments. He spoke on the West coast as well as the East, and it was in Seattle that the only adverse reaction in the whole trip occurred. His hecklers were by all accounts a strange bunch, as they were simultaneously denouncing both His Holiness and Deng Xiaoping as enemies of the people; they seem to have been supporters of the Gang of Four. His reaction was the same as in Greece: he apologised to the rest of the audience for their misbehaviour, and said that he was sure that their behaviour was the result of ignorance.

One of the most intriguing aspects of the whole tour came in Los Angeles, where the Dalai Lama met a party of Hopi elders. They had driven all night to meet him, and to point out that his arrival fulfilled an ancient prophecy of the Hopi nation, as well as one of Tibet.

According to their traditions, the world's axis passes through both their land and Tibet. At the end of a thousand years of Hopi religious practice, a great spiritual leader would arrive from the East: he would be the Sun Clan Brother, and his name would be linked with salt water. 'Dalai' means 'Great Ocean', and 'Gyatso' means ocean.

They also knew of a Tibetan prophecy: "When the iron bird flies, and the horse runs upon rails, the Dharma will travel west to the land of the Red Man."

There are many other similarities between Hopi culture and Tibetan, including some very curious ones: the Hopi word for 'moon' is the same as the Tibetan word for 'sun', and vice versa. The similarities between Hopi and Tibetan dances and rituals have been remarked upon by everyone who has seen both, and both have a fire *puja* with remarkably similar underlying symbolism and superficial form. The fire *puja* is so nearly identical that on his next visit in 1980, the Dalai Lama was able to participate with four American Indian chiefs in the ritual.

By the end of the visit to the United States, the Dalai Lama had visited a total of twenty-five American cities, and seen for himself how the richest nation in the world lived. The United States, for their part, had seen someone quite unlike anyone else they had ever seen before. He was a politician free from the taint of politics; a religious leader free from the taint of sectarianism; a refugee free from the taint of self-pity; as an unidentified member of an audience at a public speech said to a reporter, "a Buddha, maybe". Even the press felt his power: in several places, the organisers of various meetings expressed their amazement at seeing even American reporters respectful and polite, a phenomenon usually unheard of.

He had originally hoped to combine the visit to the United States with one to Canada, but there had proved to be too many demands on his time in the US. Consequently, a second North American trip was arranged for October 1980. On his way he called in to pay a courtesy call on the new Pope, John-Paul II, and on the 10th he flew on from Italy to Canada.

His reception was little short of ecstatic. The Tibetan community in Canada was overjoyed to see him, and the publicity in the American media the previous year meant that public awareness of who he was and what he represented was much greater. The public lectures were frequently filled to capacity, and although the Canadian central government did not make any official gestures, several local government organisations made him very welcome indeed.

The result of these two North American visits was that the position that most nations took concerning him was reversed: as

Tenzin Geyche put it, "Before, they did not dare to let him in; now, they did not dare to keep him out." The Chinese had been livid, denouncing imperialist intervention in internal Chinese affairs at the tops of their voices, but they had almost without exception been ignored. Public opinion, in every country that the Dalai Lama had visited, was firmly with him.

His next journey was to prove even more significant. The Kalachakra, or Wheel of Time, is one of the highest Tantric teachings and can only be administered by the most highly qualified Lamas. There had been a tradition in ancient India and then in Tibet of giving it without restriction to anyone who wanted it, monk or lay: as His Holiness explained, the aim was to plant certain karmic seeds in the mind of the initiate. Whether they were understood or not, they could in time grow. The number of times that this initiation had been given by the Dalai Lama in the twentieth century could be counted on the fingers of one hand, and never in all history had it been given outside Tibet or India. He accepted an invitation to deliver the Kalachakra Initiation in the United States.

At this point, an aside on the nature of *karma* is in order. It is a word widely used, but often with little understanding. A good way to think of it is as perception. Consider, for example, the way that Scrooge mistreats Bob Cratchit in Dickens' *A Christmas Carol*. As soon as he starts to consider the feelings of Cratchit and Tiny Tim, things start to go better for him. But what has changed? Very little, apart from his attitude. Here we see the 'good heart' at work; virtue really is its own reward. We see cause and effect, but not necessarily in mechanistic terms: Buddhism is more concerned with motive.

What the Kalachakra Initiation does is to plant the seeds of that change in perception, and the place that was chosen for this was the Deer Park in Madison. Named after the Deer Park at Sarnath, where the Lord Buddha first taught, it was a relatively new establishment when the Kalachakra was agreed upon, and the occupants had to work very hard indeed in order to finish it in time. The plans caused a certain amount of consternation at first, especially among the local residents who were worried about a massive influx of would-be initiates. Their fears were more than allayed, however, by the stringent precautions taken by the organisers. No one was to be admitted without pre-registration, and no private vehicles or walk-in visitors were to be allowed at all: everyone would be taken to the site by bus from pre-arranged pick-up points, and the only people who would stay overnight on the site were the Dalai Lama, his entourage, and the American organisers.

There are several stories associated with the Kalachakra Initiation, but there are two which have the quality of legend. One happened during the building of the temple: a volunteer said that he had seen a hawk flying overhead with a serpent in its talons, apparently unaware that *Khyung,* the Celestial Hawk, is usually represented in this way. Again, during the initiation itself, many people told of how a huge flock of swallows had swooped and swirled above the Dalai Lama's head as he spoke, borne on a great wind which arose from nowhere and as suddenly died.

To trace the story of the Dalai Lama's subsequent travels would occupy another book. As already mentioned, a full list is given in Appendix III, but a list of the places he visited in 1982 is instructive: Kuala Lumpur, Singapore, Jakarta, Yogyakarta, Denpasar, Melbourne, Sydney, Canberra, Brisbane and Perth (there are many South-East Asian Buddhists in Australia, about 100,000 at one estimate); Tashkent, Samarkand, Moscow, Ulan Bator and Ulan Ude, Budapest, Rome, Barcelona, Granada, Strasbourg, Paris, Toulouse, and Digne (the French government finally changed its mind); Milan, Pomia, Florence, Eibingen, Hamburg, Bonn, Stuttgart, Munich, and Frankfurt.

Each place has its own stories, and many are surprising. For example, Rome is a fiercely secular city with a communist administration; in 1982, the Mayor was pleased to accord His Holiness a civic reception.

In general, though, the public appearances follow a common pattern. What follows is based on one such appearance at the Methodist Central Hall in London, October 1981, when the Dalai Lama paused in England on his way to the Deer Park, but it draws on other talks and times.

There were well over a thousand people there. Some wore strange clothes, either more-or-less accurate approximations to Tibetan dress or garments of their own devising. There was a scattering of clerics, a contingent of ageing hippies, and a collection of 'believers' – people who latch onto the cult of the moment, and who regularly attend the fringe lectures of the mystical circuit.

The great majority of those present, though, were very ordinary-looking people. Most were in their late twenties and thirties, but there were also many older people.

The Dalai Lama spoke partly through a translator, and partly in his own English. His English is sufficiently good that he often has no need of a translator in order to understand a question, though he sometimes has difficulty in finding the right word for an answer.

To those who had read his books, the message of the prepared speech was a familiar one; it dealt with universal responsibility, the need for compassion, and so forth. But most had not read his books, and they were hearing something new; the hall was very quiet as he spoke.

When he had finished, and invited questions, they turned out to be a motley collection. One rather strident feminist wanted backing for her argument – it was not very clear what it was – but His Holiness's assurance that women had been able to own property in Tibet, that there had been women Tulkus as well as male, and that there had been both polyandry and polygamy seemed to satisfy her. Another member of the audience asked if the books by 'T. Lobsang Rampa' were authentic, and His Holiness smiled: "No" he said, "they were fiction, but they had certainly created a lot of good publicity for Tibet, even if they were not very accurate."

Other questions probed deeper. How can you love your enemy? What is the advantage? His Holiness explained that this is the best chance you have to develop tolerance. If you can learn to tolerate something, instead of losing your temper and reacting emotionally, you can keep your presence of mind and perhaps work out how to overcome the problem. You might find out some way of removing the problem itself, or you could decide to change the way that you felt about it. Either way, you were better off than if you simply raged and complained.

It was the unfailing patience with which His Holiness answered the questions that was so impressive, together with the extraordinary perception of the answers. 'Love thine enemy' is generally agreed to be a good precept; but to show how it can actually bring immediate benefits is a considerable advance on a pious platitude.

There were also numerous examples of his humour, though as usual they do not sound so funny when they are recounted. There are some people who make you laugh and smile all the time, not just with jokes but with their own *joie de vivre*. His Holiness would consider a question, wearing on his face an expression which clearly said, "You don't expect me to be able to answer that, do you?" And then he would launch into a closely-argued line of reasoning, which had the hall spellbound, brows furrowed in sympathy with His Holiness. When he had finished, he would suddenly laugh and say, "Well, that's what I think", as though what he had just said was something anyone could have thought of. The release of tension was enough to make most people laugh. Someone asked him if Buddhism was 'best', and he laughed and said that the Dalai Lama was likely to think that Buddhism was best – but it was only best for him, and something else could be best for somebody else.

When he had finished, almost everyone left the hall smiling; there was a feeling of calm in the air, but also of happiness, such as you might feel after a job well done. It is not easy to describe; it is an unmistakable experience.

The actual organisation of a visit is a complicated and protracted affair. At any one time, there are dozens or perhaps hundreds of standing invitations for His Holiness to speak to all kinds of groups all over the world, including Tibetan refugees, Buddhist centres, all kinds of conferences, universities, and so forth. The Private Office of His Holiness, in consultation with the Dalai Lama himself, picks a number of the more promising offers and contacts them. 'Promising' in this sense means a number of things: stable, well-organised, likely to benefit either a large number of people or people who would not otherwise hear His Holiness, and able to bear a share of the cost of the whole trip. Each trip has to be financially self-supporting, because the Government in Exile cannot afford any alternative.

When the replies are received from the first round of enquiries, with a choice of tentative dates and offers of accommodation, funding, *et cetera*, the second round begins. The offers are collated, and extra offers sought or rejected as necessary, and the overall plan for the trip begins to take shape.

There are certain guidelines that the Private Office tries to keep to. For instance, they prefer to have a hotel suite for the Dalai Lama, so that he can sleep in the bedroom and his bodyguards can sleep in the adjoining room, though if the centre cannot arrange or afford this they will consider alternatives. They rarely accept offers of accommodation in private houses, no matter how grand, unless they are loaned the entire house: this is for obvious security reasons, but it also avoids jealousy between rival groups which could arise if one felt that it was receiving better or worse treatment than another.

Security is a perennial problem. As well as the full-time bodyguards, usually two in number, who travel with His Holiness, the rest of the party also have security responsibilities. In some countries they are armed, but in others the police will not permit this. In the United States, it is usual to hire off-duty police as security guards; in some other countries, where they have to rely only on the official protection given them, security can be nerve-wracking. The first visit to England was like this, until the police increased their cover.

Airline tickets are normally booked Club Class or Business Class, which allows slightly more comfort and privacy than Economy Class but is not as expensive as First Class. There is a constant battle with Tibetan organisations who want to pay the extra, and several of the more protocol-minded officials of the Administration have pointed out that people will expect him to travel First Class; His Holiness points out gently that it is him they want to see, not an aircraft seat. A Kalmuk Mongol organisation in New Jersey once chartered a plane for him rather than miss the chance of seeing him.

There are still the diplomatic negotiations to be considered, though these are much less of a problem than they used to be: few countries would refuse to admit His Holiness any more. He does not have a passport, but travels with a document which says that he is under the protection of the Government of India.

There will normally be six or seven people in the party: His Holiness, his Private Secretary, a translator, one or two other aides, and two full-time bodyguards. Once all the arrangements have been made in outline for transporting, housing, and generally looking after them, the Private Office goes back to the original sponsors to apportion the cost. Difficult decisions have to be made: some want to give more than they can afford, a few can afford more than they want to give, and some simply cannot afford very much. Even at this stage, major changes may have to be made; the fact that His Holiness travels at all is a tribute to the organisational abilities of his Private Secretary and the Private Office.

The itinerant monk has a history which stretches back for centuries, but there can be few whose journeys have taken them so far or who have reached so many people. No one who has heard him speak can doubt that Tibet's loss is very much the world's gain.

13

Tibet, The Dalai Lama, and the Future

Tibet's loss has been very great indeed. It used to be a country in which starvation was unknown; now, Tibetan children grub in bins for food thrown away by the Chinese. It was self-sufficient; now, disastrous Chinese agricultural programmes involving totally unsuitable crops have contributed greatly to the shortage of food. It was a country in which life was sacred: the Chinese instituted animal hunts, giving each person a quota – cats, dogs, rats, mice, even flies – and punishing anyone who did not bring the requisite number of dead animals. Its pride was its religion, and the common people willingly paid for the great temples filled with beautiful statues and paintings; what the Chinese could not loot and sell, they desecrated and vandalised.

Such stories could be continued indefinitely. The Dalai Lama has sent three delegations into Tibet, and they all tell the same tale. His sister reports how she met a woman who made a gruel thickened with blood taken from her own arm: it was all that she had to feed her children. The great centres of learning were destroyed, including the Chakpori, the centuries-old school of Tibetan medicine, and learned lamas were killed outright or worked to death in the fields. The *drong,* the huge wild yak that was the nomad's staple, has been slaughtered by Chinese soldiers with machine guns; there are very few left in Tibet, and it only survives in the remotest areas. Tibetan slave labour builds Chinese military roads.

The Chinese point to improvements: roads, airfields, factories, mines. The roads and airfields are of course purely military, intended to help the Chinese keep Tibet under control rather than to benefit the Tibetans. Those 'improvements' may be discounted. The factories would not be recognisable as such to most Westerners; rather, they would be called small workshops. Many are totally unplanned, and may have been built just to impress a visiting party official, or bolster the figures on a report. Supplies of raw materials are so erratic that many factories only function for a few months each year. Tibetans make up the workforce, and Chinese provide the managers, and anything that is produced is sent to China. The mines are similarly mismanaged and exploited; and like the factories, they are responsible for the most appalling pollution. Tibet was a very beautiful country; parts are now scarred for centuries.

It is not worth continuing to catalogue the evidence. China itself suffered enough under Mao, and Tibet suffered still more. Deng Xiaoping has promised reforms – but Chou-en Lai promised them too, and the Tibetan people will believe them when they see them. One example of 'liberalisation' was the return of the right to make pilgrimages – but no mention was made of the fact that all pilgrims lose the right to food rations, and all food is rationed. Besides, the Tibetans remember the era of 'Let a Thousand Flowers Bloom'; no one wants to do anything which will subject him to attack when Chinese policy reverses again. In 1983, over one and a half thousand Tibetans were arrested for 'criminal acts and sedition'. At the time of writing, only a few had been executed with a bullet in the back of the head – but at least the Chinese did not force their families to come along and watch, and even applaud, as they did at the public executions in Lhasa in the 1970s.

The Chinese know that they have been unsuccessful. When the Dalai Lama's first delegation arrived in 1979, one Chinese general is reputed to have said to another, "There goes twenty years of political indoctrination". Fly-posters urging freedom for Tibet appear frequently in Lhasa, though the penalty for posting them is almost certain death. The Chinese say that when they arrived, the standard of living of Tibetan peasants was no better than that of animals: the Tibetans reply that if that is true, then they would like to live like animals again, because their present life is worse. On those rare occasions when Western journalists are admitted, only the blind and the corrupt could believe the party line; the majority report a situation little short of disastrous.

The most valuable gift that a visitor can give any Tibetan is a picture of His Holiness; recognising this, the Chinese only admit one picture per visitor. The Dalai Lama's birthday was celebrated in Lhasa in 1983; several of those who took part have since disappeared. No one who has any knowledge of Tibet and the Tibetan people can doubt for an instant that the overwhelming majority want His Holiness back more than anything else in the world.

The Chinese have made several overtures to the Dalai Lama to return, but these are neither as specific nor as numerous as their propaganda says. In any case, His Holiness is not prepared to go back unless he can be sure that it will do some good. Many believe that he would be kept a prisoner or worse; as Jamyang Norbu wrote in *The Tibetan Review,* "I can easily think of a nightmarish scenario where 'a liberated serf violently deranged at the unspeakable sight of the reactionary Dalai bandit should, in a fit of righteous revolutionary wrath, regrettably but understandably take a shot at his previous feudal oppressor' – of course, to be subsequently and conveniently mown down by the bullets of Chinese security men".

The Dalai Lama is understandably reticent about the conditions under which he might return, for fear of prejudicing any negotiations, but he has suggested one possible route: an internationally supervised plebiscite or referendum of the Tibetan people, by which the Chinese agree to be bound. They would be presented with various options, including Chinese rule with or without himself as a constitutional Head of State. Apart from this, speculation as to the circumstances in which he might return.is just that – speculation. There are, however, several possibilities that are discussed within the Tibetan administration.

The first is that China may voluntarily relinquish Tibet. This is unlikely, but not impossible. As His Holiness says, China may have swallowed Tibet but they have completely failed to digest it. Sooner or later they must realise that they will never do so. The blame for past 'mistakes' could be laid at Mao's door, or if he is too high to be reappraised, it could be found that he was 'misled' – by Chou-en Lai, the Gang of Four, or anyone else. With such a scapegoat, face is saved, and a withdrawal is possible. One problem with this approach is that even in the improbable event of its happening, the Chinese would be unlikely to withdraw completely from Tibet, just from the 'Tibet Autonomous Region' or 'Outer Tibet', which does not include Kham or Amdo, or the greater part of the population.

The second possibility finds little acceptance except among a few hard-liners. It is that Tibet should accept outside help in throwing out the Chinese. The Russians are known to be interested, but this might only substitute one occupying force for another. There is a modest historical precedent, in that there were several CIA men among the Tibetan guerillas of the 1960s, and there are some fascinating stories of CIA operatives who had identified with the Tibetan cause going into battle with rosary in one hand and machine-pistol in the other, muttering the mantras of wrathful deities. Taiwan, often mentioned as a potential ally, could prove just as dangerous a friend as the Russians: the Taiwanese are the remains of Nationalist China, and they are every bit as interested in pressing a Chinese claim to Tibet as are the communists. Few if any Tibetans trust them.

The third possibility, every Tibetan hopes will come to pass, is that the Chinese empire will decay as it has decayed before, and the Tibetans will be able to throw them out unaided. This may sound far-fetched, but it is by no means impossible: the situation in China is far from stable, and in Tibet there are stories of Chinese generals selling arms to the Tibetans (especially in Kham) and taking bribes. Whilst this merely represents a return to old Chinese values, many Tibetans feel that it is significant: in the hard-line Maoist days, no one took bribes. His Holiness himself has said that it would be wonderful to return to a free Tibet, just as his predecessor returned in 1912.

Another possibility, which His Holiness is again known to favour, is the establishment of a United States of Asia. This would be a confederation of various Asian countries on equal terms: Tibet, Mongolia, Turkestan, Manchuria, and perhaps Burma, Taiwan, and other countries. China would have much to gain from such a federation, not least security without war, but their past record of imperialism makes this course of action very unlikely. There would have to be individual armies, and power would have to be shared: a mere re-constitution of the Celestial Empire under a new name would not be acceptable to any except China. An intriguing aside is the possibility of a Mongolian-Tibetan federation after the decay of the present Chinese empire; such an alliance might rapidly achieve super-power status, and relegate China to obscurity.

There is also a maverick possibility, which is said by those who have had close dealings with the People's Republic of China to have a certain appeal to the Peking government. It is that Lhasa could become a 'Vatican State' of Buddhism, with His Holiness at its head, just as the Pope heads his own miniature state within secular Italy. Both the advantages and the drawbacks of this scheme are obvious; it does not seem very likely.

Whatever may happen, His Holiness believes that he will return to Tibet, and so do the majority of his people. They do not know how, and they do not know when. They know that they will have to rebuild a country that has been shattered by a foreign invader, that has been stripped of many resources, and whose people have been slaves for decades. They believe that they can do it. And with the Buddhist monk Tenzin Gyatso at their head, it is hard not to share in their belief.

Appendix I

The Constitution of Tibet

WHEREAS it has become increasingly evident that the system of government which has hitherto prevailed in Tibet has not proved sufficiently responsive to the present needs and future development of the people

AND WHEREAS it is deemed desirable and necessary that the principle of justice, equality and democracy laid down by the Lord Buddha should be reinforced and strengthened in the government of Tibet

AND WHEREAS it is deemed essential that the people of Tibet should have a more effective voice in shaping their destiny

NOW, THEREFORE, His Holiness the Dalai Lama has been pleased to ordain, and it is hereby ordained as follows:

CHAPTER I
PRELIMINARY

Commencement – Article 1. This Constitution shall come into force on the day appointed in this behalf by His Holiness the Dalai Lama.

Nature of Tibetan Policy – Article 2. Tibet shall be a unitary democratic State founded upon the principles laid down by the Lord Buddha, and no change in the present Constitution shall be made except in accordance with the provisions hereinafter specified.

Principles of Government – Article 3. It shall be the duty of the Government of Tibet to adhere strictly to the Universal Declaration of Human Rights and to promote the moral and material welfare of the people of Tibet.

Constitutional Invalidity – Article 4. (1) Any law, ordinance or regulation or any administrative order which is repugnant to any provision of this Constitution shall be null and void to the extent of the repugnancy.

(2) The Supreme Court shall be specifically empowered to decide whether laws, ordinances, regulations or administrative orders violate the terms of this Constitution.

Recognition of International Law – Article 5. All laws, ordinances and regulations in force within the territories of the State shall conform to the generally recognized principles of international law, and the legal status of aliens shall be regulated by laws in conformity with the international rules and treaties.

Renunciation of War – Article 6. In accordance with its traditions, Tibet renounces war as an instrument of offensive policy and force shall not be used against the liberty of other peoples and as a means of resolving international controversies and will hereby adhere to the principles of the Charter of the United Nations.

Citizenship – Article 7. The National Assembly shall make such provisions, as may be necessary, with respect to the acquisition or loss of Tibetan nationality and such other matters relating to it.

CHAPTER II
FUNDAMENTAL RIGHTS AND DUTIES

Equality before the Law – Article 8. All Tibetans shall be equal before the law and the enjoyment of the rights and freedoms set forth in this Chapter shall be secured without discrimination on any ground such as sex, race, language, religion, social origin, property, birth or other status.

Right to Life, Liberty and Property – Article 9. No person shall be deprived of life, liberty or property without due process of law.

Right to Life – Article 10. Every person shall have the right to life, provided that deprivation of life shall not be deemed to contravene this Article when it results from the use of force which is no more than absolutely necessary (*a*) in defence of any person from unlawful violence, (*b*) in order to effect a lawful arrest or to prevent the escape of a person lawfully detained or (*c*) in action lawfully taken for the purpose of quelling a riot or insurrection.

Right to Liberty – Article 11. (1) No person who is arrested shall be detained in custody without being informed, as soon as may be, of the grounds for such arrest, nor shall he be denied the right to consult and to be defended by a legal practitioner of his choice and to have adequate time and facilities for the preparation of his defence.

(2) Every person who is arrested and detained in custody shall be produced before the nearest court having jurisdiction within a period of twenty-four hours of such arrest excluding the time necessary for the journey from the place of arrest to the court of the magistrate and no such person shall be detained in custody beyond the said period without the authority of a magistrate.

(3) Every person who has been arrested or detained in contravention of this provision of this Article shall have an enforceable right to compensation.

Safeguards in Judicial Proceedings – Article 12. (1) Every person shall be entitled to a fair and public hearing within a reasonable time by an independent and impartial tribunal established by law. Judgement shall be pronounced publicly but the press and public may be excluded from all or part of the trial in the interests of public morality, public order or national security where the interests of juveniles or the protection of the private life of the parties so require, or to the extent strictly necessary in the opinion of the court in special circumstances where publicity would prejudice the interests of justice.

(2) Every person charged with a criminal offence shall be presumed innocent until proved guilty according to law.

(3) Every person charged with a criminal offence shall have the free assistance of (*a*) a legal practitioner, when the interests of justice so require, if he has not sufficient means to pay and (*b*) an interpreter, if he cannot understand or speak the language used in court.

Protection in respect of Conviction for Offences – Article 13. (1) No person shall be convicted of any offence except for violation of a law in force at the time of commission of the act charged as an offence, nor be subjected to a penalty greater than that which might have been inflicted under the law in force at the time of the commission of the offence.

(2) No person shall be prosecuted and punished for the same offence more than once.

(3) No person accused of any offence shall be compelled to be a witness against himself.

Prohibition of Inhuman Treatment – Article 14. No person shall be subjected to torture or to inhuman or degrading treatment or punishment.

Prohibition of Slavery and Forced Labour – Article 15. (1) No one shall be held in slavery or be required to perform forced or compulsory labour.

(2) For the purpose of this Article, the term 'forced or compulsory labour' shall not include (*a*) any work required to be done in the course of detention under the sentence of a court of law, (*b*) any service exacted in case of an emergency or calamity threatening the life or well-being of the community, (*c*) any service of a military character or (*d*) any work or service which forms part of the normal civic obligations of a nation.

Prohibition of Employment of Children – Article 16. No child below the age of fourteen years shall be employed to work in any factory or mine or engaged in any other hazardous employment.

Religious Freedom – Article 17. (1) All religious denominations are equal before the law.

(2) Every Tibetan shall have the right to freedom of thought, conscience and religion. The right includes freedom to openly believe, practice, worship and observe any religion either alone or in community with others.

(3) Freedom to manifest one's religion or beliefs and to deal with any matter relating to religious or charitable purpose either alone or in community with others shall be subject only to such limitations as are prescribed by law and are necessary in the interests of public safety, for the protection of public order, health or morals, or for the protection of the rights and freedoms of others.

Other Fundamental Freedoms – Article 18. Subject to any law imposing reasonable restrictions in the interests of the security of the State, public order, health or morality, all citizens shall be entitled to:

(*a*) freedom of speech and expression;
(*b*) assemble peaceably and without arms;
(*c*) form associations or unions;
(*d*) move freely throughout the territories of Tibet;
(*e*) the right to a passport to travel outside those territories;
(*f*) reside and settle in any part of Tibet;

(g) acquire, hold and dispose of property;

(h) practise any profession or carry on any occupation, trade or business.

Right to Property – Article 19. No person shall be deprived of his property save by authority of law and for public purpose on payment of just compensation.

The Right to Vote – Article 20. All Tibetans, men and women, who have attained the age of eighteen and above shall have the right to vote. The vote shall be personal, equal, free, and secret, and its exercise shall be deemed to be a civic obligation.

Disqualification of Vote – Article 21. (1) A person shall be disqualified to vote if he is of unsound mind and stands so declared by a competent court.

(2) A person shall not have the right to vote if he is so disqualified by any law.

Right to hold Office – Article 22. All Tibetans of either sex shall have the right to hold public offices, whether elective or otherwise, on conditions of equality in accordance with the requirements of law.

Obligations of Nationals – Article 23. All Tibetans shall fufil the following constitutional obligations:

(a) bear true allegiance to the State of Tibet;

(b) faithfully comply with and observe the Constitution and the laws of the State;

(c) to pay taxes imposed by the State in accordance with the laws; and

(d) perform such obligations as may be imposed by law in the event of a threat to national security or other public calamity.

Enforcement of Rights – Article 24. Every citizen whose rights and freedoms as set forth in this Chapter are violated shall have the right to approach the Supreme Court, Regional Courts and such other courts as the National Assembly may by a law designate for the enforcement of those rights and freedoms enumerated in this Chapter and the court shall be entitled to pass such orders as are necessary to protect those rights.

CHAPTER III

OF LAND

Land-holding – Article 25. (1) All land shall belong to the State and shall be made available on payment of annual rent as may be fixed from time to time for building, agricultural and other purposes according to need.

(2) The State shall prevent the concentration of land-holding in order to promote economic and social justice.

(3) No land shall be transferable by the holder or be used for any purpose different from that for which it was granted without the permission of the State.

Social Welfare – Article 26. (1) The State shall endeavour to secure that the ownership and control of the material resources of the community shall be so distributed as best to subserve the common good and that the operation of the economic system does not result in the concentration of wealth and means of production to the common detriment.

(2) The system of taxation shall be so devised that the burden is distributed according to capacity.

(3) The State shall direct its policy toward securing that the citizens, men and women equally, have the right to an adequate means of livelihood and that there is equal pay for equal work for both men and women.

Education and Culture – Article 27. (1) The State shall endeavour to promote education so that educational facilities are available to every child above the age of six and that free primary education for a period of seven years is provided.

(2) The State shall pay special attention to the young and promote technical and professional and higher education. Such education shall be generally available and accessible on the basis of merit and that scholarships shall be also available on the basis of merit to those unable to pay for such education.

(3) All educational establishments shall be under the control and supervision of the State.

(4) The State shall endeavour to preserve and promote national culture and to support researches both in arts and sciences.

Health – Article 28. (1) The State shall endeavour to promote adequate health and medical services and to provide that such services would be available free to those sections of the population which are unable to pay for them.

(2) The State shall endeavour to provide necessary facilities and institutions for the care of the aged and the infirm.

CHAPTER V
OF EXECUTIVE GOVERNMENT

Executive Power – Article 29. (1) The executive power of the State shall be vested in His Holiness the Dalai Lama on his attaining the age of eighteen and shall be exercised by him either directly or through officers subordinant to him in accordance with the provisions of this Constitution.

(2) Without prejudice to the generality of the foregoing provisions, His Holiness the Dalai Lama as the Head of State shall –

(a) accredit or withdraw diplomatic representatives in foreign countries and receive foreign diplomatic representatives, and ratify international treaties with previous approval, in appropriate cases, of the National Assembly or the Standing Commission of the National Assembly;

(b) grant pardons, respite or remission of punishment or suspend, remit or commute the sentence of any person convicted of any offence;

(c) confer honours and patents of merit;

(d) promulgate laws and ordinances having the force and validity of laws;

(e) summon and prorogue the National Assembly;

(f) send messages to the National Assembly and address it whenever he, in his discretion, considers it necessary; and

(g) authorize the holding of a referendum in cases provided for by this Constitution.

(3) Nothing in this Article shall be deemed to alter or affect in any manner the power and authority of His Holiness the Dalai Lama as the Supreme Spiritual Head of the State.

Ministers and the Kashag – Article 30. (1) His Holiness the Dalai Lama shall from time to time appoint such number of Ministers as may be required. Out of the said Ministers His Holiness the Dalai Lama shall nominate a Prime Minister and not less than five other Ministers to be members of the Kashag.

(2) No Minister shall be a member of the National Assembly.

(3) Any person appointed as a Minister shall on such appointment, in case he is a member of the National Assembly, vacate his seat in the National Assembly.

(4) Before any Minister enters upon his office, His Holiness the Dalai Lama shall administer to him the oath of office and of secrecy in accordance with the form and procedure prescribed by law.

(5) The Kashag shall aid and advise His Holiness the Dalai Lama in the administration of the executive government of the State.

(6) The salaries and allowances of the Ministers shall be such as the National Assembly may from time to time by law determine.

Meetings of the Kashag – Article 31. (1) His Holiness the Dalai Lama shall preside over the meetings of the Kashag and in his absence such meetings shall be presided over by the Prime Minister or by the seniormost Minister present.

(2) His Holiness the Dalai Lama may invite any other Minister or Ministers to attend such meetings of the Kashag.

Promulgation of Laws – Article 32. His Holiness the Dalai Lama shall promulgate laws within a fortnight of their transmission to the Kashag after their final adoption by the National Assembly. Provided always that His Holiness the Dalai Lama may ask the Assembly to reconsider the law or any provision thereof before expiry of this period, and the National Assembly shall reconsider it in accordance with the message of His Holiness the Dalai Lama.

Submission to Referendum – Article 33. His Holiness the Dalai Lama may in his discretion or on the recommendation of the Kashag refer any proposed legislation to a referendum and if the proposed legislation is approved by the majority of the electors, His Holiness the Dalai Lama shall promulgate it within the period specified in the last preceding article.

Dissolution of the National Assembly – Article 34. His Holiness the Dalai Lama may dissolve the National Assembly after consulting the Kashag and the Speaker of the National Assembly. Provided always that in such a case a general election shall be held in not less than forty days, after the dissolution.

Conduct of Business of Government – Article 35. (1) All executive action of the Government of Tibet shall be expressed to be taken in the name of His Holiness the Dalai Lama.

(2) With the previous approval of His Holiness the Dalai Lama, the Kashag shall make rules for the more convenient transaction of the business of the Government of Tibet, and for the allocation among Ministers of the said business, and thereafter submit such draft proposal to His Holiness the Dalai Lama for approval.

Council of Regency – Article 36. (1) There shall be a Council of Regency to exercise executive powers in the following circumstances:

(a) until such period as the reincarnate Dalai Lama becomes of age to assume the powers of his predecessors;

(b) until such period as His Holiness the Dalai Lama has not assumed the powers of his predecessors;

(c) in case of any disability which prevents His Holiness the Dalai Lama from exercising his executive functions;

(d) in case of the absence of His Holiness the Dalai Lama from the State;

(e) when the National Assembly, by majority of two-thirds of its total members in consultation with the Supreme Court, decides that in the highest interests of the State it is imperative that the executive functions of His Holiness the Dalai Lama shall be exercised by the Council of Regency.

(2) The Council of Regency shall consist of three members elected by the National Assembly, one of whom shall be an ecclesiastical representative. Provided that a member of the National Assembly shall vacate his seat if elected a member of the Council of Regency.

(3) Any Minister, if elected a member of the Council of Regency, shall cease to hold office.

(4) A person when elected a member of the Council of Regency shall take the oath of office before the National Assembly in accordance with the form prescribed by law.

(5) Whenever any member of the Council of Regency, as a result of death or otherwise, is unable to discharge his functions, the National Assembly shall elect a new member.

(6) If a member of the Council of Regency is required to be removed from office while the National Assembly is not in session, the Assembly's Standing Commission in consultation with the Kashag may deprive the said member of his functions and later recommend to the National Assembly the removal of such person from office. The National Assembly may remove the said member if it considers proper and on removal shall elect a new member in the same session.

(7) If two or all three members of the Council of Regency is required to be removed from office while the National Assembly is not in session, the Assembly's Standing Commission in consultation with the Kashag may summon an Emergency Assembly and recommend to the National Assembly the removal from office of such persons. The Assembly may remove all or such of these members as it considers proper. The Assembly shall also on such removal elect in the same session new members in place of those removed.

(8) The duration of each Council of Regency will be of the same period as that of the National Assembly.

(9) The Council of Regency, in consultation with the Kashag, Ecclesiastical Council and the Standing Commission of the National Assembly, will conduct the search for the reincarnation of His Holiness the Dalai Lama. The Council will then submit its findings and opinion on the determination and installation of the

reincarnation to the National Assembly for the adoption of a resolution.

(10) The Council of Regency shall have no power to alienate any part of the territory of the State or enter into any international agreement in relation to the independence of the State except with the previous approval of the majority of the electors expressed in a referendum held in accordance with the provisions of this Constitution and such other laws as may be enacted in this behalf by the National Assembly.

Ecclesiastical Council – Article 37. (1) There shall be an Ecclesiastical Council to administer the affairs of all monasteries and religious institutions in the State under the direct authority of His Holiness the Dalai Lama.

(2) The Ecclesiastical Council shall consist of not less than five members directly appointed by His Holiness the Dalai Lama from time to time.

(3) The Ecclesiastical Council, with the previous approval of His Holiness the Dalai Lama, will have the responsibility and power to administer all religious affairs.

CHAPTER VI

OF LEGISLATIVE AUTHORITY

Legislative Power – Article 38. All Legislative power shall vest in the National Assembly subject to the assent of His Holiness the Dalai Lama.

Composition of the National Assembly – Article 39. (1) The National Assembly shall consist of –

    (a) 75 per cent of members directly elected by the people in the territorial constituencies;

    (b) 10 per cent of members elected by the monasteries and other religious institutions in accordance with the laws enacted in this behalf;

    (c) 10 per cent of members elected by Regional and District Councils in accordance with the laws enacted in this behalf; and

    (d) 5 per cent of members nominated directly by His Holiness the Dalai Lama. Such persons shall be selected for their distinguished services in the field of art, science or literature.

(2) For the purpose of sub-clause 1*(a)* the State shall be divided into territorial constituencies. Each constituency shall be made up of an equal proportion of those entitled to vote. The number of members to be allotted to each constituency shall be determined by an Electoral Commission appointed by His Holiness the Dalai Lama in this behalf.

Duration of the National Assembly – Article 40. (1) Each National Assembly, unless sooner dissolved, shall continue for five years from the date appointed for its first meeting and no longer and the expiration of the said period of five years shall operate as a dissolution of the House.

(2) There shall be a Standing Commission of the National Assembly while the Assembly is not in session.

(3) The National Assembly shall prepare proposals on the duties, powers and number of members of the Standing Commission and present such proposals to His Holiness the Dalai Lama for approval.

Qualifications for Membership of the National Assembly – Article 41. No person shall be qualified to be elected to the National Assembly unless he *(a)* is a Tibetan national who has attained the age of 25 and *(b)* is not subject to any disqualifications as may be prescribed in this behalf or under any law made by the National Assembly.

Sessions of the National Assembly – Article 42. (1) His Holiness the Dalai Lama shall from time to time summon the regular National Assembly to meet at such time and place as may be appointed in this behalf, but six months shall not intervene between its last sitting in one session and the date appointed for its first sitting in the next session.

(2) Subject to the provisions of this Constitution His Holiness the Dalai Lama may *(a)* prorogue the National Assembly or *(b)* dissolve the National Assembly.

His Holiness the Dalai Lama's Address and Messages to the National Assembly – Article 43. (1) At the commencement of the first session after the general election and at the commencement of the first session of each year His Holiness the Dalai Lama shall address the National Assembly and inform it of the causes of its summons.

(2) His Holiness the Dalai Lama may send messages to the National Assembly, whether with respect to a Bill then pending in the Assembly or otherwise, and the Assembly shall with all convenient dispatch consider any matter required by the message to be taken into consideration.

Special Sessions – Article 44. (1) Special sessions of the National Assembly may be summoned by His Holiness the Dalai Lama, at the request of the Kashag or of the majority of the members of the Assembly.

(2) All special sessions of the National Assembly shall be opened and closed by a decree of His Holiness the Dalai Lama.

Right of Access of Ministers – Article 45. Every Minister shall have the right to speak in, and otherwise take part in the proceedings of the National Assembly and of any committee of the National Assembly of which he may be named a member but shall not be entitled to vote.

The Speaker of the National Assembly – Article 46. (1). The National Assembly at its first session after the general election shall elect two members of the Assembly to be respectively the Speaker and Deputy Speaker thereof, and so often as the office of the Speaker and Deputy Speaker becomes vacant, the Assembly shall elect another member to be Speaker or Deputy Speaker, as the case may be.

(2) The Speaker or the Deputy Speaker shall vacate his office if he ceases to be a member of the National Assembly or is removed from his office by a resolution of the Assembly by a two-thirds majority of all the members of the Assembly.

(3) There shall be paid to the Speaker and the Deputy Speaker of the National Assembly such salary and allowance as may be fixed by the National Assembly by law.

Privileges of Members of the Assembly – Article 47. (1) No member of the National Assembly shall be liable to any proceedings in any court in respect of anything said or any vote given by him in the National Assembly or any committee thereof, and no person shall be so liable in respect of the publication by or under the authority of the National Assembly of any report, paper, or proceedings.

(2) When the Assembly is in session no member thereof shall be prosecuted or arrested for civil or criminal offences without the previous authorization of the

Speaker of the National Assembly unless he is arrested in the act of committing an offence.

(3) In other respects, the privileges of the members of the National Assembly shall be such as may from time to time be defined by the National Assembly by law.

Oath or Affirmation by Members – Article 48. Every member of the National Assembly shall, before taking his seat, make and subscribe before the Speaker, or some person appointed in that behalf, an oath or affirmation according to the form prescribed by law in this behalf.

Voting in the Assembly – Article 49. (1) Save as otherwise provided in this Constitution all questions at any sitting of the National Assembly shall be determined by a majority of votes of the members present and voting, other than the Speaker or person acting as Speaker. The Speaker, or person acting as such, shall not vote in the first instance but shall have and exercise a casting vote in the case of an equality of votes.

(2) The National Assembly shall have power to act notwithstanding any vacancy in the membership thereof, and any proceedings in the Assembly shall be valid notwithstanding that it is subsequently discovered that some person who was not entitled so to do, sat or voted or otherwise took part in the proceedings.

(3) The quorum of a meeting of the National Assembly shall be one-fifth of the total number of members of the Assembly.

(4) If at any time during a meeting of the National Assembly there is no quorum it shall be the duty of the Speaker, or person acting as such, either to adjourn the Assembly or to suspend the meeting until there is a quorum.

Vacation of Seats – Article 50. (1) If a member of the National Assembly is elected a member of the Council of Regency or a Minister or becomes subject to any of the disqualifications mentioned in the next succeeding Article, or resigns his seat by writing under his hand addressed to the Speaker, his seat shall thereupon become vacant.

(2) If for a period of sixty days a member of the National Assembly is absent from all meetings thereof without permission of the Assembly, the Assembly may declare his seat vacant. Provided that in computing the said period of sixty days no account shall be taken of any period during which the Assembly is prorogued or adjourned for more than four consecutive days.

Disqualification for Membership – Article 51. (1) A person shall be disqualified for being chosen as, and for being, a member of the National Assembly –
  (a) if he holds any office of profit under the Government of Tibet, other than an office declared by the National Assembly by law not to disqualify its holders;
  (b) if he is of unsound mind and stands so declared by a competent court;
  (c) if he is an undischarged insolvent;
  (d) if he is not a Tibetan national, or is under any acknowledgement of allegiance or adherence to a foreign State; or
  (e) if he is so disqualified by or under any law made by the National Assembly.

Decision on Questions as to Disqualifications of Members – Article 52. If any question arises as to whether a member of the National Assembly has become subject to any of the disqualifications mentioned in the last preceding Article, the question shall be referred to the Chief Justice of the Supreme Court and his decision shall be final.

Penalty for Sitting and Voting before making Oath or when Disqualified – Article 53. If a person sits or votes as a member of the National Assembly before he has made and subscribed an oath or affirmation, or when he knows that he is not qualified or that he is disqualified for membership thereof or that he is prohibited from so doing by the provisions of any law made by the National Assembly, he shall be liable in respect of each day on which he so sits or votes to a fine of ......

Salaries and Allowances of Members – Article 54. Members of the National Assembly shall be entitled to receive such salaries and allowances as may from time to time be determined by the National Assembly by law.

Introduction and Passing of Bills – Article 55. (1) No Bill dealing with the imposition, abolition, remission, alteration or regulation of any tax, or the regulation of the borrowing of money or the giving of any guarantee by the Government of Tibet shall be introduced or moved except on the recommendation of the Kashag. Provided that an amendment making provision for the reduction or abolition of any tax shall need no such recommendation.

(2) A Bill shall not be deemed to make provision for any of the matters specified in the last preceding Clause by reason only that it provides for the imposition of fines or other pecuniary penalties, or for the demand or payment of fees for licences or fees for services rendered.

(3) A Bill involving expenditure for the Government of Tibet shall not be passed by the National Assembly without the recommendation of the Kashag.

(4) Subject to the provisions of the last preceding Clauses, any member of the National Assembly may introduce any Bill or move any Resolution or propose any amendment to any Bill.

(5) All Bills or Resolutions moved by a private member and all Bills proposed by the Kashag if so required shall be referred for consideration to committees especially appointed for the purpose.

Annual Financial Statement – Article 56. (1) The Kashag shall in respect of every financial year cause to be laid before the National Assembly a statement of the estimated receipts and expenditure for that year.

(2) The estimates of expenditure embodied in the statement shall show separately *(a)* the sums required to meet expenditure charged upon the revenues of the State under the next succeeding Clause; and *(b)* the sums required to meet other expenditure proposed to be made from the revenues of the State.

(3) The following expenditure shall be deemed to be charged on the revenues of the State:
- *(a)* expenditures necessary for the office and dignity of His Holiness the Dalai Lama;
- *(b)* the salary and allowances of the Speaker and Deputy Speaker of the National Assembly;
- *(c)* the salaries, allowances and pensions payable to the Judges of the Supreme Court;
- *(d)* debt charges for which the Government is liable including interest, sinking fund charges and redemption charges.

(4) So much of the estimates as relates to expenditure charged upon the revenues of the State shall not be submitted to the vote of the National Assembly, but nothing in this Clause shall be construed as preventing the discussion in the National Assembly of any of those estimates.

(5) So much of the said estimates as relates to other expenditures shall be submitted in the form of demands for grants to the National Assembly and the Assembly shall have power to assent or to refuse to assent to any demand, or to assent to any demand subject to a reduction of the amount specified therein.

Rules of Procedure – Article 57. The National Assembly shall make rules for regulating, subject to the provisions of this Constitution, its procedure and conduct of its business.

Restriction on Discussion – Article 58. No discussion shall take place in the National Assembly with respect to the conduct of any Judge of the Supreme Court in the discharge of his duties upon a motion for presenting an address to His Holiness the Dalai Lama praying for the removal of the Judge as hereinafter provided.

Promulgation of Ordinances by His Holiness the Dalai Lama – Article 59. (1) If at any time, while the National Assembly is not in session His Holiness the Dalai Lama is satisfied that circumstances exist which render it necessary and urgent for him to take immediate action, he may, after consultation with the Standing Commission of the National Assembly, promulgate such Ordinances as the circumstances appear to him to require.

(2) An Ordinance promulgated under this Article shall have the same force and effect as an Act of the National Assembly, but on the proposal of the National Assembly every such Ordinance may be amended, altered or repealed by His Holiness the Dalai Lama.

Assent to Bills – Article 60. When a Bill has been passed by the National Assembly, it shall be presented to His Holiness the Dalai Lama, and His Holiness the Dalai Lama shall declare either that he assents to the Bill, or that he withholds assent therefrom. Provided that His Holiness the Dalai Lama may, after the presentation to him of a Bill for assent, return the Bill to the National Assembly with a message requesting that it will reconsider the Bill or any specified provisions thereof and, in particular, will consider the desirability of introducing any such amendments as he may recommend in his message.

Courts not to enquire into the Proceedings of the National Assembly – Article 61. (1) The validity of any proceedings in the National Assembly shall not be called in question on the ground of any alleged irregularity of procedure.

(2) No member of the National Assembly in whom powers are vested by or under this Constitution for regulating procedure or the conduct of business or for maintaining order in the National Assembly shall be subject to the jurisdiction of any court in respect of the exercise by him of those powers.

CHAPTER VII
OF THE JUDICATURE

Constitution of the Supreme Court – Article 62. (1) There shall be a Supreme Court consisting of a Chief Justice and, until the National Assembly by law prescribes a larger number, of not more than three other Judges.

(2) Every Judge of the Supreme Court shall be appointed by His Holiness the Dalai Lama and shall hold office during the pleasure of His Holiness the Dalai Lama unless sooner removed by two-thirds majority of the National Assembly and assented to by His Holiness the Dalai Lama. Provided that in the case of appointment of a Judge other than the Chief Justice, the Chief Justice shall always be consulted.

(3) No person shall be qualified for appointment as a Judge of the Supreme Court unless he is a Tibetan national and has been for at least five years a Judge of a Regional Court or of two or more such courts in succession, or has been for at least ten years an enrolled advocate of a Regional Court or of the Supreme Court. Provided that for a period of five years from the commencement of the operation of this Constitution His Holiness the Dalai Lama may dispense with the requirements of this clause in the case of any or all appointments under this Article.

(4) Every person appointed to be Judge of the Supreme Court shall, before he enters upon his office, make and subscribe before His Holiness the Dalai Lama an oath or affirmation according to the form prescribed by the National Assembly by law in this behalf.

Salaries, etc., of Judges – Article 63. (1) There shall be paid to the Judges of the Supreme Court such salaries, allowances and pensions as may be specified by the National Assembly by law in this behalf.

(2) The salaries, allowances and other privileges of the Judges of the Supreme Court shall not be reduced or altered to their detriment during their term of office.

Jurisdiction of the Supreme Court – Article 64. (1) The Supreme Court shall be the highest appellate court and shall be the exclusive head of the judicial administration of the State and shall exercise all such powers as are necessary for the discharge of its functions in accordance with such rules and regulations as may be made by it with the previous approval of His Holiness the Dalai Lama.

(2) An appeal shall lie to the Supreme Court from any judgement, decree or final order of a Regional Court or tribunal whether in a civil, criminal or other proceeding if it satisfies the conditions which shall be laid down by the National Assembly by law in this behalf. Provided always that an appeal shall lie as of right to the Supreme Court if the case involves a substantial question of law as to the interpretation of this Constitution.

Special Leave to Appeal – Article 65. Notwithstanding anything in this Constitution or any other law specifying the conditions subject to which an appeal shall lie to the Supreme Court, the Supreme Court may, in its discretion, grant special leave to appeal from any judgement, decree, sentence or order in any cause or matter passed or made by any court or tribunal.

Rules of Court – Article 66. Subject to the provisions of any law made by the National Assembly, the Supreme Court may from time to time, with the approval of His Holiness the Dalai Lama, make rules for regulating generally the practice and procedure of the Court.

Obtaining Opinion of the Supreme Court – Article 67. If, at any time, it appears to His Holiness the Dalai Lama that a question of law or fact has arisen or is likely to arise which is of such a nature and such public importance that it is expedient to obtain the opinion of the Supreme Court upon it, he may refer the question to that Court for consultation and the Court shall, after such hearing as it thinks fit, report to His Holiness the Dalai Lama its opinion thereon.

CHAPTER VIII
OF REGIONAL GOVERNMENT

Regions of the State – Article 68. (1) The entire territory of the State shall be divided into..... regions as follows:

  (a) .....

(2) The extent of each region shall be determined by the National Assembly with the approval of His Holiness the Dalai Lama.

Regional Governors – Article 69. (1) In each region there shall be a chief executive officer directly appointed by His Holiness the Dalai Lama, who shall be styled the Governor of the Region.

(2) There shall also be a Deputy Governor in each region to be elected by the respective Regional Councils and approved by His Holiness the Dalai Lama.

(3) The Governor and Deputy Governor shall hold office for such term as may be determined by His Holiness the Dalai Lama in consultation with the National Assembly.

(4) During the absence, illness or other inability of the Governor, the Deputy Governor shall execute the office and functions of the Governor.

(5) The salaries of the Governors and Deputy Governors shall be fixed by the National Assembly and shall not be reduced during their respective terms of office.

Constitution of Regional Councils – Article 70. (1) There shall be a Regional Council in each region consisting of such number of members as may be determined by His Holiness the Dalai Lama in consultation with the National Assembly.

(2) The members of the Regional Council shall be elected by persons qualified to vote for the election of members of the National Assembly.

(3) The election shall take place at such times as the Governor shall direct in consultation with the Kashag.

(4) Each Regional Council shall continue for three years from the date of its first meeting and shall not be subject to dissolution save by effluxion of time.

Sessions of Regional Council – Article 71. The Governor of each region shall by notification fix such times for holding the sessions of the Regional Council as he may think fit. Provided that there shall be a session of every Regional Council at least three times in every year, so that a period of four months shall not intervene between the last sitting of the Council in one session and its first sitting in the next session.

Chairman of the Regional Council – Article 72. The Governor and, in his absence, the Deputy Governor of the Region shall preside over the meetings of the Regional Council and the Governor shall make rules for the conduct of its proceedings in consultation with the Kashag and in accordance with such laws as may be enacted in this behalf by the National Assembly.

Powers of Regional Councils – Article 73. Subject to the provisions of this Constitution and the laws enacted by the National Assembly, the Regional Council may make regulations in relation to matters coming within the following classes of subjects:

   (a) public health and sanitation, including the establishment, maintenance and management of hospitals and charitable institutions;
   (b) primary and secondary education subject to such laws as may be enacted by the National Assembly;
   (c) local works and undertakings within the region;
   (d) roads, bridges and other constructional works;
   (e) social welfare and public assistance;
   (f) irrigation, agriculture, animal husbandry and small-scale industries;
   (g) the imposition of punishment by fine for enforcing any regulation of the region made in relation to any matter coming within any of the classes of subjects enumerated in this Article; and
   (h) any other subject in respect of which the National Assembly may by any law delegate the power of making regulations to the Regional Council. In case of a conflict between a regulation made by a Regional Council and a law passed by the National Assembly, the latter shall prevail.

Submission of Reports – Article 74. At the end of each year the Governor of the Region shall submit to the Kashag a detailed report regarding the work done by the Regional Council and all such reports shall be laid before the National Assembly.

CHAPTER IX
REORGANIZATION

Reorganization of Public Departments – Article 75. As soon as possible after the commencement of this Constitution His Holiness the Dalai Lama shall appoint a Public Service Commission to make recommendations for such reorganization and readjustment of the departments of the public service as may be necessary.

Public Service Commission – Article 76. After the provisions of this Constitution have come into operation His Holiness the Dalai Lama shall appoint a Permanent Public Service Commission with such powers and duties relating to the appointment, discipline, retirement, and superannuation of public officers as His Holiness the Dalai Lama may, in consultation with the National Assembly, determine.

CHAPTER X
AMENDMENT OF THE CONSTITUTION

Procedure for Constitutional Amendment – Article 77. (1) This Constitution or any provision thereof may be amended, altered or varied by an Act passed by a two–thirds majority of the total number of members of the National Assembly and assented to by His Holiness the Dalai Lama.

(2) His Holiness the Dalai Lama may direct that any such amendment be submitted to a referendum, and any such amendment shall not come into force unless it has been ratified by a two–thirds majority of the electors qualified to vote for elections to the National Assembly.

(3) Nothing in this Article shall be deemed to confer any power or authority on the National Assembly to affect in any manner the status and authority of His Holiness the Dalai Lama as the Spiritual Head of the State.

Appendix II

The Escape Party, 1959

Family Members

1   Gyalyum Chenmo (the Great Mother)
2   Mrs Tsering Dolma (elder sister, now deceased)
3   Ngari Rinpoche, now Tendzin Choegyal (youngest brother)

Tutors

4   Khabje Yongzin Gadhen Tri Ling Rinpoche (Senior Tutor)
5   Khabje Yongzin Trijang Rinpoche (Junior Tutor)
    (*Khabje Yongzin* means 'All-saving Teacher')

Personal Attendants

6   Su-pon Khenpo Lobsang Jinpa (Master of the Food)
7   Zim-pon Khenpo Thubten Thonyo (Master of the Wardrobe)
8   Choe-pon Khenpo Thubten Sonam (Master of Religious Implements)
9   Zim-yok Thubten Thapkey (Assistant to Zim-pon Khenpo)
10   Choe-yok Thubten Jamyang (Assistant to Choe-pon Khenpo)

Cabinet Ministers

11   Sa-wang Surkhar Wangchen Gelek
12   Sa-wang Liushar Thubten Tharpa
13   Sa-wang Shasur Sonam Topgyal

Other Important Government Officials

14   Chee-khyab Kenpo Gadang Lobsang Rigzin (the Lord Chamberlain)
15   Ta Lama Chogten Thubten Norsang
16   Dron-nyen Chemog Phala Thubten Wodhen (Master of Protocol)
17   Kusung Dapon Takla Phuntsok Tashi (Master of the Bodyguard)

Appendix III

Places Visited by His Holiness

1967

September 25th – October 19th	Japan
November 11th – November 15th	Thailand

1973

September 29th	Rome
September 30th – October 6th	Switzerland
October 7th–8th	The Netherlands
October 9th	Belgium
October 9th–10th	Ireland
October 10th–13th	Norway
October 13th–17th	Sweden
October 17th–20th	Denmark
October 20th–30th	United Kingdom
October 30th – November 5th	West Germany
November 5th–6th	Austria

1974

Switzerland

1978

October 4th–9th	Japan

1979

June 12th	Mongolia
	Switzerland
August 3rd–6th	Greece
August 6th – September 10th	Switzerland
September 10th – October 20th	United States

1980

October 8th–10th   Rome
October 10th–31st   Canada
October 31st – November 13th   Japan

1981

June 29th – July 3rd   United Kingdom
July 3rd – July 27th   United States

1982

July 27th–29th   Malaya
July 29th – August 1st   Singapore
August 1st–6th   Indonesia
August 7th–21st   Australia
September 11th–13th   USSR
September 14th–26th   Mongolia
September 26th–27th   Hungary
September 27th–28th   Rome
September 28th – October 4th   Spain
October 4th–16th   France
October 16th–25th   Italy
October 24th – November 4th   Germany

Selected Bibliography

Andrugtsang, Gompo Tashi, *Four Rivers, Six Ranges (A True Account of Khampa Resistance to Chinese in Tibet),* Information Office of H.H. the Dalai Lama, Dharamsala, 1973.

Avedon, John F, *An Interview with the Dalai Lama,* Littlebird Publications, New York, 1980.

Bell, Sir Charles, K.C.I.E., C.M.G., *Portrait of the Dalai Lama,* Collins, London, 1946.

Choedon, Dhondub, *Life in the Red Flag People's Commune,* Information Office of H.H. the Dalai Lama, Dharamsala, 1978.

Dalai Lama, The VI, *Songs of the Sixth Dalai Lama,* trans. and with an introduction by K. Dhondup, Library of Tibetan Works and Archives, Dharamsala, 1981.

Dalai Lama, The XIV, *An Introduction to Buddhism,* Tibet House, Delhi, 1965.

———, *My Land and My People,* Potala Corporation, New York 1977.

———, *The Opening of the Wisdom Eye,* The Theosophical Publishing House, Wheaton, Illinois, 1974.

———, *Short Essays on Buddhist Thought and Practice,* Tibet House, Delhi, no date.

———, *Universal Responsibility and the Good Heart,* Library of Tibetan Works and Archives, Dharamsala, 1980.

David–Neel, Alexandra, *Initiations and Initiates in Tibet,* trans. Fred Rothwell, University Books, New York, 1959.

———, *With Mystics and Magicians in Tibet,* Penguin Books, London 1936.

Gashi, Tsering Dorje, *New Tibet,* Information Office of His Holiness the Dalai Lama, Dharamsala, 1980.

Harrer, Heinrich, *Seven Years in Tibet,* trans. Richard Graves, Pan Books, London, 1956.

Information Office of His Holiness the Dalai Lama, Dharamsala:
 Collected Statements, Interviews, and Articles of His Holiness The Dalai Lama, 1982.
 From Liberation to Liberalisation, 1982.
 Glimpses of Tibet Today, 1978.
 Tibet under Chinese Communist Rule, A Compilation of Refugee Statements 1958–1975, 1976.
 Tibetans in Exile, 1981.

Norbu, Namkhai, *The Necklace of Gzi, A Cultural History of Tibet,* Information Office of H.H. the Dalai Lama, Dharamsala, 1981.

Snellgrove, David, and Richardson, Hugh, *A Cultural History of Tibet,* Weidenfeld and Nicholson, London 1968.

van Walts van Praag, M.C., *Tibet and the Right to Self Determination,* Information Office H.H. the Dalai Lama, 1979.

Magazines and Periodicals
The Tibetan Review, Delhi, Tsering Wangyal ed., monthly
National Integration, Tibet Issue, Independence Number, 1964, Delhi.

Index